MONEY MATTERS
A CRITICAL LOOK AT BANK ARCHITECTURE

MONEY MATTERS
A CRITICAL LOOK AT BANK ARCHITECTURE

Published by McGraw-Hill
in association with the Museum of Fine Arts, Houston, and
Parnassus Foundation

McGRAW-HILL PUBLISHING COMPANY
New York   St. Louis   San Francisco   Auckland   Bogotá
Caracas   Hamburg   Lisbon   London   Madrid   Mexico
Milan   Montreal   New Delhi   Oklahoma City
Paris   San Juan   São Paulo   Singapore
Sydney   Tokyo   Toronto

Library of Congress Cataloging in Publication Data

Money matters: a critical look at bank architecture.
     p. cm.
   "Published by McGraw-Hill in association with Parnassus Foundation
and the Museum of Fine Arts, Houston."
   Includes bibliographical references.
   ISBN 0-07-030533-1. — ISBN 0-07-030535-8 (pbk.)
    1. Bank buildings — United States.   2. Bank buildings — Canada.
I. Parnassus Foundation. II. Museum of Fine Arts, Houston.
NA6241.M66   1990
725′.24′0973 — dc20   89-28362
                                                     CIP

1234567890 KGP/KGP 9543210

ISBN 0-07-030533-1 {C}

ISBN 0-07-030535-8 {P}

We would like to thank the following individuals and institutions for
permission to reproduce in the catalog works in their collection or
under their copyright protection: Collection Centre Canadien d'Archi-
tecture/Canadian Centre for Architecture, Montréal; McCord Museum
of Canadian History, Montréal; the Berenice Abbott Archive, Commerce Graphics Ltd; Toshiyuki Kobayashi, Tokyo; Citicorp Art Collection, New York; the Fay S. Lincoln Photograph Collection, Historical
Collections & Labor Archives, Pennsylvania State University; the
Historical Society of Pennsylvania; the Maryland Historical Society; the
New-York Historical Society; Julie Pratt, and John Szarkowski.

*The editors for this book were Joel Stein and Caroline Levine, the
designer was Naomi Auerbach, and the production supervisor was
Dianne L. Walber. It was set in Auriga by Progressive Typographers.*

Printed and bound by Arcata Graphics/Kingsport.

*For more information about other McGraw-Hill materials,
call 1-800-2-MCGRAW in the United States. In other
countries, call your nearest McGraw-Hill office.*

CONTENTS

4. CANADIAN BANKS
MID AND LATE VICTORIAN 57

5. AMERICAN AND CANADIAN BANKS
BEAUX-ARTS CLASSICISM 67

6. AMERICAN AND CANADIAN BANKS
PRAIRIE STYLE 79

7. AMERICAN AND CANADIAN BANKS
TWENTIES AND THIRTIES 211

8. AMERICAN AND CANADIAN BANKS
MODERNISM AND LATE MODERNISM 225

STATEMENT

Parnassus Foundation was formed in December 1986 for purposes that include the encouragement of original creative work in the arts and humanities. Important aspects of the Foundation's activities are its interest in initiating, developing, and co-sponsoring projects that are appealing and provocative; its willingness to assume a share of the managerial and administrative responsibilities to facilitate the appropriate presentation.

The Museum of Fine Arts, Houston seeks to present an exhibition program that is broad in scope and challenging to the museum's varied audiences. In order to sustain exhibitions of high quality that cut across disciplines and involve teams of professionals, museums often depend upon the support and cooperation of private foundations. The museum is pleased to be associated with Parnassus Foundation in this unique interdisciplinary exhibition on the subject of photography and the architecture of Canadian and American banks.

PETER C. MARZIO, DIRECTOR
The Museum of Fine Arts, Houston

PROLOGUE

The notion of putting together a collection of images organized to capture the power of bank architecture goes back a long way with me. It has its genesis in the special feelings that played out over a number of decades, including many years of active engagement in the investment banking business. These feelings might be variously described as awe, fear, skepticism, disdain, familiarity, and affection for the men and buildings of banking; for the places where the money is, as well as the people who guard it.

The real power of a commercial bank does not usually lie with its owners but in the place that the bank occupies in the community and the functions it performs there. Most if not all of the persons I have known who were or became high officers of a banking company had devoted their entire careers to banking; the rules and formulae that they spoke about seemed to have been handed down to them as part of a special heritage.

Bank buildings, I surmised, were often conceived and created to preserve and dignify that special tradition, and to foster respect for the practitioners — the bankers — whose role in such institutions would require an oath of allegiance to "fiduciary responsibility," eschewing the greed of the moneylender as well as other malevolent opportunistic traits. To be sure, bank buildings convey symbolic meaning and often serve to impress upon our consciousness something about the virtues and power of money.

Indeed, it is not surprising that some of the images in the collection published here reveal allusions to ancient Greek temples, and others call forth visions of Italian renaissance palazzi, for scholars have noted the historical association (going back to much earlier societies) of *money* and *banking* with loci of central authority, whether civil or sacred. In calling attention to the evocative, even mythic, character projected by many of these bank buildings, we are invited to raise questions and to speculate about the social and cultural attributes of money.

These photographs and the essays that follow were planned as a cross-disciplinary project intended to explore the interrelationships among architecture, photographic art, aesthetics, and history. The project evolved in unexpected ways, so that the result can be likened to an unfolding Chinese scroll, telling its story from multiple points of entry and perspectives, in words and pictures, markings and commentary, details and broad brush. Its elements include the work of eleven distinguished photographers who were commissioned for their creative abilities and for the quality of their vision. It was anticipated that contemporary photographs might serve as visual counterpoint to the historic buildings. Each of the photographers and each of the essayists deals with his or her interpretive world, differentiated in some ways from the reality of the bank buildings that are described. Taking note that neither individual photograph nor specific text can be relied upon to describe this reality with any final precision, one hopes there will be pleasure and insight in crossing over from one vantage point to another. As in the analogy of the scroll, this collection of images and texts forms a constellation of data telling a story that is both lively and true.

RAPHAEL BERNSTEIN
Parnassus Foundation
July 14, 1989

ACKNOWLEDGMENTS

The exhibition and associated publication, *Money Matters: A Critical Look at Bank Architecture,* are the result of the combined efforts of Canadian and American professionals. We wish to thank Anne W. Tucker, Gus and Lyndall Wortham Curator of Photography at the Museum of Fine Arts, Houston, who selected and advised the photographers; Susan Wagg, architectural historian in Montreal who selected the bank buildings; Robert Nisbet, Albert Schweitzer Professor emeritus of Humanities, Columbia University, who provided the perspective of his profession; and Brendan Gill, who addresses the subject in the introduction to this book with his characteristic insight and artistic breadth.

We are grateful to officers of the banks photographed who graciously shared their knowledge of banking and the history of their institutions. In particular, we recognize Gaylord Freeman, former Chairman of the First National Bank of Chicago and Lloyd P. Johnson, Chairman and Chief Executive Officer of Norwest Corporation. We would also like to thank H. G. Kehlenbeck, President of Pacific National Bank, Nantucket; Kenneth E. Wilcox, President of Norwest Bank, Owatonna; and Mavis Kaminsky, Manager, Canadian Imperial Bank of Commerce, Innisfree, Alberta.

We wish to thank bank staff members and others for technical assistance and information, especially Diane Fraser, Bank of California; Susan Cunningham, East Cambridge Savings Bank; John Neff and Dan Mills, First National Bank of Chicago; Sandra Wingfield, Bank One, Dallas; Robert Fournier, Pacific National Bank, Nantucket; Victor Pepenelli, PSFS; Vera Babcock and John S. Patterson, RepublicBank; David G. Edmonds, Society Corporation; Libby Tallean, Dollar Bank; Sherrin Grout, Columbia State Historic Park, California; Jacqueline Woods, Bank of Canada, Ottawa; and Richard Maidment, Bank of Nova Scotia; Allanna Little, Canadian Imperial Bank of Commerce Head Office; Freeman Clowery, Yolaine Toussaint, and Robert Frank, Bank of Montreal Head Office; Gordon Rabchuk, Royal Bank of Canada Head Office; and Mildred Pulleyblank, Toronto Dominion Bank Head Office.

For advice and assistance in research, we acknowledge and thank James Borcoman and Ann W. Thomas, The National Gallery of Canada, Ottawa; Martha Langford, Martha Hanna, and Susan Lagasi, Canadian Museum of Contemporary Photography, Ottawa; and David Harris, Canadian Centre for Architecture, Montreal; Stanley G. Triggs, Notman Photographic Archives; Conrad Graham, McCord Museum of Canadian History; Robert L. Kirschenbaum, Pacific Press Service; Neil Harris, University of Chicago; Carol Marley, Irena Murray, and Marilyn Berger, McGill University Library; Margaret Brown, Washington, D.C.; Judith Middleton, Charleston; William and Mary Martha Sherts, Southport; Betsy Woodman, Newburyport; and Dennis Walsh. Additional thanks for professional advice go to C. William Brubaker, Perkins & Will; William L. Livingston, Gensler & Associates; Douglas C. McKinnon, Gerald D. Hines Interests; Thomas J. Parish, Norwest Properties, Inc.; and to Danny Samuels, Robert G. Hecht, Louis Skidmore, William Stern, Joe Aker, and Paul Hester. And for their professional generosity and curatorial expertise we are indebted to Richard Pare and John Szarkowski.

Scholarly guidance and encouragement were critical to the development of manuscripts. For their support and counsel, we thank S. Allen Chambers, Jr., Kenneth A. Randall, Deryck W. Holdsworth, and Martha White Paas. We wish to note the exceptional work of editors Diana Menkes and James T. Rogers as well as Anne Feltus and Carolyn Vaughan.

Photographs by Serge Hambourg and John Pfahl were printed by Edward Burtynsky and his staff at Toronto Image Works. These exhibition photographs, as well as Mr. Burtynsky's, were printed on Century Print paper donated by Konica Canada.

Skillful professionals in many departments of the Museum of Fine Arts, Houston, have dedicated themselves to the preparation, organization, and presentation of this exhibition and catalogue. While extending our appreciation to every contributing staff member, we recognize the particular efforts of Barbara Michels, Maggie Olvey, Carrie Springer, Betty Gerhardt, and Mathilda Cochran.

Special thanks and appreciation are offered to Jeanette Neal, Executive Director of Parnassus Foundation, whose attention, judgment, and good humor were ever present and much relied upon.

RAPHAEL BERNSTEIN
Parnassus Foundation

PETER C. MARZIO
The Museum of Fine Arts, Houston

INTRODUCTION

Brendan Gill

During the past century and a half, certain generic types of structures — among them banks, churches, courthouses, firehouses, and railroad stations — have asserted as if by right a predominant architectural presence in our towns and cities. I picture them as shouldering their way forward with the cocky air of those who, not without reason, regard themselves as indispensable. Nearly always, the communities upon which this presence has been imposed have consented eagerly to it, and why not? What more practical way to manifest civic pride than by a conspicuous display of bricks and mortar—better still, of marble and bronze? Moreover, the bigger the bank, church, or railroad station, the more ambitious (and therefore, it was silently assumed, the more virtuous) the citizens who had contrived to bring it into existence. Whatever else one might say about such structures, they were at the very least notable feats of self-congratulation.

When it happened that a new building was much admired, it was also much imitated, and this led to the development of strong family resemblances within a given generic type. A bank that echoed Hadrian's Pantheon led to a hundred similar pantheons; one Gothic church spire against the urban sky caused the sky to bristle with Gothic spires as St. Sebastian bristled with arrows. This being so, one might have expected (confidently in times past, less confidently today) that a stranger strolling along any one of our innumerable Main Streets would be able to identify by its appearance alone the purpose for which a particular building had been designed: on that corner he would catch sight of what was surely a bank, across the way he would catch sight of what was surely a church, and so on. But this was not always the case, or not quite the case. For the buildings I am speaking of also possessed a tendency to resemble one another *outside* the generic type to which they belonged; as a result, my imaginary stranger might well have mistaken a firehouse tower for the tower of a railroad station, a courthouse for a bank, a bank for a basilica. Different as they were in function — within this set of walls, one worshipped Almighty God, within that set one worshipped the Almighty Dollar — they were often bizarrely alike in respect to style and scale.

A reason for this blurry blending of architectural identities is that the various types of buildings that traditionally make up the hearts of our cities have been designed less to serve a practical purpose than to serve as a symbol of that purpose. It is a primary requirement of symbols that they be easily recognized, which means that at some period in their history they must enjoy a measure of popular acceptance — must be, in effect, fashionable. Architects dislike being accused of inaugurating fashions or, what is worse, of following them, but history makes it clear that the accusation is a just one. Over the centuries, we observe in architecture a seemingly irrational process, in the course of which old styles are continuously deposed and new styles take their place. It is a process that threatens to trivialize the intellectual pretensions of architects — are their buildings no better than so many frocks and bonnets when it comes to embodying aesthetic principles? That is a question often asked of architects but rarely answered, except by hot-tempered huffings and puffings inside the profession.

Almost without exception, the generic types that I have mentioned have been forced to obey that iron law of fashion which states that change — not progress, but change — is inescapable. In one of his most celebrated poems, Tennyson defends the logic of this (at first glance) illogical precept; he argues that from time to time we must replace the old with the new "lest one good custom should corrupt the world." In architecture, we need never fear that any particular school of thought will prevail for long; whether or not it is a case of the profession observing aesthetic principles, it is certainly the case that in a single lifetime an architect may find himself passing through half a dozen differing styles, each of which he embraces in good faith, or at the least without overt hypocrisy. (In our time, one thinks at once of Philip Johnson, leaping with such incomparable agility from Mies to Postmodern and then on — perhaps tomorrow? — into the gravityless moonscape of Deconstructivism; in his day, Stanford White leapt with an equal lack of embarrassment from brown-shingled Queen Anne houses to houses neo-Colonial, neo-Venetian, and neo-French Renaissance.)

Of the several types of structures that have been accustomed to dominate our Main Streets, one or two in recent years have come close to being rendered technologically obsolete. Firehouses and railroad stations have lost much of their prominence as architectural icons, in the case of firehouses because we require fewer of them (thanks to strict fire laws, cities are far less readily combustible than they used to be) and because the structures that house them have grown smaller in scale as the efficiency of firefighting equipment has improved — for example, we no longer build towers for the drying of fire-hoses, since contemporary hoses are made of plastic instead of canvas and do not rot from being wet. As for railroad stations, they are no longer our chief means of transportation from city to city and are therefore no longer relevant as symbols; even when the stations are still in use, we tend to diminish their psychological importance to us by shunting their natural functions away into odd corners and renting out their original grand spaces for profit-making retail purposes. In such cities as Baltimore, St. Louis, Chicago, and Los Angeles, the railroad station tower that one saw rising above neighboring rooftops bore an enormous clock-face on each of its four sides (in the nineteenth century, wristwatches being non-existent and pocket watches a luxury, public clocks were a precious urban amenity). Again and again it has happened that the clocks have ceased to tell time, and the failure to perform this function becomes a sort of secondary symbol, sadly calling attention to the failure of the primary one.

The other three types of dominant structures remain robustly themselves in their natures, though not, following the Tennysonian edict, in their styles. The façades of the courthouses designed and built in recent years are far less convincingly symbolic of their age-old task of administering justice than the austerely bepillared Greek and Roman temples in granite and marble whose vogue was largely halted by the financial catastrophe of the Great Depression. Both structurally and symbolically, our courthouses today lack the awesomeness of their predecessors; partly but not wholly for budgetary reasons, they have come to resemble conventional corporate office buildings, where a vast amount of litigation, civil and criminal, must be confronted and got through. Lofty abstractions of the kind once carved on courthouse walls ("Equal justice under law" and the like) have given way to an ever more hasty and stressful manufacture of "product," which as it increases in amount decreases in quality.

Houses of worship continue to be built — at the moment, economists class organized religion as a growth industry — and not only for Catholic, Protestant, and Jewish congregations. (As I write, the first Moslem mosque ever to rise in New York City is under construction on a valuable corner site in upper Manhattan.) Architects struggle to invent novel variations on designs that have been more or less stable for many hundreds of years; whether for good or ill from an aesthetic point of view, the degree of approval with which these variations are received by the communities in which they are set down is nearly always in proportion to their lack of novelty. This is perhaps a consequence of the fact that as physical entities houses of worship must express to a greater extent than either courthouses or banks an immediately identifiable symbolic value. Architects are not inclined to tamper rashly with a structure that many of their fellow-citizens believe to be sheltering not merely representations of God but God Himself.

I mentioned banks first in my list of the generic types that have dominated the architecture of our towns and cities and yet I arrive last at discussing them. The fact is that, like the celebrated bank robber Willie Sutton, I am irresistibly attracted to these institutions, but some inbred caution prompts me to approach them by stealth. Be that as it may, it is certainly the case that in recent years banks have enjoyed a greater freedom than either courthouses or churches to modify and sometimes even to abandon altogether their traditional forms. For obvious commercial reasons, they have wished to remain conspicuous, and novelty, whether in respect to the design of new buildings or in respect to the remodeling of old ones, is an obvious way to accomplish that goal. Moreover, since innovation in their banking practices is one of the things that banks constantly boast of in their advertising, it is only natural for innovation in all aspects of banking to put on the dignity of a principle — the very principle enunciated by Tennyson, though few bankers and still fewer advertising agencies are likely to be familiar with His Lordship's lapidary words.

How radically banks have altered their so-called public image during the past fifty or sixty years can be measured by a similarly radical alteration in the appearance of their premises. As late as the 1920s, although banks flirted with those cosmetic changes in style dictated by fashion, essentially they continued to depend upon the architectural symbolism employed in the eighteenth century by Sir John Soane in England and in America a few decades later by Benjamin Latrobe, William Strickland, and others. The intention of this symbolism, which drew mostly upon ancient Greek and Roman sources, was above all to convey a sense of security, for until the New Deal of the 1930s such governmental safeguards as the Federal Deposit Insurance Corporation didn't exist; even in prosperous times, and of course especially in hard times, banks would fail and people's savings would be wiped out. This unfortunate possibility had to be disguised, if not expunged, by what amounted to cunning stagecraft. Whether a given bank was sound or unsound, it took care to put up what was literally a good front—a façade that, whatever happened to lie behind it, proclaimed an impregnable fiscal integrity.

As anyone studying the photographs in this book will observe, our Greek and Roman architectural heritage was employed until fairly recent times to intimidate us and, at the same time, to reassure us. Whether we approached a bank in order to deposit money or to borrow it, we were made to feel humbly grateful—indeed, that we were allowed to cross the threshold of the arcanum at all was in itself a reason for congratulation. Passing between majestic stone pillars and then through mighty gilded bronze portals, we would find ourselves at last inside a lofty chamber, vaulted and domed, floored and wainscotted in marble, and ringed round with tiny altars, each of which was set within a cage of slender, protective bars and presided over by a resident priest, usually male and usually wearing a habit of dark blue serge. How lucky we were to be there! In an awed whisper, we would make our wants known and then hope for the best.

By the time a studious turner of pages has reached the end of this book, he will have observed the carrying out of at least two revolutions. In the first revolution, the bank as a temple, whether in classical, Romanesque, or other dress, gives way by the middle of this century to the bank as a seraglio, wearing as little dress as possible and bedecked with flowering plants; instead of having its privacy preserved by thick walls of granite, this saucy new sort of bank invites the world to assume the role of voyeur, peering through great sheets of glass at whatever activities may be taking place inside. The grim Puritan conviction that financial transactions are a serious matter, not to be entered into lightly or ill-advisedly, has yielded to a conviction—no, not so much as a conviction but, rather, a vague, unreasoned, contented impression—that if something should ever go wrong in respect to local, national, or international monetary matters, somebody somewhere would surely set it right.

One of the earliest, as well as probably the most famous, of these seraglios was the Manufacturers Trust Company building, erected in 1954 on the corner of Fifth Avenue and West Forty-third Street, in New York City. What a bewitching shocker it was, especially to those of us who had long given our patronage to a bank that stood a block further up Fifth Avenue and that for several generations had been satisfied to do business in a remodeled brownstone mansion of no very great size. (Set in the basement floor of the bank was a heavy iron grating; I used to kneel and put my ear to the grating and hear in a stone-paved tunnel far below the gurgling of one of the long-buried streams of Manhattan.) The new bank, with its voluptuous masses of flowers, an abstract sculpture by Harry Bertoia, and an airy absence of tellers' cages, was an immediate success. The bank appeared to be beckoning suggestively to passersby to come in and borrow money and in the passersby came, not awestruck and humble as in times past but eager to be caressed and seduced.

The Manufacturers Trust Company building helped to usher in a revolution that seemed at the time certain to have lasting consequences. Not so, for of course there is no such thing as a lasting consequence, and in the past decade or so we have witnessed the birth of a new revolution, more subtle but no less violent than its predecessor. In the style that bears the slovenly name of Postmodern, banks have abandoned the voluptuous seductiveness of the seraglio in favor of a return to grandeur. But Postmodern grandeur is only a pastiche of the real thing; in example after example, it is nearly always an inferior work mocking a superior one in the name of paying it homage. The preposterous exaggeration of the scale on which it is designed and the over-ripe richness of the materials employed in its construction parody — and display what may well be an unconscious contempt for — the original upon which it is based.

To my mind, the parodistic nature of the new grandeur is bound to have its effect upon the ordinary bank customer, who will have passed willingly enough from being cowed and grateful to being showered with embraces and who now glances about him with a certain arrogance as he crosses an eight-story-high main banking floor and thinks to himself, "H-m-m! Not bad at all!" But alas for the bank that believes it has won his loyalty! For this spoiled and willful creature recalls that the bank under construction across the street will boast an *eighteen*-story-high atrium and, as a weekly door prize, a white Cadillac Coupe De Ville convertible. He can scarcely wait to make the switch.

In our latest bank buildings, the symbols of the profession of banking as it used to be practiced have been rendered obsolete; nevertheless, the actual physical presence of banks in the hearts of our cities is more dominating than ever. They greatly overshadow their former companions — the churches, courthouses, railroad stations, and firehouses of an earlier time — and this is in part because, with few exceptions, they are no longer freestanding, self-contained structures but a portion — in most cases, a very large portion — of immense skyscraping office towers. One always expected to encounter bank buildings on a gigantic scale in New York City, Chicago, and our other metropolises; today one finds them as well in such comparatively small cities as Hartford, Milwaukee, and Des Moines.

Gigantism is a malady that our bankers appear to regard as a sign of health. They are not alone among businessmen in arriving at this peculiar judgment, and I mustn't make too much of it as a contemporary phenomenon. It was suggested at the start of this essay that our ancestors made a practice of putting up buildings far bigger than they had need for; the egotism that caused them to do so came to seem, with the passing of years and the expansion of commerce, an act of simple prudence. By a similar stroke of good fortune, what I currently perceive to be architectural follies may one day be hailed as manifesting exceptional foresight on the part of their designers and builders. Nor do I fear being found wrong *by* history:

on the minefield of prediction I have been blown up not once but many times.

The banks whose likenesses we possess in this book can be read in many ways, and not least as if they were novels instead of structures of stone, steel, and glass. Plots benign and sinister promise to unfold as we gaze upon the superb photographs gathered here; behind the pillars, the high windows, the big doors, how many private melodramas have taken place and will no doubt continue to take place! Led on from page to page, we wait for the pictured walls to speak. For bending foward and listening hard, we hear, do we not, something more interesting to us than the chink of coins, the hushed rustle of dollar bills?

MEN AND MONEY: REFLECTIONS BY A SOCIOLOGIST

Robert Nisbet

"You can tell what's informing a society by what the tallest building is," the late scholar Joseph Campbell said in a television interview with Bill Moyers. "When you approach a medieval town, the cathedral is the tallest thing in the place. When you approach an eighteenth-century town, it is the political palace that's the tallest thing in the place. And when you approach a modern city, the tallest places are the office buildings, the centers of economic life."

Architecture, whether of banks or churches or of great houses and public buildings, has always had a pioneering role in the history of culture and civilization. It was the rise of the Gothic style in church architecture in the early twelfth century that proved to be the vanguard of the immense revival of the thirteenth century. As Henry Adams wrote, the ribbed vaults, pointed spires, and flying buttresses served as a very metaphor for theologians, philosophers, and scientists. A few hundred years after the Gothic era, landscape architecture in England ushered in, with its romantic revolt against the geometric, classical gardens of the seventeenth century, the whole Romantic Age in modern literature.

The social scientists Nathan Glazer and Mark Lilla, in their introduction to *The Public Face of Architecture,* have this to say: "Architecture, by its very nature, is a public matter. Whenever we consider buildings in their aesthetic, economic, or moral dimensions, we must be prepared, at the same time, to treat those dimensions in public terms: to see that buildings can also serve as public art, or as civic monuments, or as contributions to the social life of the city." Glazer and Lilla conclude that, although all architecture is created for "consumption" by its owners, the primary purpose of much architecture is to speak to the broad range of "anonymous public that walks or drives by the façade, crosses the building lobby, or waits in the doctor's office."

Bank architecture sits intentionally within this definition. Banks have a special character that sets them apart in our society. They cross the boundaries between privately owned business and public service, operating as custodians of other people's money. Created by private capital to serve a pragmatic function for its owners, bank architecture at the same time turns a public face to its community in a vigorous attempt to communicate, persuade, assure, impress, and convince.

In establishing their status in the community, banks are free to indulge in architectural statements of their choosing. Seeing what values banks choose to visualize gives us an idea of which values society holds in priority. Contemporary attitudes regarding money, respectability, security, and corporate aesthetics are reflected. Banks, particularly central offices, occupy places of great importance in our cities. They are often the tallest buildings anchoring the urban skyline, and they overshadow churches and government buildings as the most eyecatching structures. Bank architecture thus communicates the importance of banks as institutions, assuring us of their stability, prosperity, and permanence and inviting us inside to do business.

Against this backdrop of architecture as message, one sees at the Place d'Armes in Montreal a telling juxtaposition: on one side the Church of Notre Dame, across from it the Bank of Montreal. Each building conveys a message about the social forces that underlie it. The church institutionalizes a religion; the bank institutionalizes the concept of the banker as a high priest of finance.

What the two buildings have in common is a dependence on faith. Without the faith of communicants on the one hand and depositors on the other, neither church nor bank will endure. Not the strongest of sacraments or the most durable of reserves will sustain churches and banks against the erosive effects of skepticism and disbelief. Indeed, it was loss of faith that led to the Protestant Reformation in the sixteenth century—loss of faith in the Roman Church that had before been one with the whole of Western civilization. And it was loss of faith that led to the epidemic of bank failures at the beginning of the Great Depression in 1931. When I taught Western European history, I took some pleasure each year in likening the Reformation to a run on a vast bank, a panic engendered by loss of trust in spiritual reserves.

Banks are about money as churches are about divinity. Money is never an isolated phenomenon, any more than human perceptions of the divine are. Even in purely economic terms, money—however covetable in its own right—is inseparable from its role as denominator of competing values in the social order. It is as denominator that we know money best. By its nature money is the resolver of the problems instigated by competing goods—bushels of wheat and works of art, for example. Money translates qualitative differences into simple variations of quantity.

Money is one of the primary forces behind the rise of civilization, in ancient Egypt as well as contemporary Africa. Money's specific importance to the release of the currents that mark the rise of civilization in an area is of course its role as denominator among qualitatively different goods. Money is the lubricant of commerce and trade. But money's importance to civilization goes further. It falls among the varied means of human exchange that are crucial to the growth of the mind in the individual and to cultural interactions in the social order.

But the importance of money transcends the economic sphere. It must be seen as a part of the large world of symbolism that exists in any civilization. As the French historian Fernand Braudel wrote: "Money everywhere contrives to insert itself into all economic and social relationships. This makes it an excellent indicator: [through it] a fairly accurate assessment can be made of all human activity, even the most humble."

The human activities reflected by the function of banks change slowly over time as societies change. In the earliest years of North American banks, the societies of the U.S. and Canada were predominantly agrarian. Bray Hammond described the situation in his book, *Banks and Politics in America from the Revolution to the Civil War:* "When the first American bank was established, at the end of the Revolutionary War, the American business world was engaged almost wholly in the export and import trade and in domestic merchandising. It was a well-to-do, intelligent, compact, energetic, and influential minority, comprising maybe a tenth of the population. The great majority was agrarian. Alexander Hamilton was spokesman of the one, Thomas Jefferson of the other.

"Eighty years later, at the beginning of the Civil War, the business world had steam and credit at its command. . . . Business was no longer a matter of dealing in merchandise almost wholly, but a matter of manufacturing innumerable kinds of things by new processes incomparably more productive than the old; it was a matter of railway and steamship transport, of mining, of the telegraph, of power printing, of banking, insurance, brokerage, and investments."

In the early years, banks — of which there were few — had nothing like the influence or prestige of the modern bank. Their position reflected the dominant agrarian view that people should be frugal and avoid debt. Benjamin Franklin, in his *Way to Wealth,* embodied the concept in an aphorism: "He that goes a-borrowing goes a-sorrowing." Hamilton expressed the opposing view: "Most commercial nations have found it necessary to institute banks; and they have proved to be the happiest engines that ever were invented for advancing trade."

Throughout the eighteenth century and into the nineteenth the two points of view contended. Business enterprise championed banks because they provide the credit that is crucial to enterprise. Agrarians were hostile or wary, believing (in the words of John Taylor) that "banking in its best view is only a fraud whereby labour suffers the imposition of paying an interest on the circulating medium." Hammond again: "Enterprise won, it got banks by the thousand, and it devoted Americans to dollars." By the middle of the nineteenth century, banks had attained the position they occupied until well into the twentieth century as financiers of the burgeoning economy and seats of might. Their imposing architecture reflected their influence and prestige.

The two world wars of the twentieth century brought about profound changes in society. Woodrow Wilson began the transformation chiefly within the context provided by World War I. But it was by no means the war alone that spurred him to his work of centralizing political power. He was an ardent prophet of the state. From him supremely came the politicization, the centralization, and the commitment to bureaucracy of American society during the years since the U.S. entered the war in 1917.

Wilson only began this evolution, and what he did was chiefly apparent during the two years the U.S. was at war with Germany. But the wartime powers assumed by the national government proved to be durable seeds. By 1939 Wilsonian centralization and collectivization were, under Franklin Roosevelt, as pervasive as they had been during the Great War. Ever since, there has been a unitary, unilinear pattern of development to be seen, only rarely punctuated by sign of reversal, that has centralization of government as its embedded goal.

There is, however, another side to this trend. Repeatedly in history the combination of war and political centralization has led to a fraying effect upon the social fabric. Threads are loosened by the tightening of power at the center. Dr. Johnson once told Boswell of a man he knew who "hung loose upon society." Loose in the sense of the loose cannon, the ship that slips its hawser, the dog its leash, the individual his accustomed moral restraints.

Without doubt there are a great many loose individuals in American society today — loose from marriage and the family, from the school, the church, the nation, job and moral responsibility. What sociologists are prone to call social disintegration is really nothing more than the spectacle of a rising number of individuals playing fast and loose with other individuals in relationships of trust and responsibility.

As Alexis de Tocqueville saw it, in such a situation money becomes the common denominator of human life. It acquires an "extreme mobility," and "everybody is feverishly intent on making money. . . . Love of gain, a fondness for business careers, the desire to get rich at all costs . . . quickly become ruling passions under a despotic government." Government is the primary force in it all. Such government weakens where it strengthens: weakens normal social authority as it strengthens itself through laws, prohibitions, and taxes.

Others, however, including Edmund Burke and Thomas Carlyle, have made the economic factor central in the process of loosening ties and multiplying loose individuals. It was the vast debt of France, Burke insisted, that formed the background against which "a great monied interest had insensibly grown up, and with it, a great power. . . . The monied power was long looked on with rather an evil eye by the people. They saw it connected with their distresses, and aggravating them." Carlyle, responding to what seemed to him a "spiritual emptiness" of his age, cited the "cash nexus" as the main force. Cash payment, he wrote, "is the sole nexus between man and man."

The loose individual is a familiar figure in our age. The economy, among many other components of society, is rich in such figures. I take "economy" in its large sense to include in our day evangelists of the television ministries, who alone form an economic system of profit and loss running into the billions; the baseball, football, and basketball stars; the university — once as noneconomic in function as a monastery, but no longer — and the now-thick crowd of former public officials who, whether in lecture fee, corporate directorship, book authorship, or consulting business, demonstrate how often and quickly the revolving door turns.

It is also interesting to look at the economy proper, site of property and profit in the old sense. Some fifty years ago the distinguished Harvard economist Joseph Schumpeter, in his *Capitalism, Socialism and Democracy,* laid out clearly the essential processes leading to the business and financial scene of the present. Schumpeter referred to an evaporation of property: more particularly, an "Evaporation of Industrial Property" and an "Evaporation of Consumer Property," both reflecting a historical trend of tidal proportions that had been going on in the West and especially in America over the past century.

The effect of the evaporation of industrial property—looking at the matter solely from the property-holder's viewpoint—was the substitution of the "soft" property of shares of stocks and bonds for the "hard" property of land, buildings, and machines that the property-holder had once managed as well as owned and had been very much a part of in its operation. Independently of volition such a property-holder had a distinct stake in society, a role of social responsibility based on day-to-day mingling with managers, workers, and consumers.

Very different is the "evaporated" property owner, typically possessing shares of stock existing in their own seemingly detached, stock-market world, independent of their owner's will beyond the buying and selling of the shares. There is far less stake in society in this kind of property. After all, a single safe-deposit box can hold many millions of dollars of property, the whole requiring little of the attention and responsibility that are mandatory when property exists in the forms of land, buildings and machinery. An atmosphere of not only impersonality but also irresponsibility is encouraged by evaporated property.

It is evident that as a result of the two evaporations, we have the foundation prepared for a very different kind of capitalism from that of a century ago. More and more, capitalism tends to exalt the monetary unit over the type of property that theoretically alone gives the monetary unit its value.

The evaporation of property Schumpeter describes had its effective beginning in World War I in America. In ways they had never known before, the war introduced Americans to money and the ease of its creation. The decision by Wilson to finance the war by bonds rather than taxes had a measurable effect on the American mind. For the great majority until then such matters as stocks, bonds, and other debentures were arcane in the highest degree. One made money as one's father and grandfather had, by saving and investing in hard, tangible property. There was never a great deal of cash around in the economy, and credit was for most Americans something to be avoided like the plague. Jobs were hard to get, and when one got one, one stayed with it to the end. Land, rural or urban, was clutched by its owners as though life depended on it. It was the supreme form of capital. One lived off one's capital through interest and rent, and only fools dipped into their capital.

The vast excitement of 1917–1919 changed or began the change in this style of living. Of a sudden, spendable money increased immensely as the result of almost total employment, generally at high wages. Profits were generous too.

These were, of course, people whose immediate thought was to spend war-made money to buy the kind of property—industrial or consumer or both—their fathers had known, to save and to invest in growth industries. But there were others who, beginning in the 1920s, made it evident that the old style of business, finance, and living was not for them. The result was a substantial contribution to what became known as the "Roaring Twenties," a decade of escalating stock-market values such as the world had never seen and of the birth of dreams in which the old-fashioned ways of making money—hard work, saving, investment, production of needed and wanted goods—were scattered to the past, with the new ways of slickly managed buyouts, mergers, inside deals, and the like taking over.

The Depression and New Deal reform stopped, but did not kill, the new ways of making money.

World War II did exactly what the first world war had done, but on an immensely greater scale. And the postwar years proved to be a period of business and financial expansion without precedent. No real depression interrupted things this time. Schumpeter's principles of evaporation of property — of conversion of the hard to the soft, of tangible ownership and management of plant to parcels of highly negotiable shares, of commodity to service, and, withal, an ever-growing financial liquidity, with oceans of cash and instant credit lying around for quick use — all these new forces moved like a single great avalanche across the financial terrain.

In such circumstances the loose individual flourishes. In an epoch of high liquidity, incessant turnover of shares, and fast-moving takeovers, mobility on the part of the operator is imperative. Looseness of economic muscle is indispensable. "Conservative" was once an accolade to a bank or a brokerage house. Today it is anathema.

George Bernard Shaw seemed to have something of the sort in mind when he wrote, in his preface to the play *Major Barbara:* "The universal regard for money is the one hopeful fact in our civilization. . . . The two things [money and life] are inseparable: money is the counter that enables life to be distributed socially." Shaw was far from being a capitalist; he was at heart something of a permanent revolutionist. He knew that money has been historically one of the surest solvents of immemorially old barriers to individual advancement such as kinship, ethnicity, religion, and social class.

Money puts a high premium on elites, which are the modern successor to historic social classes. In an elite there is no nonsense about ancestry, honor, family, and the like. Elites rest on two things: individual talents and quick rewards in money. Our society is full of elites: artists, writers, musicians, professional athletic stars, Nobel Prize winners, National Academy scientists, bankers, chief executive officers of corporations, politicians, and so on and on. Inevitably we measure the cultural affluence of a given society by its richness in elites.

There is a further point to stress here, albeit all too briefly: the role of the modern state with respect to banks (as well as such other quasi-public institutions as churches, universities, and trade unions). I refer to the pulverizing effect the modern state has had on all major groups intermediate to the individual and the state. In its grasp for power the state reacts jealously to all bodies, like the church and the bank, whose authority springs from the social allegiances of their members — communicants and depositors.

Closely allied to the state's drive toward centralization of power is the thrust in modern Western history toward individualism. A functional relation has existed between centralization of power and individualization of society. As the state expanded its power, the authorities of the component groups of the traditional social order weakened, and in their weakening the social fabric opened up, as it were, with individuals taking a more and more prominent place. In turn, as individualist currents made their way against the corporate unities of religion, the economy, and the culture, the expansion of the sovereign state was made easier.

In closing, there is one more aspect of money, somewhat somber perhaps, that deserves to be mentioned. I have pointed to the signal influence of money in the rise of modern individualism. But the detachment of individuals from classes and castes that lies behind the rise of individualism can yield up states of alienation as well as freedom. They are two sides of the same coin. We regularly celebrate the Free Individual in our national ceremonies, but moralists are beginning to be equally aware of the alienated, loose individual. The cash nexus invariable encourages some degree of loosening of social ties. "Though in Holy Wedlock he and she go, Each maintains a separate ego," wrote a somewhat jaundiced observer of the social scene years ago. The sports fan loves teams but increasingly gets free agents. "Have grant, will travel" is the motto of more and more professors in the universities. And nowhere are money and its glitter more vivid to the eye than in the cathedrals of the televangelists.

History is cyclical. It is very likely that we in the Western world are at present in the phase of undue monetarization of the social order, of the liquidity and mobility of relationships that are chiefly governed by money. If so, it is more than likely, on the basis of past experience, that historical forces—perhaps inscrutable—are already at corrective work. But who knows? It is, in any event, notable that while we seek to reduce the influence of money on human values and relationships, to diminish the role of the Loose Individual on Wall Street and Main Street, across the world Mikhail Gorbachev is seeking almost desperately through perestroika to instill monetary values in the marketplace in order to end the tyranny of bureaucracy.

A CRITICAL LOOK
AT BANK ARCHITECTURE

Susan Wagg

·1·

AMERICAN BANKS

FEDERAL PERIOD
THROUGH
THE GREEK REVIVAL

It was the Revolutionary War that precipitated the founding in Philadelphia of the continent's first bank in the modern sense — the Bank of North America, established in 1781 by the Congress of the Confederation to help finance the war.[1] The success and prominence of this bank, which had a national monopoly during the war, stimulated the founding of others. By 1790 a bank was operating or being organized in Philadelphia, New York, Boston, and Baltimore. Two of these still survive: the Bank of New York, founded by Alexander Hamilton, and the Massachusetts Bank, which was absorbed early in this century by the First National Bank of Boston. By 1800 banking had spread to the main commercial centers of the South, to the smaller northern seacoast cities, and to trading centers as far inland as Albany. By 1820 there were over three hundred.[2]

The founders of these pioneer American banks were men of high social standing, the young country's leaders, mainly wealthy merchants and some lawyers who had organized supplies and financing for the war. With the winning of independence, they directed their energies and talents to developing the new nation, an enterprise which required a regular supply of money and credit. For this they established banks to make short-term commercial loans, serve as safe places of deposit for merchants' funds, and provide the country with paper money in the form of bank notes and other types of bank liabilities. Lending in these early days was the responsibility of the bank directors, who advanced credit to other local merchants. A room where the directors could meet to vote for or against each loan or discount — as often as twice weekly — was one of the requisites in the buildings designed to house the early banks. Frequently living accommodations were provided on the premises for the cashier, who soon evolved into the chief administrator of the bank.

The initial American banks enjoyed a status well above that of other contemporary businesses. In contrast to the pattern in Great Britain and Europe, where for centuries banking had been in private hands, the first American banks were corporations, chartered by federal or state governments.[3] Although managed by groups of individuals, they were enhanced as well as bound by governmental authority and rapidly became the most important and successful of the country's eighteenth-century business corporations. For the public, banks assumed an aura of mystery in the way they created money: "For each dollar paid in by the stockholders, the banks lent two, three, four, or five."[4] Banking was something of a mystery even to the early bankers themselves. The Boston merchants who set up the Massachusetts Bank in 1784 wrote for advice to Thomas Willing, first president of the Bank of North America. He replied, "When the bank was first opened here, the business was as much a novelty to us . . . as it can possibly be to you. It was a pathless wilderness, ground but little known to this side of the Atlantick."[5]

Similarly, when it came to designing appropriate buildings for these new and influential enterprises, American bankers and their architects or builders had few European precedents to guide them. In eighteenth-century England commerce still lacked social prestige, and only toward the end of the Georgian period did businesses begin to commission architects of note. Even then, banks did not immediately emerge as distinctive structures; for since the days of the great Florentine merchant-bankers, banking had taken place in the residence of the banker, and bank architecture in England continued to exhibit a domestic character into the early Victorian period. The Bank of England, that country's mighty public bank, which served as a model for early American banking practice, had begun as a private company. The first buildings constructed for it in the early 1730s resembled two grand Palladian houses, one wholly given over to its banking hall.[6] The monumental rebuilding, which resulted in one of Europe's architectural masterpieces, was commenced by Sir John Soane in 1788 and progressed only slowly and haphazardly through the 1820s, exerting influence initially as a series of awe-inspiring interiors.

Before the Revolution the designing of buildings in North America was undertaken by local carpenters and craftsmen or by gentlemen amateurs, all increasingly influenced by architectural books published in England, which propagated the Renaissance classicism of Italy. By the time the first banks were built, at the very end of the eighteenth century, classicism was the common architectural language in the land.

Founded during wartime, the Bank of North America had simply opened for business in the cashier's store on Philadelphia's Chestnut Street in 1782 and did not start its own building until 1847.[7] The directors of other early banks, however, were clearly eager to project an impressive architectural image and began to patronize the most talented professional architects at a time when such individuals were rare in the United States. The country's two leading early architects, Charles Bulfinch and Benjamin Henry Latrobe, both received bank commissions. Bulfinch is known to have designed seven banks during his career, all in Massachusetts;[8] Latrobe was responsible for three, including the preeminent masterpiece of early bank architecture, the Bank of Pennsylvania [4], unfortunately now demolished. Two still exist: Bulfinch's Essex Bank in Salem, dating from

1811, and Latrobe's State Bank of Louisiana in New Orleans, designed in 1820; neither is now used as a bank.

With little to guide them, pioneer bank designers took their cue from the unusual private-public nature of these New World enterprises. Some early banks thus resembled fine houses familiar to their wealthy directors, while others projected a more deliberate public image. An interesting parallel can be found in the choice of bank presidents during this initial phase. They "were either men who had attained a high rank in public life and therefore enjoyed public confidence, or they were merchants. In the former case the semipublic status of the banks was stressed; in the latter their character as business enterprises." [9]

Two beautifully maintained banks dating from the Federal period, one in Charleston, the other in Nantucket, are fine examples of the more domestic type of design, their forms derived from high-style houses modified to accommodate banking functions.

[1] *Bank of South Carolina*

Citizens and Southern National Bank of South Carolina
(Trust Department)
50 Broad Street, Charleston, South Carolina
Architect unknown

Founded: 1792
Chartered: 1801 (defunct)
Constructed: 1797–98

This is the oldest purpose-built bank in the United States which still serves a banking institution. Occupied from 1835 to 1966 by the Charleston Library Society and subsequently by the Charleston Chamber of Commerce, it was restored in 1966 by the Citizens and Southern National Bank of South Carolina and currently houses that bank's trust department.

When the Bank of South Carolina was founded in 1792, the great southern trading port of Charleston was also the country's major slave port, the fourth-largest and perhaps the most elegant city in North America.[10] The bank was organized by a group of local citizens just as the state's first bank, a branch of the federally chartered Bank of the United States, was getting underway. These were to be the only full-fledged banking institutions in the state during the decade. In 1801 the Bank of South Carolina became the first bank to be incorporated by the state.[11]

At the time the directors announced plans for constructing a banking house in 1797, the bank had been doing business on Broad Street under the residence of its cashier, Mr. Bacot.[12] Purchasing land on the same street, the conservative directors used as their model that traditional British symbol of wealth and power, the private palace. However, it was not to the palatial country seat that the Carolinians turned for inspiration, but to the town mansion; for unlike the English or even their own compatriots in Virginia, these southerners looked upon their country estates as sources of funds to support their Charleston houses.[13] The design of the Bank of South Carolina thus recalls one of the most splendid town houses in eighteenth-century America, the Georgian Palladian villa in Charleston commenced in 1765 by the colonial slave merchant Miles Brewton. Like the Brewton House the bank is a two-story red brick building with a hipped roof. In the commercial building, however, a slightly projecting, gabled three-bay centerpiece takes the place of the combustible two-tiered, partly wooden portico that graces the house, and fireproof limestone trim is used to provide contrast with the brick.[14] The plan is expanded from a typical domestic rectangle to a T-shape, with the unusual structural modification of a vaulted basement for protection against fire and theft. Indeed, in 1803 two unsuccessful robbers spent three months underground in an attempt to tunnel into the vault. The building's 30-inch-thick walls above ground have withstood bombardment during the Civil War, the earthquake of 1886, and numerous hurricanes.

The restored banking room, now used as a reception room, contains the original carved woodwork and black-and-white marble floor, although the stained glass in the fanlight is a Victorian addition. Reflecting the skilled but conservative craftsmanship which flourished in Charleston at the time, the interior does exhibit one reminder of the new order which had come to pass: two American eagles carved on the imposts of the interior arch of the main doorway. The work of unidentified local masons and craftsmen, this very early bank represents the continuation of an acclimated, high-style Georgian Palladianism updated with newer Federal detailing in the fanlighted door, the pediment, and the keystone lintels. It is the older English colonial tradition, however, that dominates.[15]

[2] ## *Nantucket Pacific Bank*

Pacific National Bank of Nantucket
51 Main Street, Nantucket, Massachusetts
Architect unknown

Chartered: 1804
Constructed: 1818

While aristocratic southern Charleston, the wealthiest city in colonial America, began to decline in the post-Revolutionary period, the towns of enterprising, commerce-minded Yankees prospered. Nantucket, a 57-square-mile island about 25 miles southeast of Cape Cod, had during the eighteenth century built up a whaling industry. The period after the Revolution and through the first half of the nineteenth century was the time of Nantucket's greatest prosperity. The Nantucket Pacific Bank was the second banking institution to be launched on the island, established and incorporated in 1804, by which time Nantucket had become the greatest whaling port in the world. The name of the bank identified the current source of the island's wealth; for Nantucketers had, in 1791, rounded Cape Horn and opened up the vast whaling resources of the Pacific. Renamed the Pacific National Bank in 1865, the institution continues to operate in the structure which was erected to house it in 1818. Before then, like the Bank of South Carolina, the Nantucket bank had previously conducted business in the house of the cashier.[16]

When completed the Nantucket Pacific Bank building was an architectural pacesetter, the "handsomest and most sophisticated of early nineteenth-century buildings in Nantucket."[17] During the preceding century, the island had developed into a Quaker stronghold where ostentation was frowned upon. The architecture of eighteenth-century Nantucket is thus exceptionally plain and unassuming. After the War of 1812, however, the whaling industry expanded and profits soared; whaling ceased being a communal enterprise and developed into a notoriously brutal business. As the wealth of Nantucketers increased in the early nineteenth century, the moral control exerted by the Quakers declined. By 1830 the formerly ascetic community had become the third largest town in Massachusetts, its principal streets lined with beautiful Federal and Greek Revival houses, many built of customary wood but a number constructed of more expensive imported bricks.

The bank building was a forerunner of the town's splendid Federal mansions. The Federal style, first established by wealthy merchants along the New England seaboard, was a development and refinement of the preceding colonial Georgian style, being a lighter, more elegant form of classicism. It drew on contemporary European trends, in particular the work of the Adam brothers in Britain, and was the dominant style of the new United States from about 1780 to 1820. Federal houses, which the bank resembles, were generally square or rectangular, brick or frame, three stories high—the bank has only two—and crowned by a low hipped roof. The elegance of the style lies in the beautifully scaled and articulated detailing, with exterior decoration concentrated primarily on the main entrance. The bank's wooden portico is typical, a graceful semicircular version with two slender Ionic columns. The curved forms of this portico are repeated in the flaring staircase with wrought-iron railings that leads up to it, in the blind arches of the main floor of the three-bay façade, and in the segmental-headed windows of the second story. The bank is, in architectural historian Clay Lancaster's opinion, "the finest example of pure Federal-style architecture in Nantucket." [18]

Occupying the most commanding site overlooking Market Square, the new building was designed to be as fireproof as it was fashionable. It is built of red brick laid in Flemish bond on granite foundations. The staircase and the trim—the blind arches and recessed panels into which the door and windows are set, the keystone lintels of the upper floor, and the two belt courses—are all of brownstone. Slate covers the roof.[19] Wood was used on the exterior solely for the portico, the door and window frames, and the cornice, which assumed the present heavy bracketed form around the time of the Civil War.[20]

The Nantucket Pacific Bank has survived the demise of the whaling industry and two major fires in 1836 and 1846, the brick of its walls helping to stop the flames of the latter fire, which leveled most of the commercial area. At this time the width of Market Square was increased as a fire-resisting measure, which gave the bank increased prominence. The buildings fronting on upper Main Street, following the example of the bank, were rebuilt mostly of fireproof brick with brownstone trim and slate roofs.

Perhaps no other bank in history can claim to be the site of the discovery of a comet, an occurrence which took place in 1847 just after the second fire. The astronomer was Maria Mitchell, daughter of the cashier of the bank, who lived with his family on the upper floor. Maria's discovery from her rooftop observatory made her world famous.

[3]   *First Bank of the United States*
120 South Third Street, Philadelphia, Pennsylvania
Samuel Blodget, Jr.

Chartered: 1791 (defunct)
Constructed: 1795–97

While the earliest commercial banks exerted enormous local influence, the most powerful bank in the young Republic was the Bank of the United States, established in 1791 by the new federal government. Three commercial banks were active when the Constitutional Convention met in 1787, and a majority of delegates were friendly to banks; but these poorly understood yet obviously powerful institutions provoked divisions and controversy that endure to this day. So strong was the opposition that the convention rejected a proposal to give Congress the power to charter financial corporations. However, Alexander Hamilton, the first secretary of the treasury, felt it essential to establish a national bank to give the new government a means of handling its financial needs, of assisting the country's economic growth, and of bringing order to banking. In Hamilton's opinion, the very survival of the nation, composed as it was of thirteen jealous, combative, and fiercely independent states, depended on the creation of a stable banking system. Thomas Jefferson and James Madison, two of the most violent opponents of the banks, strongly disagreed. These equally dedicated statesmen distrusted banks, and that mysterious entity, credit, and were fearful of excessive power accruing to the federal government.

Eighteenth-century America was agrarian. Benjamin Franklin conjectured after the Revolution that for one artisan or merchant there were at least a hundred farmers, a population which was sustained by ideals of frugality and avoidance of debt.[21] To these Americans, banks — run by and serving the wealthy — were anathema in a nation founded on democratic principles, with a system of government created to forestall the concentrations of power and privilege that were a despised feature of the Old World. Yet Hamilton won his battle to establish a federal bank in the first major test of the American Constitution, the debate concerning the authority of Congress to charter his proposed bank. Bray Hammond, the great historian of American banking, has observed: "Alexander Hamilton prepared America for an imperial future of wealth and power, mechanized beyond the handicraft stage of his day, and amply provided with credit to that end. Thomas Jefferson represented the yeomanry and designed for America a future of competence and simplicity, agrarian, and without the enticing subtleties of credit."[22]

The Act incorporating the first Bank of the United States was signed into law in 1791. Patterned by Hamilton on the long-established Bank of England, this bank was unlike any present-day North American bank, for it served not only as the financial arm of the government but competed with the country's commercial banks. It was given a twenty-year charter and authorized to establish branches, which ultimately numbered eight — in Boston, New York, Baltimore, Charleston, Norfolk, Washington, Savannah, and New Orleans. Among the institution's stockholders were George Washington, Harvard College, the state of New York, and thirty members of Congress.

Notwithstanding Jefferson's low opinion of banks and bankers, he had a profound influence on early bank design. As a gifted amateur architect, he perceived that architecture could express the ideals upon which a country was founded and help to ensure its survival by promoting a sense of national identity. Advocating the rejection of the British classical tradition that had served colonial America and persisted in the Federal style, Jefferson looked to the revolutionary Neoclassicism of contemporary France and to the architecture of ancient Rome. He insisted that the first public buildings of the United States should not only in size, form, and elegance look beyond the present day but express to the world the new way of life, based on liberty and equality.[23] His exemplar for public architecture was his own design for the Virginia State Capitol (1785–89), which he modeled on the Roman Republican temple at Nîmes, known as the Maison Carrée. Jefferson described this temple, which he had visited, as possibly "the most beautiful and precious morsel of architecture left us by antiquity . . . it is very simple, but is noble beyond expression, and would have done honor to any country." [24] The Virginia Capitol marked the first time that the temple form had been used for a public building of importance anywhere in the modern world.[25]

Jefferson's advocacy of architectural excellence and of the columnar style of antiquity influenced the designs of the first of the buildings undertaken in Washington — the President's House and the Capitol — and also, undoubtedly, of the first Bank of the United States in Philadelphia, which served as the country's temporary capital from 1790 to 1800. The federal bank had begun operating in 1791 in Carpenter's Hall, the colonial guild hall in which the First Continental Congress had met in 1774. In 1795 construction commenced on a "New Banking House," which was open for business in mid-1797.[26]

Since the Bank of the United States was the government bank, the projection of its public character was the overriding consideration in its design. The putative architect was an energetic New Hampshire native, Samuel Blodget, Jr. After making a fortune in the East India trade in Boston, he astutely moved to Philadelphia in 1789 and by 1792 was involved in the development of Washington, where he began speculating in real estate. He entered the United States Capitol competition, which had been initiated on Jefferson's advice, and cannily submitted a preliminary study partially inspired by Jefferson's beloved Maison Carrée. Although Blodget appears to have dropped out of the competition, in 1793 he was appointed superintendent of buildings, representing the commissioners of the Federal City.[27] A year earlier George Washington had characterized him as "certainly a projecting genius." [28] His connections in Washington and Philadelphia undoubtedly explain his involvement with the Bank of the United States.

Recent scholars question Blodget's actual authorship of the design, but whoever the individual was, he lacked Jefferson's unique familiarity with French Neoclassicism and Roman forms and was unable to shake off the influence of Palladianism. The ultimate source of the three-story design is the palatial porticoed Anglo-Palladian country house that served in the eighteenth century as a model for various types of large buildings, including the original banking hall of the Bank of England. Fiske Kimball proposes that the bank's designer knew the Royal Exchange in Dublin, an imposing structure designed by Thomas Cooley and completed in 1779, which suggests that the design may have been ghosted by James Hoban, architect of the President's House, who had designed a hotel for Blodget in 1793.[29] Hoban was an Irishman who had worked on the Dublin Exchange before emigrating to Philadelphia in 1785. The magnificent hexastyle Corinthian portico, giant pilasters, and balustraded roofline (although not the dome) of the Exchange appear in the American design, producing a building of unprecedented grandeur, the first monumental classical bank in the United States.

With its façade of American white marble and the arms of the United States emblazoned on the pediment, the new building was immediately praised as the masterpiece of Philadelphia.[30] Despite the Palladian dependency that is obvious to modern-day observers, the bank was described in a contemporaneous publication as "a truly Grecian Edifice," the proportions of the portico "nearly corresponding to the front of the celebrated Roman temple at Nismes; the Pediment supported by six columns of the order of Corinth, with the decorations they bore at Palmyra and Rome when architecture was at its zenith in the Augustan age."[31] If Jefferson's vision of a national style of architecture was as yet unrealized, it was believed at the time to have been achieved. Moreover, its image of public grandeur, if not its actual appearance, was soon to be emulated by other banks.

[4]

Bank of Pennsylvania
(Demolished)
Second Street, Philadelphia, Pennsylvania
Benjamin Henry Latrobe

Chartered: 1793 (defunct)
Constructed: 1798–1800

The Bank of the United States, while imposing, was not significantly different in design from the President's House, for example, nor was the interior unusual in any way. Between 1798 and 1800, however, a truly original bank building, now sadly gone, was constructed by a gifted professional architect, Benjamin Henry Latrobe, who had arrived in America from England in 1796. He was cultured and well-travelled, familiar with advanced European Neoclassicism and Soane's brilliant work at the Bank of England. Yet he was also highly sensitive to New World aspirations and needs, perhaps because his mother had come from Pennsylvania. Thus when he began to design in the United States, he was free of the persistent colonialism which marked the work of native Americans, including even Jefferson, and also of the urge to implant copies of recent European buildings.

In his design for the Bank of Pennsylvania, an institution established by the state in emulation of the first Bank of the United States [3], Latrobe carefully analyzed the requirements of developing American banking procedures of the time. These included a main banking room, directors' room, stockholders' room, fireproof vaults, and various offices. Having practiced in Richmond, Virginia, for seven years, he was familiar with Jefferson's state capitol and sympathetic to his ideas. Yet this newcomer, the most sophisticated architect America had yet seen, did not follow Jefferson's example and recreate a classical temple on American soil; in fact, he rejected the directors' entreaties to copy the Parthenon.[32] Rather he used classical Greek and Roman forms creatively to produce a highly specialized banking structure, something as new as the enterprise it housed.

The exterior of the Schuylkill marble building was a direct statement of the internal arrangement. A square central block, above which rose the stepped stages of a shallow dome crowned by a cupola, contained a great circular banking hall. Joined to this central block were two gable-roofed end wings, each fronted by a portico. In one of these wings was the public entrance, opening onto a barrel-vaulted vestibule, with offices to each side and the money and security vault above. In the other wing was the stockholders' room on the ground floor with the directors' room above. The portico, which faced a small garden, served as the bank officials' entrance.

The centerpiece and spatial focus of this elegantly simple design was, literally and symbolically, the dramatic domed banking hall, lighted by the glazed cupola. Although Soane had completed his domed Bank Stock Office for the Bank of England by 1794, before Latrobe left for the United States, this was the first domed banking chamber to appear in the New World. An exhilarating space, it is believed to have been finished in a scheme of pale yellow, blue, and white, with a minor accent of dark russet in the frieze.[33] Other banking rooms were pedestrian by comparison, for Latrobe had, like Soane, harnessed space for expressive, not simply functional, purposes.

Another new aspect of Latrobe's design was its structure, composed entirely of masonry vaults, an advanced European system which made possible the banking chamber and provided a great improvement in fireproofing. Moreover, this immensely strong structural technique projected qualities of strength and security appropriate to a bank.

The Bank of Pennsylvania, destroyed by the government in the 1860s, established Latrobe as the most accomplished architect in the United States. Of his years in Philadelphia he wrote: "I have changed the taste of a whole city." [34] In addition to its other innovative qualities, Latrobe's Neoclassical bank represented a break with the prevailing Federal style. Moreover, its Ionic porticoes marked the first appearance of a Greek order in American architecture. This stylistic first would have profound consequences for the future of bank architecture.

[5] ## Second Bank of the United States
420 Chestnut Street, Philadelphia, Pennsylvania
William Strickland

Chartered: 1816 (defunct)
Constructed: 1819–24

Between 1791, when the first Bank of the United States [3] was chartered, and 1811, when its charter expired, the number of banks in the country rose to ninety. During these twenty years the bank had had an excellent record, fulfilling its creator Hamilton's expectations. In a report to the Senate in 1809, Secretary of the Treasury Albert Gallatin stated that "the affairs of the Bank of the United States, considered as a moneyed institution, have been wisely and skilfully managed." [35] Yet antagonism to this, the country's largest corporation, did not abate. Inveterate agrarian opposition to this "powerful urban capitalistic institution" was augmented by state banking interests, jealous of the federal bank's privileged position and resentful of its restraining influence.[36]

The country in 1811 was undergoing rapid development and diversification. The cotton gin, water-powered manufacturing, steamships, roads, and soon canals were beginning to bring about immense change. The population had increased within two decades by almost six million, and half the vast territory beyond the Mississippi had been acquired by President Jefferson in the Louisiana Purchase of 1803. As the country grew and business expanded, the demand for banks — highly profitable businesses themselves — accelerated. Joining forces with the traditional agrarians, the proponents of state banks and easy credit managed to exert sufficient pressure on the Eleventh Congress that the charter of the first Bank of the United States was not renewed.

The bank's building in Philadelphia and most of its assets were purchased by Stephen Girard, one of the bank's largest stockholders and the wealthiest merchant in the Quaker city. In 1812 Girard started his own bank, keeping on the former officers and employees at the same salaries. The Bank of Stephen Girard remained private and unincorporated during the owner's lifetime, Girard using his personal power to withstand the dual threat of Philadelphia's chartered banks and state banking legislation.

With the Bank of the United States and its branches eliminated in 1811, the number of small banks multiplied, increasing to nearly 250 in the next five years. These new banks were improperly supervised, and the result was widespread bad banking practice, a flood of worthless paper money, and frequent panics. Local banks were simply unequal to the task of looking after the demands of government, trade, and industry, and of financing the War of 1812. The economic situation grew so dire that even long-standing opponents of a national bank such as President James Madison changed their opinion. In 1816 Congress passed an act establishing a second Bank of the United States in Philadelphia, still the financial and cultural center of the country. Among those appointed directors was Girard, the second largest stockholder after the government. Since the Bank of Stephen Girard now occupied the first Bank's building, the second Bank, like its predecessor, opened for business in Carpenter's Hall. Two years later the directors published a notice inviting architects to submit designs for a building, to be a rectangle of equal or unequal sides, faced with marble, with "a portico on each front, resting upon a basement or platform of such altitude as will combine convenience of ascent with due proportion and effect." The directors also wanted the edifice to exhibit "a chaste imitation of Grecian Architecture, in its simplest and least expensive form."[37]

Philadelphians' enthusiasm for Greek forms had been growing in the early nineteenth century in large part because of a brilliant, influential young man, Nicholas Biddle, who became a director and then president of the second Bank of the United States. In 1806 Biddle had been the first cultivated American to visit Greece, then under Turkish rule, and he fell in love with ancient Greek architecture, much as Jefferson had with the Roman Maison Carrée at Nîmes two decades earlier. Thereafter for Biddle "the two great truths in the world [were] the Bible and Grecian architecture."[38] In 1814 he had a paper published promoting Greek forms as the most suitable inspiration for an American architecture. It has been suggested that the learned Biddle, although not yet a director, was responsible for the competition program for the second Bank.[39]

Latrobe, who had served as Architect of the Capitol from 1803 to 1817, was extremely eager to secure this prestigious commission. He lost out, however, to a former pupil, William Strickland, whose father, as a bricklayer and master carpenter, had worked on Latrobe's Bank of Pennsylvania [4]. That bank had been an original creation and not a copy, but Strickland sought as close a copy of an ancient Greek temple as was practicable, basing his design on illustrations of the Parthenon found in Stuart and Revett's *Antiquities of Athens*.[40] The unsuccessful design submitted by Latrobe, although similar in many ways, featured a high attic which projected above the roof, disturbing the temple form of the whole. Not surprisingly, the directors found Strickland's design more "classic."[41]

Although Strickland's exterior was sufficiently Grecian to meet the directors' requirements, he omitted the Parthenon's lateral colonnades in the interest of interior light and space. While the building was still under construction, Strickland wrote that in selecting the Parthenon "as a model for a building such as a Bank, requiring a peculiar internal arrangement and distribution of space and light, it becomes a difficult task for an architect to preserve *all* the characteristics of a Grecian temple, whose original design and appropriation was solely for the worship of the gods, and for the deposition of public treasure."[42] Antique references in the interior were thus largely limited to decorative details. Strickland provided an elegant sequence of rooms, including a central barrel-vaulted banking hall, spacious but low enough to be contained within the classical gable line of the roof.

Standing on its platform, an isolated monument, the austere marble edifice was immediately acclaimed as one of the chief architectural glories of the new Republic. For many it was the most beautiful building in the land. Its enormous appeal lay in the way its architecture was so perfectly attuned to the mood of America at the time. "Of all governments," remarked a Maine congressman in 1824, seeking to characterize appropriate public buildings, "a republic ought to appear with sober pomp and modest splendour. Not the dazzling radiance of the throne is here reflected; but the mild lustre, the serene majesty, of the sovereign people."[43]

The second Bank of the United States was the first public building in America patterned on a Greek temple. In a democracy, however, temples were to be no one's exclusive preserve. Greek forms were soon seen as the perfect means of expressing the proud nationalism and political idealism of the country, and Greek Revival became the national style that Jefferson had called for. By 1838 a character in a James Fenimore Cooper novel remarked: "The public sentiment just now runs almost exclusively and popularly into the Grecian school. We build little besides temples for our churches, our banks, our taverns, our court houses, and our dwellings. A friend of mine has just built a brewery on the model of the Temple of the Winds."[44]

The branch offices of the second Bank, twenty-five by 1830, emulated the architectural image of the parent institution. Of necessity smaller and simpler, often located at the very edge of the wilderness, they were an important means of spreading the taste for Greek Revival architecture throughout the land. The Bank of Indiana, for example, which had a branch office in every leading town of the state, adopted the same Corinthian front for all.[45] Even when the second Bank's charter was allowed to expire in 1835 and detractors referred scathingly to "the Greek temple in Chestnut Street," the classical image remained so appealing to bankers that it continued to be invoked well into the twentieth century.

Under Nicholas Biddle the second Bank fulfilled a role in the economy similar in many respects to that of the Federal Reserve Banks and the Bank of Canada, although it was also run as a profit-making institution. According to Hammond, the brilliant Biddle "carried the art of central banking further than it had so far been developed even by the Bank of England." The bank "provided as uniform and satisfactory a monetary system as any country in the world possessed, and better than most, especially with the vast territorial extent of the United States taken into account."[46] Nevertheless, as with the first Bank, opposition continued, and when Andrew Jackson was elected the seventh President of the United States in 1829, a determined foe of banks became leader of the nation.

While Jackson himself was an agrarian whose fierce hatred of banks resulted from personal experience, the country he governed was not the agrarian Arcadia envisioned by Jefferson but the budding industrial nation dreamed of and prepared for by Hamilton. No longer struggling to survive, Americans were pouring their energy into the development of the vast lands and resources at their disposal. Eager entrepreneurs demanded more banks and abundant credit. For them, the restraints imposed by the federal bank were intolerable. Other heightened emotions added fuel to the fire: the self-made businessman's hatred of the old monied aristocracy, which the arrogant Biddle personified; continuing sectionalist aversion to federal powers; and a general nostalgic agrarian antipathy. A new factor was ambitious New York. With the completion of the Erie Canal, it became the country's commercial center, resentful of Philadelphia's financial primacy.[47]

[6]   *Bank of Louisville*
                320 West Main Street, Louisville, Kentucky
                        James Harrison Dakin

Chartered: 1833
Constructed: 1835–37 (building not occupied by bank)

As the historian Hammond observes, although the phraseology of the Jacksonian attack on the bank was agrarian, the substance was entrepreneurial.[48] The early banking history of Kentucky bears this out. Initially banking had not been popular in agrarian Kentucky, admitted as the fifteenth state in 1792. So great was the antipathy that the first chartered bank had to seek incorporation as an insurance company in 1802. Only three years later the charter was repealed, categorized as "monopolistic, aristocratic, privileged, and thoroughly inimical to free institutions."[49] Yet in 1806 the state established the Bank of Kentucky, which enjoyed a monopoly until 1818, when the legislature, responding to the expansive mood of the times, incorporated forty new banks in one Act. All failed within a year.

In 1833 the legislature incorporated another group of banks, among them the Bank of Louisville. The bank's building, designed by the American-trained architect James Dakin, was one of the most original and distinguished creations of the Greek Revival period.[50] The focus of Louisville's historic financial district, this institution became the financial seat of power for the state. During the Civil War the president of the bank refused to release funds to either side, an event which was a major factor in Kentucky's neutrality during the conflict. Since 1972 the building has housed the Actors Theatre of Louisville, one of the country's leading companies.[51]

Monumental temple banks with two octastyle porticoes modelled on the second Bank of the United States [5] were not only expensive undertakings, but were not always suited to a particular site. An early practical adaptation, based on a smaller Greek prototype, involved setting two columns within the projecting side walls of the building. Solomon Willard had used this distyle in antis arrangement for the Boston branch of the second Bank of the United States as early as 1824. Dakin used the formula for his one-story Bank of Louisville, setting the columns in a recessed porch. Like Latrobe, however, he used his ancient forms imaginatively. His two slender Ionic columns rise between end piers that are slanted or battered in an Egyptian manner, giving the granite façade a powerful, secure, pylonlike quality. The soaring columns and inclined walls draw the eye upward to a fanlike acroterion, composed of a Greek honeysuckle motif, of sufficient scale to crown the building so that a costly pediment could be omitted. Though hardly widespread, there was current interest in Egyptian forms and motifs, and Dakin drew on his knowledge of this exotic style to create a bank façade that is noticeably distinctive and original.

The interior banking hall, which now serves as a grand lobby for the Actors Theatre, is as impressive as the façade. Above the central portion of the oblong room is an elliptical domed ceiling, deeply coffered, with an oculus, originally covered by stained glass, to provide additional light. Two pairs of freestanding columns and ten pilasters support a rectangular architrave upon which the curved base of the dome appears to rest lightly. The magnificent ceiling was the most elaborate Louisville had seen; in fact, a plasterer of the day observed that such expensive work had never been done even in Baltimore.[52]

In 1836, as Dakin's Bank of Louisville was under construction, the charter of the second Bank of the United States was allowed to expire. Yet if the destruction of the federal bank, engineered by President Andrew Jackson and his supporters, meant the demise of economic prudence and governmental restraints, it also meant that tremendous forces were unleashed, spurring the rapid development of the vast country.

·2·

CANADIAN BANKS

LATE GEORGIAN
THROUGH
THE 1850s

In contrast to the United States, Canada remained relatively undeveloped during much of the nineteenth century, hindered by her formidable terrain and climate. The first permanent European settlers in this northern land were the French, who lost their empire to the British in 1760. The first significant catalyst in the development of modern Canada was the American Revolution, which created political exiles — Tories to Americans, Loyalists to Canadians. These refugees spelled the beginning of settlement on the upper St. Lawrence River and the Great Lakes, while adding to colonization that was already underway in Nova Scotia.

At the end of the Revolutionary War there were four remaining British possessions in North America: Quebec, Nova Scotia, Newfoundland, and Rupert's Land, the latter controlled by the Hudson's Bay Company. In 1791 the Crown divided the vast province of Quebec into Upper and Lower Canada, roughly corresponding to today's provinces of Ontario and Quebec, allowing mainly French-speaking Quebec to retain its distinctive seigneurial system of land ownership, French civil law, and the special status of the Roman Catholic Church.[1] Upper Canada received English law and institutions, although both provinces had representative government. The Loyalist influx also resulted in the division of Nova Scotia into four provinces: a smaller Nova Scotia, New Brunswick, Prince Edward Island, and Cape Breton, which was reattached to Nova Scotia in 1820.

After 1815 and the cessation of the Napoleonic Wars, these initial British North American settlers were joined by an increasing number of immigrants who came directly from the motherland, where a severe economic depression and the Scottish Clearances were causing widespread unemployment and distress.[2] These newcomers made the remaining North American colonies more British than they had ever been before.[3]

While the majority of French Canadians continued in their customary agricultural pursuits, many of the English-speaking settlers were merchants. Strategically located Montreal, at the center of the St. Lawrence trading system and the base of the fur trade, owed its rapid nineteenth-century growth to this small but powerful group of merchants, many of Scottish origin, who quickly made the city the financial and commercial capital of the Canadas. Like their American counterparts, these early traders required banks to facilitate business. Most pressing was the need for a reliable circulating medium, since specie — gold and silver — was in desperately short supply.

[7] *Bank of Montreal*
(Demolished)
St. James Street, Montreal, Quebec
Architect unknown

Founded: 1817
Chartered: 1822
Constructed: 1818–19

Canada's first permanent bank was established in 1817 as a private company, designated the Montreal Bank, by nine of the city's leading merchants. George Moffat and George Garden respectively represented the fur-trading interests of the Hudson's Bay Company and its rival the North West Company. Horatio Gates was a former New Englander with a successful American trade and valuable banking connections in the United States. Another founder, Austin Cuvillier, a well-to-do importer, was French Canadian. John Richardson, the Scottish-born guiding spirit of the enterprise, had been a privateer during the Revolution and subsequently became the dominant partner of a leading Montreal mercantile and financial house, Forsyth, Richardson & Co. In 1792 and 1808 he and other merchants had unsuccessfully tried to establish a bank in Lower Canada.[4] Richardson's third attempt was an enduring success, for in 1822 a royal charter was granted incorporating the company as the Bank of Montreal, the name it carries to this day.[5]

The model for this first Canadian bank (and of the other pioneers, who followed its example) was Alexander Hamilton's Bank of the United States [3], which had a proven record in the New World environment.[6] Whereas Hamilton's creation was destroyed by politics, the more conservative Canadians "took the best of American experience for a pattern and stuck to it."[7] Consequently the Canadian banking system is more truly the child of Hamilton than is the present regionalized American system. Indeed, the Bank of Montreal quickly set up agencies in Quebec City and in the two leading towns of Upper Canada, Kingston and York (later Toronto). Although not strictly branches, these offices presaged a major distinguishing feature of the modern Canadian banking system — nationwide branching.

The Montreal Bank opened for business in 1817 in rented premises with the resolve that "a piece of Ground should be purchased and a building erected thereon from the funds of the Bank, for the more convenient carrying on of the Business."[8] Accordingly a fine site was purchased on the corner of St. James and St. François Xavier streets adjacent to the city's public square, Place d'Armes. Upon this piece of property was erected, between 1818 and 1819, the first purpose-built bank in Canada, an action that would establish St. James Street as the financial heart of Canada until the latter part of the twentieth century.

For its time and place the Montreal Bank was an outstanding building. John Bland, former Macdonald Professor of Architecture at McGill University, refers to it as "the building that capped the period of early nineteenth-century British-American architecture."[9] A detached rectangular edifice constructed of "best quality" local limestone ashlar, the bank had a low hipped roof and a Doric portico sheltering the main entrance.[10] There was a fine cornice, and rusticated quoins marked the corners. It was quite different from the general run of commercial structures in the city—undecorated attached stone buildings with steep roofs protected by high parapeted fire walls. There were three stories above ground, "with a Stable, Ice House and privy with a good stone wall all around the said Lot."[11] The banking chamber and directors' offices occupied the ground floor, which was 16 feet high; the cashier lived on the floor above, and the top floor was given over to a garret. The vaults were located in the basement, which was vaulted with four arches. Although the architect (if any) is unknown, Andrew White, a carpenter-joiner, was the builder and Robert Smith the stone cutter.[12] To give the bank—in particular the banking floor—special distinction, four relief panels of Coade's Artificial Stone depicting "Commerce, Agriculture, Navigations, Arts & Manufactures" were set above the ground-floor windows of the main façade.[13] Although the building was demolished in the 1870s, the panels survive in the present Montreal head office building.

This restrained classical building was a sober greystone relative of the elegant Federal town houses in brick or wood that abounded in northern American coastal cities, themselves variants of a British eighteenth-century prototype.[14] The low hipped roof was of a kind remarked on at the time as being "American style."[15] Such a blending of local, American, and British elements was typical of early Loyalist architecture in Montreal, of which this first Bank of Montreal head office was the preeminent commercial example. Its Anglo-American classicism and smooth masonry set the building off sharply from the existing French pattern of rubble-stone building, making it a major architectural symbol of the new, post-Conquest order. In a travel book published in London in 1824 it was described as "by far the finest edifice, either public or private, in the Canadas."[16]

[8]   *Bank of Upper Canada*
                    252 Adelaide Street, Toronto, Ontario
                    William Warren Baldwin

Chartered: 1822 (defunct)
Constructed: 1825–27

Lacking a direct outlet to the sea, Upper Canada (now Ontario) was merely an economic tributary to the lower province during the early nineteenth century. In 1817, however, the same year that the Montreal Bank opened for business, agitation for banks began both in Kingston, the colony's largest trading center, and in smaller York (incorporated as the city of Toronto in 1834), the political capital.[17] The petitioners were none too soon, for by 1818 the Montreal Bank had established agencies at Kingston and York. The initial winners were the politically well-connected promoters of the Bank of Upper Canada in York, which was finally chartered in 1822 and commenced building in 1825.[18] The architect was probably an amateur, Dr. William Warren Baldwin, a director involved in the planning of the building.[19] For forty-four years this was the central financial institution for the province.

Baldwin had been born in 1775 in Ireland into the minor landed gentry and practiced both medicine and law in Upper Canada. Through marriage he became one of the largest landowners in York and designed two houses for his country estate, as well as the city's courthouse and jail.[20] The bank was the creation of the powerful political oligarchy to which Baldwin was related, disparagingly referred to by contemporaries as the Family Compact, which controlled Upper Canada until the 1830s.[21] This local aristocracy was fiercely loyal to Britain, believing in British institutions and a hierarchical society, hostile in the extreme to the republican United States. Their architectural tastes, too, were British—and ambitious. It was hoped, for example, that John Soane, the distinguished architect to the Bank of England, might design the legislative building and residence for the governor, a commission which, unfortunately for North America, was not fulfilled.[22]

The Bank of Upper Canada, like the Montreal Bank [7], was based on a domestic prototype. It resembled a fine freestanding house, akin to the scaled-down Anglo-Palladian country houses Family Compact members built for themselves on their parklike town properties. Containing the apartment of the cashier as well as banking rooms, the bank was located next to the gardens of the Chief Justice's house in what was then a fashionable residential area. Of finely cut grey limestone, the bank is a rectangular block, seven bays long, with a slightly projecting three-bayed center. The original roof and dormers were concealed behind a cornice and semibalustraded parapet. A flight of stone steps, partially protected by a portico, leads to a handsome double-doored entrance which contains a semicircular fanlight and is flanked by slender windows lighting the hall. For security these could be covered by heavy pine inner doors. The building's spare late-Georgian style was updated in the 1840s by the professional architect John Howard, who added a new stone portico containing four Roman Doric columns, the paired pilasters flanking the main door, and the cast-iron railing which crowns the portico. A mansard roof was added in the 1870s.

Although it is somewhat difficult now to appreciate the building's original appearance, the design of the Bank of Upper Canada, unlike the Bank of Montreal, reflects the Old World, either as recalled by William Baldwin or through the intermediary of one of the contractors who had worked in England.[23] Yet the austerity of both these early Canadian buildings is a response to local conditions. An early traveller to Montreal had remarked on this plainness of style, finding "any exuberance of ornament . . . inconsistent with a climate so severe as that of Canada."[24] Nevertheless, the Bank of Upper Canada was one of the grandest structures in early York, with its unpaved streets. One of the town's few stone buildings, this lordly edifice was a perfect reflection of the taste and aspirations of the powerful colonial clique that created it. The structure is now the oldest surviving purpose-designed bank in the country.[25]

[9]   *Commercial Bank of the Midland District*

13–15 Wellington Street West, Toronto, Ontario
William Thomas

Chartered: 1831 (defunct)
Constructed: 1843–45

Thanks to the power of the Family Compact, no other group in Upper Canada was able to secure a local charter for a decade after 1822. Moreover, discriminatory legislation passed in 1824 forced the temporary retreat of the Lower Canadian banks. Although the Bank of Upper Canada was an important agent in the development of the province, it was fiercely resented by more republican elements in the population and by merchants in rival cities who wished to establish their own banks. The latter included two groups of Kingston's leading citizens in the 1810s and 1820s.

Kingston, situated at the junction of the St. Lawrence River and Lake Ontario, was strategically located for both defensive and commercial purposes. Founded by a small group of Loyalists in 1784, it grew rapidly into the largest town in the province, serving as the major transshipment center for goods moving to and from Montreal and as a major British naval and military station.

Patriotic and self-interested Kingston merchants, who were prevented from establishing their own banks, understandably continued to be distressed that the banking profits of their prospering community were enriching the Bank of Upper Canada, through its Kingston office, and latterly the Bank of Montreal, which had reestablished an agency in 1829 in connection with the financing of the Rideau Canal and other public works. In 1831, after a bitter legislative battle, a charter was obtained for the Kingston-based Commercial Bank of the Midland District, which very quickly was regarded as the equal of its long-time rival in York and a worthy competitor of the Bank of Montreal.[26] Soon it had branches or agencies in every important city and town in the province. Three years into the economically buoyant 1840s, the Commercial Bank purchased a lot on Wellington Street in Toronto and commenced a handsome building to replace their existing branch.

William Thomas, a talented architect who had arrived from England early in 1843, was given the commission.[27] He had been involved in a wide range of speculative building, related in style to the work of John Nash, in Leamington Spa, a famous Regency watering place in Warwickshire.[28] Thomas's design for the Commercial Bank implanted something of this Regency urbanity in Toronto, for his source was the urban terraces of late-eighteenth- and early-nineteenth-century England, which were more appropriate models for fast-growing Toronto than the older Anglo-Georgian isolated-house-in-a-garden tradition that had inspired the Bank of Upper Canada.

Although designed to be freestanding, Thomas's bank is nevertheless a manifestly urban composition. The three-story structure is set back very slightly from the street behind a cast-iron fence contained within stone piers. Moreover, only the main façade is important; it alone was faced in grey Queenston limestone. Architectural detailing was reserved for this front, extending only minimally around the corners, since contiguous buildings would have been anticipated. The organization of this façade is not focused on a grand central doorway, as in Georgian compositions, but consists of a three-bay center framed by end bays, each containing an entrance.[29] This lateral arrangement is largely responsible for the urban quality of the building, since it implies the continuity of the street. Thomas embellished his main façade with carved Greek Revival decorative details and with a delicate cast-iron balcony carrying an anthemion motif. In British North America the impact of the Greek Revival on bank architecture was superficial.[30] No major banks employed the Greek temple form so beloved by Americans.

The location of the Commercial Bank on Wellington Street near King and Yonge streets, some considerable distance from the Bank of Upper Canada, signified this area as Toronto's emergent financial and commercial district.[31] Indeed, the Bank of Upper Canada felt impelled to move west in 1861, occupying an existing building at the corner of Yonge and Colborne streets for the few years that remained before its collapse in 1866.

[10] *Bank of Montreal*

119 St. James Street, Montreal, Quebec
John Wells

Founded: 1817
Chartered: 1822
Constructed: 1845–47

The 1830s, the decade in which the Commercial Bank had been chartered, was a time of considerable political agitation in British North America. Many of the newer immigrants had brought with them liberal or reform ideas from Britain or were inspired by the Jacksonian United States. The expanding population grew resentful of rule by small minority groups backed by the Imperial government, as exemplified by the Family Compact. In addition, there was friction in Lower Canada between the French and the English with their differing views: the former a conservative, agricultural people anxious to hold on to their cherished language and traditions, the latter aggressive and money-minded, supporters of commerce and progress. As grievances grew and reform movements developed, armed rebellion broke out in 1837 in both Upper and Lower Canada.

The result was the establishment of responsible governments in the colonies and, in 1841, the union of Upper and Lower Canada into the United Province of Canada. By this latter move it was hoped (vainly, as it turned out) that the French might eventually be assimilated into a wholly British Canada. Although Kingston served briefly as the first capital of the United Province, the government moved to Montreal in the spring of 1844. By that time the Bank of Montreal had outgrown its head office and in 1845 a splendid adjacent site overlooking Place d'Armes had been purchased, a building committee appointed, and a notice placed in the Montreal *Gazette* advising architects that a fifty-pound premium would be awarded for the best submission of ground plan and elevation for a new bank. In addition, the cashier had written to the bank's correspondent in Edinburgh "for the purpose of obtaining the Elevation of the principle Banking Houses in that City & Glasgow." [32] At the annual June meeting, the president noted that the directors hoped for "a structure of convenient dimensions, and classical taste, that will do credit to the Stockholders of the oldest Bank of British North America and be an ornament to the Capital of the Province." [33]

In August, the building committee recommended awarding fifty pounds to two of the entrants, Messrs. Wells and Springle, but stated that this did not mean that either of the submissions would be followed. [34] In her research on the building history of the Bank of Montreal, Michelle Nolin-Raynauld found no further references to plans until a description that appeared in *Le Minerve* (Montreal) on January 15, 1846. Here an engraving entitled "Bank of Montreal. (With the Dome.)" depicts the porticoed, domed seven-bay façade of the edifice that was eventually completed in 1847 and also shows relief sculpture in the pediment that was not put in place until 1867. [35] The brief accompanying text gives the dimensions of the exterior and of the banking hall, states that the façade will be ornamented by a portico and six Corinthian columns, and identifies the architect as John Wells. [36]

It has been assumed, at least since the publication of Merrill Denison's two-volume history, *Canada's First Bank,* that the executed design of the Bank of Montreal was closely modelled on the Commercial Bank of Scotland, completed in 1846 in Edinburgh. Designed in 1844 by the prominent Scottish architect David Rhind, this grand edifice was, if not the most original, certainly the most ornate and expensive-looking bank built in the 1840s in Britain. It so impressed the directors of the Bank of Montreal, Denison writes, that they made it the prototype for their new head office, commissioning John Wells as the "supervising architect." [37] While the influence of the Scottish bank seems clear from the visual evidence, searches by both Mme. Nolin-Raynauld and Bank of Montreal Archivist Freeman Clowery have turned up no documentation to prove this link.

Although the façades of the two buildings, completed within a year of one another, do share many similarities, they are not identical. Wells, a native of Norfolk, England, had come to Montreal about 1830 and proceeded to build up a respectable practice in the city. Not surprisingly, his design for the Bank of Montreal, which was constructed of local grey limestone, is less ornately mid-Victorian than Rhind's creation. It is characterized by a late-Georgian restraint, undoubtedly a response to local taste and available masonry skills but also a reflection of Wells's age — he was nineteen years older than Rhind — and East Anglian origins. The Montreal bank lacks the Edinburgh bank's rusticated walls and balustrading, for example, while the intended pediment sculpture (if the 1846 engraving is indicative) would also have been simpler. In the Montreal building traditional pedimented windows replace Rhind's less orthodox round-arched and rectangular openings. The most remarkable differences are the typically Georgian hipped roof and the dome that crown the Bank of Montreal. The Scottish bank has no such terminating features; rather, its roofline is concealed by a balustrade. Yet it is the combination of a giant portico and dome, reminiscent of the Pantheon — preeminent monument of the Roman Empire — that gives the Montreal bank an imperial grandeur, symbolizing both its dominance in colonial banking and its location in the new provincial capital. The engraving in *Le Minerve* suggests that the idea for the nonstructural dome was locally generated, while Mme. Nolin-Raynauld reveals that it was only in September 1846, while the building was under construction, that the directors finally approved its erection. [38] Unfortunately, this supremely expressive external feature was constructed of wood and had to be removed after a few bitter winters. It was replaced more substantially, however, by McKim, Mead & White early in the twentieth century.

The completion of the new Bank of Montreal meant that historic Place d'Armes, dominated for nearly two decades by the early Gothic Revival Church of Notre-Dame, was now the site of another significant monument, one described in an 1870 visitor's guide as the finest public building in the city.[39] To this day, these two temples, the one dedicated to God, the other to Mammon, face each other across the city's oldest public square.

·3·

AMERICAN BANKS

MID AND LATE
VICTORIAN

From the 1790s onward, banks in the United States tended to specialize, catering to different groups of customers even within the same city. The first banks had been the creations of wealthy merchants engaged in foreign mercantile trade, who were supporters of Alexander Hamilton's Federalist party. Soon, however, banks were founded to serve their political enemies, the Republicans. (Jefferson, since he could not do away with them, was in favor of making all banks Republican.) The industry quickly became more democratic and diversified as banks were established to look after the needs of smaller businessmen such as farmers, shop-keepers, and "mechanics," the latter term denoting manufacturers and craftsmen. The name of the institution — for example, Merchants Bank — signalled the type of customer the bank wanted to do business with. Banks were also founded to finance public improvements like roads, canals, and schools.

With the demise of the regulating federal bank in 1836, an era of unrestrained banking set in. Proliferating state banks, all of them issuing bank notes, would dominate the industry until the Civil War. Multiplication rather than consolidation was the order of the day. Some states were more lax in their banking legislation than others. Indiana's banking law of 1853 was so permissive that ninety-four new banks opened in the first three years after passage, fifty-one of them failing before the third year was out.[1] The epithet "wildcat bank" was coined early in this period to characterize banks purposely located in remote places (where the wildcats were), so that customers could not easily appear and demand their banknotes be redeemed in coin.[2] Banks outside the larger centers generally occupied single-story frame structures with one or two rooms, while some never opened any building at all. One bank president kept his funds in a potato barrel in the cellar of his farmhouse; a blacksmith-cashier used a box under his anvil as a vault.[3]

Failures and panics did little to stem Americans' appetite for banks, although some states' constitutions forbade incorporated banking for a time, or strong opposition kept it out. As late as 1852 there were no incorporated banks actively operating in seven of the thirty-one states, in the territories of Minnesota and Wisconsin, or in the District of Columbia. For all its drawbacks, however, free banking suited the *laissez-faire* mood of the time, contributing significantly to westward expansion and to the development of the fabulous resources of the vast continent. As Hammond writes, "bank credit was to Americans a new source of energy, like steam."[4]

[11]   *Farmers' and Exchange Bank*
141 East Bay Street, Charleston, South Carolina
Jones & Lee

Chartered: 1852 (defunct)
Constructed: 1853–54

As diversity and individualism came to characterize banking in the years before the Civil War, there was a concurrent awareness of nonclassical styles that could be used to set off a bank from its competitors. Indeed, as early as 1808 the prescient Latrobe had designed a building (no longer extant) embellished with neo-Gothic details for the Philadelphia Bank, the first in that city to serve middle-class tradesmen. An outstanding mid-century example of the need for a distinguishing image is the Farmers' and Exchange Bank in Charleston, chartered in 1852 and a late-comer to South Carolina's banking capital. Designed by a local architect, Francis D. Lee,[5] it is in the rare Moorish Revival style, which enjoyed a brief popularity along with related Near Eastern, Indian, and Oriental modes during the late 1840s and the 1850s. It is a style less associated with commercial architecture than with pleasure palaces such as hotels, theaters, and that wildly exotic mansion, P. T. Barnum's "Iranistan," built in 1847 in Connecticut and inspired by Nash's Royal Pavilion in Brighton. The Charleston bank's arresting qualities were nationally acclaimed, however, when it was singled out in *Harper's New Monthly Magazine* for its style and coloration—alternating bands of pale Jersey and dark Connecticut brownstone.[6] The foreign image was perhaps intentional, meant to advertise the bank's dealings in exchange, which was the method of financing not only the international commodities trade but of trade between the economically specialized regions of the United States.

Situated in Charleston's financial district in a row of banks which formerly stood on the west side of East Bay Street between Broad and Queen, the small two-story structure succeeded in holding its own against the imposing Doric portico of the Planters' and Mechanics' Bank (destroyed to make way for a parking lot) next door. Three double-doored entrances contained within striking horseshoe arches opened into a paved vestibule which led into a spacious, two-story banking room, "'finished in the most elaborate manner, Moorish arches, panels, brackets, arabesques . . . fresco painting . . . lighted by a glass paneled ceiling.' "[7] This must have been one of the most individualistic banking rooms of the time. Yet the symmetrical arrangement of the solid masonry façade came from the classical tradition, providing the dignity and sobriety appropriate to a bank later described as "one of the financial strongholds of the state and city."[8]

♦ ♦ ♦

In 1853, the year the Moorish Farmers' and Exchange Bank was begun, the Grecian edifices on New York's Wall Street were being described in *Putnam's Monthly* as "grim temples."[9] America and American taste had changed dramatically. In just four decades the country had emerged as a leading manufacturing nation, its export-import trade increasing sevenfold. The paper wealth resulting from Andrew Jackson's fiscal policies had created a "calico aristocracy," as *Putnam's* called the new rich of the mid-century, a group whose tastes were very different from those of the Republic's early social leaders.[10] Along with the demand by this newly rich merchant class for lavish display, there was a simultaneous realization that Greek-inspired temples were not suited to increasingly congested cities. Their self-contained plans and elevations were inflexible, their columns screened out light, and construction was expensive.

Emerging in the late 1840s, a more suitable formula for buildings was that based on the formal Italian Renaissance palace or *palazzo*. The English architect Charles Barry had drawn attention to this mode with his Traveller's Club (1829–32) and Reform Club (1837–41) in London and his Athenaeum (1837–39) in Manchester. These works had an enormous impact on architectural design throughout the British Isles and North America. Two Renaissance Revival palazzos were commenced in the United States in 1845: the Athenaeum, a club in Philadelphia designed by John Notman, and Stewart's Store on New York's Broadway.[11] Within five years the palazzo mode, suitable for grand freestanding buildings as well as ordinary attached street façades, had become overwhelmingly popular for commercial architecture and remained so for a quarter of a century.

The first palazzo bank, now demolished, was designed in 1847 by John Notman for the Bank of North America in Philadelphia.[12] Palazzo banks began to appear in New York, on the Bowery and on Broadway, by 1850–51. Extraordinarily versatile, the flat-roofed palazzo was extensible, provided well-lit interiors, and could be either cheaply or expensively built. Although the basic composition of the elevations was simple, an unprecedented richness was possible. In fact, it has been noted that the historical place or period which provided inspiration was not as essential in the creation of these commercial palaces as the impressive appearance.[13] Renaissance Revival (also called Italianate) forms, however, predominated up to the Civil War, the tendency being toward greater elaboration and richer effects.

Farmers and Mechanics Bank
427 Chestnut Street, Philadelphia, Pennsylvania
John M. Gries

Chartered: 1809 (defunct)
Constructed: 1854–55

A distinguished Renaissance Revival palazzo was erected in 1854–55 on Chestnut Street in Philadelphia for the highly regarded Farmers and Mechanics Bank, which had been chartered in 1809 to extend banking facilities to a hitherto ignored group, agricultural and mechanical entrepreneurs. The charter stipulated that a majority of the thirteen directors be farmers, mechanics, or manufacturers actually employed in their profession; and in fact the initial board included three merchants, a saddler, a farmer, a paper manufacturer, an iron manufacturer, a currier, a bookseller, a watchmaker, a hatter, a brewer, and an attorney.[14]

By the 1830s the Farmers and Mechanics Bank had prospered to the point that many others sought connection with it as a correspondent. In the early 1850s it vied with the Bank of Pennsylvania for first place in the city, and, after the collapse of the latter during the Panic of 1857, it became fiscal agent to the state. The design of its new edifice, three stories high and abutted on both sides, was based on the rich Venetian version of the palazzo. This treatment allowed the architect, John M. Gries of Philadelphia, to create an elaborately carved marble front that reflected the bank's growing wealth and position. Bracketed cornice and windows, Corinthian pilasters, figurative keystones, and relief panels ornament the façade, which contrasts sharply with the austere Greek Revival second Bank of the United States [5] across the street.

Crowning the façade of the new building, prominently carved on a panel in the center of the parapet, are a plow and an anvil. Originally the main front had three doorways, but the end ones were later converted to windows. The central door gave access to a passage leading to a rear sky-lighted three-story banking room with an arched ceiling. Iron, an increasingly important building material at this time, was used extensively throughout the building.

♦ ♦ ♦

By the middle of the nineteenth century, iron was sufficiently cheap and available in the United States to make its widespread use practicable. Used initially for various structural and ornamental elements, it became popular for entire façades, which could be mass-produced in sections at foundries, shipped by boat or rail, and speedily erected. Soon, "Ferromania" swept the country.[15] By 1858 cast-iron fronts prefabricated in New York had reached clients in Savannah and Charleston, Chicago and San Francisco, even Havana. Until conflagrations in the early seventies proved it inferior to traditional masonry, cast iron seemed ideal for all kinds of commercial and industrial buildings, since the great strength of iron in compression made not only large windows possible but also open interiors with more usable floor space when the material was used for slender supporting columns.

The new technology was immediately attractive to America's growing population of bankers, for in addition to its appealing economy and presumed fire resistance, iron could be cast to emulate the richest and most aristocratic styles of the past.[16] The palazzo and cast iron were ideally suited, since sections of repeating Italianate arches could be joined together vertically and laterally to create buildings of varying size. A fine example is the cast-iron Renaissance Revival edifice commenced for the Bank of Columbus probably in 1859, but which remained partially unfinished until after the Civil War.

[13]   *Bank of Columbus*
1048 Broadway, Columbus, Georgia
Architect unknown

Chartered: 1856 (defunct)
Constructed: c. 1860

The location of Columbus on the Chattahoochee River provided water-power for a thriving textile industry and an outlet to the Gulf of Mexico, so that by the time the war broke out its unusually advanced (for the South) industrial development made it one of the major producers of war goods in the Confederacy. The Bank of Columbus was presided over by William H. Young, who had founded one of the great textile mills of the South, Eagle Mill, at Columbus. Venturing from New York to Georgia's western wilderness at the age of seventeen, Young personified the self-made entrepreneurs who were transforming the country during this period.[17] When the Civil War broke out, his bank subscribed $135,000 to the Confederate loan and lent an additional $35,000 to the State of Georgia, while over $2 million in gold and silver coin was deposited in the bank vault during the hostilities.[18] Young also equipped, at his own expense, a Confederate cavalry company, of which his eldest son was commander.

Young himself is credited with idea for the stylish iron-fronted building, the largest of its kind in Georgia.[19] Young's choice of iron was perhaps influenced by a disastrous fire that destroyed a whole business block in Columbus in the 1840s. Who designed the bank's two iron façades and where they were manufactured have not been definitely established, although family recollections indicate that the iron elements were ordered from England by Young.[20] The completion date, too, is unclear. The Bank of Columbus had begun acquiring the land along Broadway for the building as early as 1856 and appears to have conducted business in the partially finished structure from 1860 until it declared bankruptcy in 1866 as a result of the war.[21] John S. Lupold, an historian at Columbus College, has seen an engraved bank note issued by the Bank of Columbus in 1862 depicting the completed building, but this may have been anticipatory.[22]

Regardless of its final completion date, the unusually large building—three stories and a block-long façade—was clearly intended from the first to provide rental space in addition to banking premises. The Bank of Columbus is, in fact, an early example of the form that bank architecture would increasingly assume following the Civil War: a multipurpose building, in this case a business block, housing a bank, rentable offices, and frequently shops.

William Young's striking cast-iron palazzo was not only sizable but extraordinarily elegant for this remote manufacturing town, where utilitarian commercial structures had been the norm. Rectangular in shape, it presents a short seven-bay iron façade to Broadway, Columbus's main business street, and a matching, longer metal façade to Eleventh Street. A corner entrance originally existed, as well as two additional doorways, later changed to windows. On the long front an imposing off-center main entrance is distinguished by a broken pediment supported on tall Corinthian columns fronting an elaborate inner door frame. On the two upper floors the iron fronts consist of repeating round-arched windows with acanthus-ornamented keystones and flanking engaged fluted Corinthian columns. A taller, related arcade is used for the ground floor. Differing entablatures demarcate the floors, with a bracketed cornice used to finish off the whole. The treatment of these façades, although complex, is austere when compared with the extravagant ornamentation possible with cast iron, and this restraint contributes to the building's lasting beauty.

Known locally for generations as the White Bank, the structure suffered a major fire in 1957 and was threatened with demolition in the 1970s. In the mid-1980s it was renovated by two local architects, Robert G. Hecht and Edward C. Burdeshaw, and William Headley, a contractor. Newly painted in tones of grey, a treatment more in keeping with the antebellum practice of painting iron buildings in light stone colors, the beloved old landmark continues to serve its original purpose, housing a bank and prestigious office space.[23] The restoration project received an award from the Georgia Trust for Historic Preservation in 1987.

[14]   *Southport Savings Bank*
People's Bank (Southport Office)
226 Main Street, Southport, Connecticut
Adapted from design by Henry Austin

Chartered: 1854
Constructed: 1863–65

Despite Ferromania and the popularity of the palazzo, the simple front-gabled Greek Revival dwelling, which also suited narrow lots, proliferated throughout the East, South, and Middle West, and continued to be built into the eighties, often updated by the addition of Italianate details. In Southport, Connecticut, a prosperous farming community and busy port with a rich heritage of Greek Revival architecture, the Southport Savings Bank erected a handsome building in 1863–65 based on this popular pattern.

By 1860 Southport was called the Onion Capital of America, and during the Civil War the federal government contracted with local growers to provide this sturdy vegetable for the Union Army to help prevent scurvy.[24] The new savings bank occasioned by this onion-based prosperity was located near the foot of Main Street, close to the bustling waterfront and Southport's business center, "accessible to shipowners, shop keepers, the farmer patronage, and commercial traders."[25] It stood opposite the older Southport Bank, a porticoed building in the Greek Revival style built in 1833.[26]

Situated then, as now, in semiresidential, semicommercial surroundings, the Southport Savings Bank was the work of local builders Sherman & Jelliff. No architect was needed, since the original specifications, which survive, state that the structure was to be built "according to the specifications and plans and the Elevation" of the Danbury [Connecticut] Bank and that it was "to be finished in similar style . . . and of similar materials; excepting in dimensions and other particulars to be stated." [27] The major differences between the two banks involve their roofs and main building materials, the Southport building being more conservative in design and more lavish in materials.

The Danbury Bank, designed in 1855 by New Haven architect Henry Austin, was a fashionable palazzo, three bays wide and two stories high, with a low (virtually invisible) hipped roof and projecting horizontal cornice. Surviving illustrations show the main elevation with a ground floor pierced by two semicircular-arched doorways, each reached by a flight of steps, and a similarly treated window in the center embellished with a hood molding. Three square-headed windows with bracketed sills appear on the upper floor.[28] The Southport Savings Bank was organized in the same manner, except that the clients preferred their roof to have a pitch "like the Episcopal church and to be of slate and running the length of building (& not hipped . . .)." [29] The resultant triangular gable end, embellished with a bull's-eye window, maintained Greek Revival tradition but was framed by an emphatic Italianate bracketed cornice.

It was stipulated that the walls of the bank "instead of being laid with good common hard brick and rubbed and painted . . . may be laid with the best of Croton Front Brick . . . so as to present a true and handsome face on the outside of the walls, and so finished without painting." [30] Brownstone was used on the street front for the door and window trim — hood moldings being added to the two doorways, for a plaque bearing the bank's name, and for the two flights of steps.

While the rich hues of deep-red brick and brownstone and the lusher detailing of the Southport Savings Bank are part of the mid-Victorian reaction against the "grim temples" of the Greek Revival, the restraint and harmony of its retrospective composition reflect the classical discipline which was so firmly established in the building tradition of old New England communities. An unacknowledged source for the design may be John Haviland's bank[31] illustrated in his widely used builders' guide, *An Improved and Enlarged Edition of Biddle's Young Carpenter's Assistant,* published in 1837. Haviland's front-gabled Greek Revival façade is similarly fenestrated and also features a bull's-eye window in the gable end. The conservatism expressed by both the cautious style and the domestic pattern of the Southport bank perhaps reflects local resistance to the changes which industrialization and urbanization were making in American life, those very things which William Young's activites in Columbus were promoting. The *Southport Chronicle,* which began publication in the 1860s, provides evidence of such an attitude.[32] Even today this affluent residential suburb seems magically untouched by time. The beautifully maintained savings bank building still serves its original purpose, although today it functions as the Southport office of the People's Bank following a merger in 1955.

♦　♦　♦

If the Civil War stimulated Northern economies such as Southport's, it also provoked important changes in the country's banking system, which since 1836 had been left to the vagaries of the various states. With commercial banks issuing the only paper money in circulation, an intolerable situation existed when the war broke out. At that time the country's paper money supply comprised not only the notes of countless solvent banks (the worth of which varied) but also the spurious notes of nonexistent banks, genuine notes with forged signatures or with raised denominations, altered or old notes of failed banks, and quantities of counterfeits. On top of this, no local banks were strong enough to arrange the financing of the war for the Union government.

In 1861 Salmon P. Chase, Lincoln's secretary of the treasury, conceived a plan to finance the war that brought the federal government back into the country's banking system. The National Currency Act passed in 1863 provided for a system of federally chartered and regulated national banks to be established in local communities.[33] They would issue government-bond-backed currency of uniform design that would be of equal value throughout the country. To expedite development, in 1865 Congress passed a bill taxing new state bank-note issues, with the result that numerous state banks transferred to national charters and state bank notes ultimately disappeared. Essentially unchanged until the Federal Reserve System was put in place in 1913, the national banking system did not in fact eliminate the decentralization so dear to Americans. Rather it combined, many thought, the best features in the country's collective banking experience. In the words of Civil War financier Jay Cooke, it provided "the unity of action and general control, and the uniformity of currency—which were the best features of the United States Bank—with the diffusion of issue and freedom in local management which characterize the State system." [34]

Unfortunately, the currency legislation was not structured to meet fluctuating seasonal or regional monetary needs. Statutory restrictions severely limited credit needed to rebuild the South, and limits on real estate lending kept national banks from effectively supporting migration to the West. Growing numbers of small, non-note-issuing state-chartered banks met these needs, while the national banks grew more in size than in number. Nor was the problem of periodic financial panics solved. Yet the dual banking system that took root continues as a powerful political and economic force. The creation of a stable, uniform currency was obviously of critical importance to the nation's growth. Indeed, one enthusiastic supporter of the legislation had written to Secretary Chase in 1864 that "if the Civil War resulted in nothing else than providing the country with a uniform currency it would not have been fought in vain." [35]

[15]   *Dollar Savings Bank*

Dollar Bank
Fourth Avenue and Smithfield Street, Pittsburgh, Pennsylvania
Isaac H. Hobbs & Son

Chartered: 1855
Constructed: 1869–71

Unlike the note-issuing banks which were the focus of the Civil War banking legislation, mutual savings banks were established for working-class wage earners, a group that was of no interest to commerical banks. Patterned on the savings banks and provident institutions already operating in Scotland and England, they began to appear in the United States by 1816. The objective of these banks and their public-spirited founders is well expressed in the articles of association of the Philadelphia Saving Fund Society, which was the first such institution to conduct business:

> To promote economy and the practice of saving amongst the poor and laboring classes of the community — to assist them in the accumulation of property that they may possess the means of support during sickness or old age — and to render them in a great degree independent of the bounty of others . . . .[36]

Such sentiments were typical of the period — a blend of paternalism and the tenets of Ben Franklin's Poor Richard.[37]

Savings banks differed considerably in their make-up from commercial banks. Their charters were perpetual, so that depositors need not worry that the institution would suddenly lose its charter and go out of business. Trustees were not allowed to receive any financial benefit, and there were no stockholders. The distributed earnings of the bank — mainly from long-term mortgage loans — were divided among the depositors. Often these institutions purposely avoided the unpopular word 'bank' in their names in order to more readily secure charters from legislatures and to appeal to their inexperienced, apprehensive clientele. This new type of bank expanded rapidly. By 1820 there were 109 in the country, and by 1900 there were 652. Savings banks caught on quickly in the northeastern states with their growing manufacturing and commercial centers but were less popular in the southern and western areas where agriculture, lumbering, and mining predominated and where the greatest need was for short-term or commercial credit.[38]

In the competitive American environment, it did not take long for the savings banks to evolve from semicharitable institutions to business enterprises. Increasingly, the thrifty working class, rather than the indigent poor, formed the clientele. For all their benevolent origins, savings banks could only prosper by attracting customers. This goal resulted in the construction, between the mid-nineteenth century and the Great Depression, of some of the most notable — and extravagant — buildings in the history of American bank architecture. A particularly eloquent example, the Dollar Savings Bank, still stands in Pittsburgh.

Situated at the junction of a great river system and an early gateway to the West, Pittsburgh developed first into a major trading city and then, with access to immense reserves of raw materials like iron ore, into an industrial center. A mutual bank was a difficult concept to sell in this profit-minded city; few thought it viable or wanted to serve as voluntary trustees or as the unsalaried president. When the Dollar Savings Bank finally did manage to open in 1855, five customers appeared with a total sum of $53 to deposit. Within ten years, however, deposits had climbed to over $1.77 million and ultimately this mutual bank outlasted all other early Pittsburgh banks.[39]

Although the Dollar Savings Bank had been founded during a period of severe depression, the Civil War contributed greatly to Pittsburgh's growth and prosperity. A month before Lee's surrender at Appomattox in 1865, a lot was chosen for a new building to replace the bank's rented office. After a long delay, a design submitted by Isaac H. Hobbs & Son was selected in 1868, construction began the following year, and the new banking house was occupied in 1871.

The country's first bank architects had worked for and reflected the educated taste of a wealthy elite. However, Isaac Hobbs, an apparently self-taught Philadelphia architect, capitalized on the opportunity to cater to the vastly expanded middle class. Primarily a designer of houses, he astutely published two pattern books of his residential designs, further publicizing and selling these through the medium of *Godey's Lady's Book,* a periodical aimed at middle-class women. Although his book *Hobbs's Architecture* was scathingly reviewed in the *American Architect and Building News,* the architect was very successful, especially in unsophisticated rural towns in Pennsylvania and New York.[40]

Only an untrained architect could have produced so enchantingly bizarre a façade, and indeed the Dollar Savings Bank is primarily façade. The colossal Composite columns (the most ornate of the Roman orders) and the overpowering, totally original entablature terminate shortly after turning the corner, resulting in a frontispiece that resembles a boom-town front decked out as a triumphal arch, which masks the lower, simply treated structure behind. The giant surround containing the main doorway, also extravagantly embellished, displays terminal figures, two lion heads, and—in the center—a giant dollar coin encircled by the bank's name. Perhaps most memorable are the two lions that recline on either side of the steps leading to the main door. The trustees intended these as symbolic guardians of the people's money, while the lofty columns were a reminder of the institution's high aims.[41]

Hobbs personally supervised the construction of the building whose cost rose $70,000 above the original estimate. Major expenses included the Connecticut brownstone used for the front and for sculpturing. The interior, especially the main banking room, was also finely finished. The local *Daily Gazette* was impressed, finding the result a "noble structure, surpassed in permanence, symmetry and beauty by no public edifice in any American city," a building which excited "awe in the mind of the beholder."[42]

[16]   *Institution for Savings in Newburyport and its Vicinity*

93 State Street, Newburyport, Massachusetts
Rufus Sargent

Chartered: 1820
Constructed: 1871

Another engaging savings bank building from the same period is the Institution for Savings in Newburyport and its Vicinity, one of the earliest savings banks in the country. The building was designed by Rufus Sargent, a native of West Amesbury, Massachusetts. Sargent had established himself as a joiner-carpenter in Newburyport by 1843, and in 1849 was listing himself in the city's directory as an "Architect." Sargent began designing in the prevailing Greek Revival style and moved on to Italianate around the late 1850s.[43]

On the occasion of the bank's opening in 1871, the *Newburyport Daily Herald* observed that it was not an imposing structure on account of its size but nevertheless was a "temple of wealth erected by elegant taste."[44] Set back like many local mansions on a large lot, the distinctive little building has a swaggering cosmopolitan air, its singular style, brownstone walls, and spacious lawn contrasting with its immediate neighbors—

reserved, white-painted wood and brick, colonial and Federal-period buildings which hugged the street.

Sargent's design for the bank is not typically Italianate: its symmetrical, tripartite composition consists of a central pavilion with projecting centerpiece flanked by lower, recessed wings. This unusual design along with the prominent Corinthian pilasters that ornament the three bays of the pavilion suggests that the self-trained architect may have spent some time in nearby Boston looking at — but not totally comprehending — the new city hall. Completed in 1865, it was a prime American example of the Second Empire style, which became the architectural symbol of the free-wheeling Grant administration. The ultimate source for this opulent manner was contemporary Paris, transformed in the fifties and sixties by Napoleon III and his great planner, Baron Haussmann, into the most admired modern city in the world. Expressive of post-Civil War prosperity and cultural ambitions, the American version brought something of the flavor of the French capital to the country, until the Panic of 1873 and the ensuing economic depression caused the style to fall from favor. Its lavishness, combined with its conscious modernity, made it a favorite for new banks, while many an urban palazzo of the fifties, including the Bank of New York on Wall Street,[45] was updated in the seventies by adding a French mansard roof, which gave two more stories of rentable space.

Although Sargent's Institution for Savings lacks the mansard roof, that hallmark of the Second Empire style, his design otherwise seems a solecistic excerpt from Boston's City Hall.[46] As originally executed, with a miniature pediment crowning the whole, the bank resembled this possible source more strongly. In 1903, however, the building was lengthened at the rear, the interior remodelled, and the pediment removed. The wooden balustrade capping the roofline was replaced in brownstone and an elegant brass and wrought-iron railing added, giving the building a somewhat more sophisticated Beaux-Arts flavor.[47] In 1980 a manifestly modern addition by the Newburyport firm of Woodman Associates was joined at the rear, which courteously does not interfere with the gemlike original structure.

If richness of ornament began to typify ambitious bank architecture in settled parts of the country, plainness prevailed on the frontier, a term which described California in the 1850s. When gold was discovered in January 1848, there were still nine days to go before Mexico ceded the sparsely inhabited territory to the United States. Gold fever brought tens of thousands to California, which in 1850 became the thirty-first state. At the California convention held that same year to write a constitution, a bitter battle was waged over the article providing for the forming of corporations, especially those that would engage in banking.

During the gold rush all that was needed to provide banking services for the miners was a safe in a well-protected building. Some prominent merchants who had come to supply the gold seekers had such safes and simply added banking to their business. Other early California bankers were assayers, who took the dust from miners in exchange for drafts on Eastern banks. Express companies also took up this aspect of banking, sometimes taking gold at the point of production in exchange for local or Eastern drafts. Express companies were especially suited to do banking in this manner, since in distributing miners' supplies they reached all the populated places in the interior.

Despite the rapid appearance of banks in California, the forty-niners had brought west with them a distrust of these institutions, based on the ruin caused by the collapse of the banking system in the 1830s. Understandably, they also distrusted paper money. The outcome of the California constitutional convention was that incorporated commercial banking was not allowed in the state: associations could be formed for the deposit of gold and silver, but not for the issuing of paper money. Gold was the trusted circulating medium in California, retarding the organization of national banks in the state and the acceptance of national bank notes.

Thus restricted, banking in California followed a peculiar pattern which enabled an early express and banking company to emerge as one of the most famous banks in the West. Its founders were two eastern businessmen, Henry Wells and William G. Fargo, who formally announced in 1852, at New York's famous Astor House, the establishment of a joint stock company that would provide financial and communications services to Californians. That year the company opened its first office in San Francisco and by 1855 had established fifty-five agencies throughout California and Oregon. In 1886 it was described as:

> . . . the omnipresent, universal business agent of all the region from the Rocky Mountains to the Pacific Ocean. Its offices are in every town, far and near; a billiard saloon, a restaurant, and a Wells & Fargo office are the first three elements of a Pacific or Coast mining town; . . . It is the Ready Companion of civilization, the Universal Friend and Agent of the miner, his errand man, his banker, his post-office.[48]

[17]   *Wells, Fargo & Co.*
Main Street, Columbia, California
Architect unknown

Founded: 1852
Constructed: 1858 (not occupied by bank)

One of the early Wells, Fargo & Co. offices can still be seen in the old gold-mining town of Columbia, which is now a State Historic Park. Gold had been discovered in the area in March 1850, and within a month the mining-camp population numbered over 6,000. In 1851, when Columbia's streets and lots were laid out, the "architecture" of the place was composed of "shakes, mud and stone, clapboard and adobe . . . having the ground for a floor and a dried bullock's hide in place of a door."[49] Wells Fargo bought out an established express business in this dismal place in 1853 but did not construct the existing brick building until 1858, by which time two fires had destroyed the old town. The brick business district of today's restored Columbia postdates these fires, suggesting nothing of the wretchedness of the early 1850s but providing a romantic locale for film companies.

Burnt out of frame structures twice, William Daegener, the first Wells Fargo agent, contracted in 1858 for the erection of a two-story brick building, which would contain the express office in front and his family's living room in the rear of the first floor, with two bedrooms above.[50] Initially, this particular office did not function as a bank, for there already existed in the town a branch of the D. O. Mills & Company bank of Sacramento, which operated in a little brick building until it failed during the panic of 1865.[51] After that time the townspeople simply made use of the imposing Boston-made safe emblazoned with "Wells Fargo & Co. Bankers" that still stands in the interior and had been in service in the express office since 1854.[52]

Understandably, fire resistance was of great concern in the design of the Wells Fargo buildings. The walls, 13 to 18 inches thick, were constructed of a poor quality local brick, and heavy iron shutters could be closed to seal the doors and windows.[53] Although simple and utilitarian in the extreme, this home and business premises of one of Columbia's leading citizens achieved local grandeur by means of a delicate second-floor balcony of iron and modest brick corbelling below the flat roofline. In fact, the façade resembles the company's first office on San Francisco's Montgomery Street, and both might be termed gold-rush palazzos. The Columbia building was continuously in use until 1914, although even by the mid-1860s gold had become difficult to find. When the last newspaper closed its doors in 1868, it signalled the end of Columbia as a mining center. It is estimated that over $55 million in gold dust was weighed on the magnificent scales that were returned to the counter in 1954 at the time the Wells Fargo buildings were restored by the State of California. [54]

[18]   *Syracuse Savings Bank*
1 Clinton Square, Syracuse, New York
Joseph Lyman Silsbee

Chartered: 1849
Constructed: 1875–76

In 1870 an amazing device went into operation in a prominent New York business building, the Equitable Life Assurance Society, which for a time was the city's tallest building, with seven stories. The device was the passenger elevator. Elevators meant that the upper floors of buildings were as desirable to tenants as the lower ones, and a taller building meant greater rental revenue. The Equitable Building was an immediate success, and this "spelled the doom of the commercial palace because it paved the way for the skyscraper." [55]

From the 1870s on, height became a powerfully expressive tool in the hands of architects, but it also created aesthetic problems. The palazzo in its Second Empire manifestation could comfortably accommodate five stories, with two of them masked by the mansard roof. Yet historically the Renaissance palazzo was a low-rise domestic mode that could not be stretched skyward indefinitely without appearing ungainly. One imaginative early solution to the problem of height appears in a savings bank in Syracuse that was designed in 1875 by Joseph Lyman Silsbee, an architect mainly remembered as Frank Lloyd Wright's first employer. A native of Salem, Massachusetts, Silsbee was educated at Harvard and the Massachusetts Institute of Technology before setting up an office in Syracuse in 1872, one of the first wave of architects to practice in that growing industrial city.

Silsbee was an ardent disciple of the influential English art critic John Ruskin, whose compelling prose cast a spell over America beginning in the 1850s. Ruskin found great virtue in the medieval Gothic architecture of Venice but saw a reflection of corruption in its Renaissance style. By the 1860s and 1870s the architecture he championed, now called High Victorian Gothic, with its moralistic overtones, vied with the worldly Second Empire as a stylistic favorite, especially for religious and educational buildings.[56] It was also a visually arresting style, characterized by colorful, often strident, materials, profuse decoration, and dramatic skylines. It was used for some exceptional banks in the 1870s designed by such notable practitioners as Frank Furness, Russell Sturgis, and Leopold Eidlitz, all profound admirers of Ruskin.[57] For high-minded savings bank directors who intended to include several floors of rentable space in the new building, Victorian Gothic was an astute choice. With its towers and pinnacles and evocations of medieval cathedrals, it could be used to celebrate verticality, which is what Silsbee did in his design. He organized his six-story structure tightly around a 30-foot-square, 170-foot-high central tower, which contained both the vaults and Syracuse's first elevator.

Then the tallest building in the city, the Syracuse Savings Bank remains an important landmark. It borders Erie Boulevard, which covers what was once the famous Erie Canal. This celebrated canal, the source of Syracuse's early wealth and a common site for major buildings of the time, obviously influenced the choice of the Venetian Gothic style. Bank publicity material records that the detailing was chosen because of "the similarity between the setting of the palaces of the Doges of Venice, which overlook that Italian city's famous canals, and the Syracuse site adjacent to the legendary Erie canal."[58]

Despite this intentional and typically Victorian association, the bank actually resembles neither a Venetian palace nor any other medieval building but rather the Dry Dock Savings Bank in New York by Leopold Eidlitz, which also dates from 1875. Eidlitz's bank (no longer extant), like the Syracuse bank, featured a prominent tower and a picturesque balcony which one wag explained away as "the place where the president comes out to address depositors when the bank breaks."[59] The Dry Dock has been called "the chief architectural ornament of the Bowery" and an early example in New York of a monumental, isolated savings bank.[60] In Silsbee's contrastingly symmetrical design, however, verticality is foremost, the tower serving to pull the building upward rather than attracting attention to the entrance at the corner.

As originally designed and constructed, the Syracuse building's main central entrance was sheltered by a Gothic porch which covered a stairway to the second-floor offices.[61] The street-level floor was rented to other banking tenants and the upper floors to local businesses. The exterior, with its variously sized and detailed windows, reflects these divisions. The multitudinous parts, however, are controlled by the symmetrical arrangement, while the architectural color is—for High Victorian Gothic—subdued.[62] Still, when completed, with its pale buff and red sandstone, multiple towers and gables, and rich Gothic detailing, the building was a spectacular sight both from afar and from the canal barges passing by.

[19] *Society for Savings*

Society National Bank
127 Public Square, Cleveland, Ohio
Burnham & Root

Chartered: 1849
Constructed: 1888–90

The buildings of the 1860s and 1870s such as the Syracuse Savings Bank were soon dwarfed by the office buildings that Chicago pioneered in the aftermath of the great fire of 1871. For such immense structures—ten, sixteen, even twenty-two stories high—the fussy, fastidiously crafted High Victorian Gothic mode was economically impracticable. These marvels of modern engineering, dependent on fireproofed metal skeleton framing, were a distinctly American architectural type, requiring something new in the way of aesthetic expression. Finding appropriate ways to handle what would soon be known as the skyscraper was to be the foremost architectural challenge of the modern age.

Among the Chicago firms making history in the 1880s was Burnham & Root, whose works include such masterpieces as the Rookery (1886) and the Monadnock Block (1892). The designing partner, John Wellborn Root, was a combination of two of the most potent forces of the Victorian era: fascination with technology and intense romanticism.[63] In the fall of 1887, the Chicago architect was planning the first skyscraper in Cleveland,[64] a ten-story building to house the Society for Savings, which had been incorporated as a benevolent society in 1849. The Society for Savings of the City of Cleveland had grown into one of the best-known, most trusted financial pillars of Ohio, and by 1890, when it occupied its new home, there were more than forty thousand depositors and over $20 million in deposits.[65]

At this time Root and his colleagues were developing several mixed-structure options between traditional load-bearing masonry and the new true skyscraper construction—an all-metal frame combined with lightweight exterior cladding. The Society for Savings Building had an extremely advanced interior steel structure: the odd-numbered floors were diagonally windbraced and the supporting columns built up from Z-bars. This technique was pioneered by Charles L. Strobel in 1886 for his Chicago, Milwaukee & St. Paul Railroad bridge at Kansas City.[66] Indeed it was to such railroad engineers that Chicago architects turned for guidance in the steel skeleton construction that made their soaring buildings possible. For Root, such advanced techniques afforded not only height and fire-resistance but the large windows needed to light an office structure. He also introduced a central light court to illuminate the glass ceiling of the ground-floor banking chamber and an inner range of offices on the floors above.[67]

Harriet Monroe noted in her biography of Root that his mind "could build temples, towers and palaces upon a hint, but it craved the hint, as Shakespeare craved his plot, for the starting-point of his dream. Usually this hint came from one or more conditions inherent in the problem: . . . and from such a seed the plant would grow and flower in Root's brain as swiftly as a magical mango-tree."[68] The hint that sparked his conception for the Society for Savings was the massive defensive towers—the donjons or keeps—of the eleventh and twelfth centuries, which he had seen on a recent trip to Europe. In these austere rectangular fortresses he found analogies to the emerging monumental form of the modern office block and a means of achieving an impregnable image for a savings bank. To further this image he used solid masonry walls "as if such things as steel beams and pillars had never been dreamed of."[69] In fact, there is an equipoise between solid walls and glittering windows, which is often not seen in photographs. Root's delight in traditional building materials ("when the fates place at your disposal a good, generous sweep of masonry, accept it and thank God")[70] and the possibilities for light afforded by modern building technology are equally apparent in the Cleveland bank.

One of the great glories of the building is the masonry. Its base is constructed of enormous blocks of Missouri granite, from which spring massive squat piers of the same material. The capitals of these circular piers are left as unadorned rough-hewn stone blocks. The bulk of the walls, however, is rock-faced red Michigan sandstone, decorated with carving at major points such as entrances and certain windows. The elemental form of Root's structure and the rugged masonry both show the powerful influence exerted on Chicago architects by H. H. Richardson, through his Marshall Field Wholesale Store, completed in 1887.

An office tower, unlike a medieval keep, is composed of multiple floors of repetitive windows, and Root's tactile masonry and ornament combated the uniformity inherent in this design. To further enliven the face he grouped the windows in differing patterns as the building progresses upwards. Large windows deeply recessed behind the granite piers distinguish the arcaded banking floor. Ornamental hanging buttresses on the main elevation indicate the two major entrances and link the lower floors to those above. Here, pairs of windows are set within two tiers of giant arches each three floors high, with the windows of the second, sixth, and tenth floors differentiated to create transitions between base, tiers, and crown. The latter is embellished with a cornice, moulding course, and four angle turrets.

The detailing is eclectic in the manner of the day. Several periods of Gothic as well as Romanesque and Renaissance forms furnished Root with motifs, producing an agreeable — to contemporaries — visual variety. At times the ornament is pure delight. The spandrels of the main entrances, for example, are filled with keys and keyholes, while a wondrously vegetative wrought-iron electrolier near the entrance wraps its graceful tendrils around the corner of the building. The whimsy evident in the exterior ornament is also apparent in the banking room, where two painted panels set the mood — a medievalizing, late-nineteenth-century-English one. The panels, executed by Root's friend the Chicago artist William Pretyman, are based on drawings by a popular English storybook illustrator, Walter Crane. They depict in a rollicking manner the legend of the golden goose, a drolly appropriate subject for a savings institution.[71] This giant red tower projected the image of a protective fortress, but it was a decidedly friendly fortress.

If Root's design in the final analysis falls short of the aesthetic unity achieved for large commercial buildings by H. H. Richardson in the eighties and by Louis Sullivan in the nineties, it has a remarkable unity of expression. Like Richardson and Sullivan, Root sought ways of investing America's new large-scale commercial architecture with the dignity and meaning which had once been reserved for palaces and churches. The Society for Savings Building is a particularly moving testament to Root's special capacity in this quest.

Princeton Bank

12 Nassau Street, Princeton, New Jersey
William E. Stone

Chartered: 1834
Constructed: 1896 (not occupied by bank)

While city skylines were being radically altered by ever-taller buildings, the country's many small suburban and rural banks were also looking for new architectural images as distinguishing as the skyscraper. A charming end-of-the-century example is the former Princeton Bank.[72] Established in 1834 by a group of local citizens, this bank had provided much of the capital for the expansion of the town during the canal and early railway era. In 1896 the directors purchased land on Nassau Street, selling their original Georgian Palladian building. The year 1896 marked the Sesquicentennial of the founding of the town's most notable feature, the College of New Jersey, which officially became Princeton University during the festivities. In that year Moses Taylor Pyne, a wealthy graduate and benefactor of the college, who favored the lifestyle of the English gentry, commissioned two half-timbered buildings for Nassau Street, Upper and Lower Pyne, which would house shops and dormitories and help to establish Pyne's vision of Princeton as a university situated on the high street of an old English town. Infected no doubt by this local fever, the Princeton Bank commissioned a New York architect, William E. Stone, to design their new building.[73]

The Nassau Street elevation of the structure, which occupies a corner site, is three bays wide, comprising two large windows and the off-center main doorway. A generous bay window faces the side street to provide further light to the banking floor. Though modestly scaled, the building was and is an eye-stopper—even more visually arresting than the black-and-white Upper and Lower Pyne.[74] In the Dutch Revival style, the bank is constructed of bright-red brick with contrasting white stone trim and features an ornate stepped Dutch gable visible from some considerable distance as it soars above Nassau Street.

The critic Montgomery Schuyler was puzzled by the style, although he liked the building. In 1910 he wrote:

> . . . Princeton is not Dutch as other settlements in "the Jerseys" are Dutch, nor was there any apparent reason why the architect of the bank should have resorted to a Dutch motive. All the same, the visitor to Princeton has reason to rejoice that he did so. For of the many buildings which have been suggested by that famous and fantastic old sixteenth century meat market at Haarlem, none is more successful or seems more in place than this.[75]

How the directors and their architect happened on this picturesque style may never be known, but it was an inspired choice, for Dutch Revival conferred a certain cachet at this time. During the eighties and nineties acres of London were covered with Dutch gabled red-brick structures, both commercial and residential, some designed by the most admired British architect of the day, Richard Norman Shaw. The bank was thus not departing so radically from the English ambience that Pyne was seeking for Princeton. Moreover, just a year earlier, a striking Dutch Revival edifice (albeit a twelve-story one) had appeared in the Wall Street area: the John Wolfe Building. Widely praised, it may well have been admired by the Princeton financiers.[76]

The colorful Dutch style so popular in London had been initiated in the United States in 1885 with a row of New York townhouses by the notable firm of McKim, Mead & White. Here the rationale was a link with Manhattan's Dutch colonial past.[77] It was one of several revival styles promoted by this prolific New York firm that drew on the country's own history, to which attention had been focused by the centennial exhibition held in Philadelphia in 1876. The colonial revivals emerged as a popular means of expressing roots, of old money rather than new, and this too may have had some bearing on the directors' choice, for the Princeton Bank's long history was inextricably bound up with that of the town.[78]

The visual drama of the style, however, probably overrode all other factors. The bank's modest size does not disturb the scale already in place along Nassau Street, as skyscrapers were doing in major cities, but the ornate Baroque pediment decorating the gable serves as an assertive, towerlike feature to advertise the building. Indeed the gable, which is also embellished with scrolls, finials, corbels, a cartouche, and banded windows, nicely performs its traditional function, as in old or New Amsterdam, adding status to a building of domestic scale. The strongly contrasting colors of the materials were still popular at the end of the Victorian era. With its moderate scale, fine brickwork, and charming ornament, the old Princeton Bank is a particularly happy example of Late Victorian revivalism.

·4·

CANADIAN BANKS

MID AND LATE VICTORIAN

By 1841, when Upper and Lower Canada were united, the divergence between American and Canadian banking was already clear. While Americans were committed to free competition and easy money, conservative British North Americans, in their intimidating land, stayed close to the basic ideas embodied in Alexander Hamilton's plan for the first Bank of the United States. With the union of the provinces came a common banking law, which removed obstacles to branching and thus enabled — and indeed compelled — banks to build more ambitious branches as they vied for local business. Still, the more restrained development of Canadian banking was echoed in the more conservative, less individualistic appearance of bank buildings, which contrasted markedly with the rich diversity found in the United States following the demise of the Greek Revival style.

The Imperial Roman temple form adopted by the Bank of Montreal [10] for its new head office in the 1840s might seem an obvious equivalent of Strickland's Greek temple of democracy in Philadelphia [5]. Yet although the half-century following the completion of the Montreal bank was marked by notable economic growth and a steady increase in the number of banks,[1] this ambitious building was not a similarly influential prototype.[2] The innovative branches for the Bank of England designed by C. R. Cockerell in the 1840s in Britain were also ignored, while the domed banking hall, long since introduced by Soane and Latrobe, did not appear in Canada until the mid-1880s. Far more important as models were the palatial town mansions and gentlemen's clubs in the classical tradition that were built in Britain during the Regency and early Victorian periods.

Falling somewhere between a private house and a public building, a gentlemen's club was an especially appropriate model in hierarchical colonial society, since the bank manager, a person of high status in the community, generally lived on the premises. Moreover, boards of directors that met in these banks were virtually exclusive clubs.

[21] *Commercial Bank of the Midland District*

243 King Street East, Kingston, Ontario
William Hay

Chartered: 1831 (defunct)
Constructed: 1853–54

One of the handsomest extant examples of the pervasive mansion or club manner is the head office built for the Commercial Bank of the Midland District in Kingston, a Great Lakes port thriving on trade with the United States during the early fifties. The decision to build such a grand edifice was probably influenced by the impressive branch erected for the rival Bank of Montreal (1845–46), designed by the talented government architect George Browne. To have been architecturally eclipsed by the Montreal bank would have been intolerable to Kingston's home institution, which originally occupied a more modest building on Princess Street.[3]

By 1853 the city of Kingston was blessed with many notable limestone buildings designed by a number of able architects and constructed by expert stone masons who had been attracted to the area since 1827 to work on Imperial defenses against the United States, including the Rideau Canal and a new Fort Henry. When Kingston was named the capital of the United Province of Canada in 1841 the exuberant city fathers embarked on an ambitious building program, which, despite the early removal of the capital to Montreal, resulted in British North America's noblest civic structure to date, Browne's Kingston city hall. In 1850 a British rival, the Bank of British North America, became a tenant in this magnificent multipurpose structure.[4]

The architect of the new Commercial Bank was the Scottish-born William Hay, who had learned his profession in the office of John Henderson in Edinburgh, a center of classicism. In 1846 Hay was hired by the immensely popular Victorian Gothicist George Gilbert Scott to serve as clerk of works on Scott's Anglican cathedral in St. John's, Newfoundland. Hay spent part of the following decade practicing in Toronto but ultimately made his way back to Edinburgh, where his most important work was the restoration of St. Giles Cathedral.[5]

For the bank Hay designed a monumental rectangular limestone structure of three stories, which presents its three-bay front to King Street, then primarily a fine residential avenue. In the center the entrance to the bank is marked by an imposing double-storied portico ornamented with clustered piers at the second-level balcony and crowned by a balustrade. The side elevation facing William Street is five bays long, with a one-story portico sheltering the doorway to the manager's apartment.[6] A ground-level balustrade separates this private front from the public street.

The stonework and detailing of these two elevations are splendidly handled and serve to announce the functions within. The ground floor, originally housing the banking offices and manager's dining room, is set off by assertive rusticated masonry and tall semicircular headed openings. Smooth ashlar marks the next floor, where the other principal rooms of the manager's apartment were located. This story features tall rectangular bracketed windows, each with a shallow balustraded balcony. The less-consequential attic story, also of smooth ashlar and separated from the floor below by a cornice, has simply treated, smaller windows. From here four neo-Baroque chimneys and an unusual central terminal element rise high above the roofline.

Although Hay's powerful exterior is characterized by the richer, more plastic classicism that appealed to current taste, it does not replicate Charles Barry's influential palazzo paradigm, which was only beginning to exert influence on British architecture when Hay left England. Instead, the odd Baroque elements and heavy scale provide the edifice with a self-assured presence. This special quality may well have been inspired by the striking body of work that Browne had left in Kingston before moving with the government to Montreal in 1844. Professor J. Douglas Stewart of Queen's University sees in Browne's buildings a heroic primitivism that is supremely expressive of Kingston's pioneering energy during her days of glory.[7] However conceived, the Commercial Bank of the Midland District symbolized with equal success this high-water mark in the city's history. Architecturally it could hold its own against any bank building in British North America at that time — with the exception of the Bank of Montreal on Place d'Armes [10].

By the late 1840s, the burgeoning settlements of Canada were demanding local banking service, then not sufficiently provided by the existing chartered banks. In response, the United Province of Canada passed free-banking legislation in 1850 with the objective of stimulating the establishment of banks in smaller towns. No branches were allowed and the minimum capital requirement was £25,000 — more than many communities could raise. Moreover, the banks' notes had to be backed by provincial government securities, a government fund-raising scheme which put these banks at a disadvantage vis-à-vis the individually chartered ones. The legislation established a dual system: the traditional chartered banks with branches and extensive capital, and the new banks, which were purely local with limited capital. In the end only five banks were organized under the free-banking law, and three of these shortly obtained regular charters. In 1866 the province's free-banking legislation was repealed, after being inoperative for a number of years.[8] To this day, the chartered banks (now federally chartered) with their nationwide branches are the key players in the Canadian banking system.

Molsons Bank

Bank of Montreal (International Service Centre)
288 St. James Street, Montreal, Quebec
George William Richardson Browne

Founded: 1854
Chartered: 1855
Constructed: 1864–66

Two entrepreneurs who did profit from the free-banking legislation were William and John Molson, sons of the founder of Molson's Brewery, the longest-lived family firm in Canada's history. The Molson family had already been issuing private currency to pay for labor and materials since 1837, but an early application for a bank charter—in 1839—had been rejected on the grounds that they were primarily brewers and distillers. With the passage of the free-banking legislation, the two brothers obtained a license in 1854 for Molsons Bank in Montreal. Despite runs orchestrated by the Bank of Montreal, of which the two Molsons had lately been directors, the new bank not only survived its first year but even paid a dividend. In 1855 the brothers' application for inclusion in the select circle of chartered banks was granted.[9]

This was an excellent time for the Molsons to start a bank. The period from 1850 to 1857 witnessed the greatest industrial and commercial growth that British North America had yet known. Although the cessation of colonial preferences in the 1840s had created an initial period of anxiety, the long-term effect was to jolt Canadians out of their dependency on Britain, forcing them to develop their vast terrain themselves. William Molson, founder and president of the bank, was actively involved in a number of railroads, the mania of the 1850s and the first and most important result of the new spirit of enterprise.[10]

When the monetary crisis of 1857 occurred, none of the chartered banks suspended. Conservatively run, Molsons Bank prospered and by 1860 was regarded as one of the soundest financial institutions in the North American colonies. In 1864 the directors acquired the property adjoining their premises for a splendid new banking house, completed in 1866. Until the prudent institution opened its first branch in London, Ontario, in 1870, all the bank's business was conducted from this Montreal building.[11]

For the new Molsons Bank the directors selected the architect George Browne by competition.[12] Constructed of buff Ohio sandstone, with entrance porch columns of highly polished reddish Peterhead granite, Browne's edifice follows the mansion-club pattern that had now become standard for Canadian banks and which he had earlier used in a more restrained fashion for the Bank of Montreal branch in Kingston. The Molsons building was designed large enough to provide "commodious chambers" on the second and third floors, reached by a separate entrance, which the bank intended to lease "to public companies." This was expected to "prove largely remunerative, inasmuch as they are thoroughly heated and ventilated, and fitted with lavatories, water closets, dust holes and bin, porter's room, &c." [13]

The design was also a trend-setting early Canadian response to the French Second Empire style. Although Browne retained the blocklike form and much of the detailing of the well-established Italian Renaissance Revival, he adopted an iron-crested mansard roof and enriched the exterior surfaces by means of projecting and receding wall planes and luxuriant ornament, which reflected the newer French-inspired trend. The use of imported colored building materials rather than local grey limestone was indicative of advanced mid-Victorian taste and also of advances in transportation which the Molsons promoted. Too, the imported materials and their profuse detailing represented a considerable expenditure — an effective means of advertising the bank's position.

Ohio sandstone, softer than eastern Canadian limestones, allowed for a virtuoso display of the stonecutters' art. William is commemorated by a carved likeness above the lintel of the main entrance door, while at cornice level is a sculpted shield bearing the Molson coat of arms, flanked by two seated female figures. The keystones of the upper windows carry the caduceus, generally associated with the medical profession, but which also — with its entwined serpents of prudence — calls attention to an essential business virtue. Carved above the fireplace of the handsome panelled boardroom is the bank coat of arms, surmounted by the family crest. The bank's shield depicts an Indian holding a bow, a beehive surrounded by bees, an oak tree with a beaver at its base, and a ship with its sail furled. These symbolize Canada, industry, the lumber and fur trades, and water transportation, respectively.[14] The ship is especially significant, for in addition to founding the famous brewery, John Molson had inaugurated steam navigation in British North America in 1809, two years after Robert Fulton's *Clermont* had made its first trip on the Hudson River.

Recently restored extensively by the Bank of Montreal to use as offices,[15] Browne's creation remains one of the jewels of the city's financial district. Although its business was entirely local until 1870, the Molsons Bank building was as imposing as any of the head or regional offices erected by other chartered banks during the sixties and seventies.

The most important accomplishment of the mid-Victorian period, however, was not the chartering of new banks and the erection of fine bank buildings, but the founding of modern Canada. Railroads, conquerers of geological and climatic barriers, provided the means of linking the vast territories, while renewed fear of annexation by the United States — precipitated by the Civil War — was among the compelling motives for union. Thus in 1867 the two Maritime provinces of Nova Scotia and New Brunswick joined together with the Province of Canada, which was subdivided into Quebec and Ontario, to form the Dominion of Canada. By 1871 British Columbia and the immense, virtually untouched Hudson's Bay Company empire of Rupert's Land and the North-Western Territory had become part of Canada, which now extended across the continent. Ultimately the provinces of Manitoba, Saskatchewan, and Alberta and a part of what came to be called the Northwest Territories would be carved out of Rupert's Land. The Yukon Territory was made separate from the Northwest Territories in 1898. A financial crisis created by inept railway construction impelled Prince Edward Island to join the Confederation in 1873, although isolated Newfoundland did not choose to belong until 1949.

Canada's first transcontinental railway, finally completed in 1885, was crucial to the welding together and growth of the newly created Dominion, much as Alexander Hamilton's stable banking system had been needed to strengthen the new United States a century earlier. In the words of Canadian historian Michael Bliss:

> The construction of the Canadian Pacific, at the time the longest railway in the world, was one of the epic feats of nineteenth-century railway building, unmatched until Russia built the Trans-Siberian line at the end of the century. The transcontinental railway's importance to Canada was so fundamental that its history has been celebrated in song and story as a Canadian national epic.[16]

Government support was essential in building the railroad, but the nearly insurmountable task of financing was the work of George Stephen, president of the Bank of Montreal when he took over the job in 1880. Although Stephen resigned from the bank the following year, his chief associate was his cousin, Donald A. Smith, who was named vice-president in 1882, president in 1887. The Bank of Montreal served as the major financial intermediary for the project, acting as fiscal agent for the Canadian Pacific Railway and furnishing the company with direct loans totalling nearly $11.5 million. The other Canadian banks played a part in financing the enterprise, but none to the extent of the Bank of Montreal.[17] This is hardly surprising, for the Montreal-based institution had become banker for the new Dominion Government, a continuation of the role it had played for the government of the Province of Canada since 1863.[18] By 1873 this bank was held to be "in a position far beyond anything known on the continent of America, and . . . one of the largest banks in the world."[19]

[23]   *Bank of Montreal*
                    30 Yonge Street, Toronto, Ontario
                    Darling & Curry

Founded: 1817
Chartered: 1822
Constructed: 1885–86 (not occupied by bank)

In 1885 the Bank of Montreal, clearly anticipating increased business resulting from the completion that same year of the transcontinental railway, commenced a larger Toronto main branch at a new location: where the main commercial street met the railway and the waterfront. Their existing Renaissance Revival building,[20] although handsome, no longer served their physical requirements or reflected their image. The new edifice, completed in 1886, was as much a landmark in the history of Canadian bank architecture as was the Montreal head office [10] four decades earlier.

To begin with, the bank took the unusual step of commissioning a talented thirty-five-year-old Canadian architect, Frank Darling, who had submitted the winning (but unbuilt) competition design for the Ontario Parliament Buildings in 1880. This was Darling's first bank (in partnership with S. G. Curry), but it was not to be in the High Victorian Gothic manner for which he became known after working in London under G. E. Street. Darling maintained the classical tradition that was still preferred for Canadian banks, but he abandoned the old-fashioned mansion-club formula, looking instead to contemporaneous British free classicism for inspiration. This individualistic manner encompassed eclectic detail and lavish ornament and the functionalism of the English Gothic Revival. Darling's ornate Ohio sandstone exterior is organized around the key element in the design — the 45-foot-high banking hall, which was of a size and scale unprecedented in Canada. This splendid octagonal chamber, double the height of its nearest rival and richly decorated, was the grandest bank interior of its day in Canada, "the first of the great banking halls that are still a preoccupation of Canadian banks and their architects."[21]

Although the main door, situated on the corner, is given an unusual and elaborate surround, the banking hall windows on the side elevations are what dominate this remarkable composition. They are set within virtual pedimented porticos of a monumental size usually reserved for front entrances and, indeed, which recall the grand Corinthian portico of the Montreal head office [10]. It is here, on the two friezes, that the bank's name is emblazoned. The exterior sculpture, by the Toronto firm of carvers Holbrook & Mollington, is uncharacteristically ebullient for a Canadian bank, expressing the pride and economic optimism engendered by the railroad. The piers flanking the banking hall windows are embellished with sculptured shields and trophies hanging from carved masks which represent the arts and industries of Canada. The stained-glass skylight atop the opulent banking hall was also replete with allegory:

> Cornucopia pour out in lavish fashion the gold and silver coin, which for centuries have been the emblem of the banker's occupation. Dragons and mythical personages in blue and crimson draperies keep guard over these treasures and defy 'the gorgons and chimaeras dire', which from other portions of the dome would ravish them away.[22]

This commission rightly served to launch Frank Darling on a long career as one of Canada's premier bank architects.

However successful Darling was, from the mid-1880s until the turn of the century, the Scottish-born Andrew Taylor was the preeminent bank specialist in Canada.[23] He designed bank buildings from Nova Scotia to British Columbia, ranging from semiresidential banks in small towns to tall office buildings in growing western cities such as Winnipeg, Vancouver, and Victoria. His firm (Taylor & Gordon) had as clients not only the Bank of Montreal, but Molsons Bank, the Merchants Bank, the Bank of British North America, the Bank of Toronto, and the Imperial Bank.

Taylor had not designed banks before coming to Canada in 1883. He began by adapting romantic Late Victorian domestic architecture to banking needs — an appropriate response, since bank managers continued to live on the premises. Initially Taylor used the picturesque, colorful English styles — Queen Anne and Dutch Renaissance — as well as the widely admired Richardsonian Romanesque of the United States. In doing so, he broke classicism's stranglehold on Canadian bank architecture for a brief decade and a half in the eighties and nineties. He embraced classicism only around 1900 while associated with the fashionable New York architects McKim, Mead & White in the enlargement of the Bank of Montreal head office [27]. Because of the fragmented character of the American banking system, no American architect could boast of similar nationwide bank commissions during the nineteenth century. Moreover, in Canada only the Bank of Montreal was then in a position to build on such an ambitious scale.

Bank of Montreal West End Branch

Guardian Trust
950 St. Catherine Street, Montreal, Quebec
Taylor & Gordon

Founded: 1817
Chartered: 1822
Constructed: 1889 (not occupied by original bank)

Among Taylor's works is the stylish Richardsonian Romanesque Bank of Montreal West End Branch erected in 1889. This building was contemporaneous with that seminal Canadian monument in the round-arched Richardsonian manner: the Canadian Pacific Railway's Montreal terminal, Windsor Station (1888–89), designed by the New York architect Bruce Price.[24] The West End Branch is situated on a corner, a desired location for banks for reasons of increased traffic and interior light. Its asymmetrical composition is organized around an attention-getting conical corner tower and includes a steeply pitched irregular roof with prominent gables on the two street fronts. Despite Richardson's influence, the building clearly reflects Taylor's High Victorian Gothic training in its picturesque functionalism and striking polychromy. Composed of three shades of red Corsehill and Ohio buff sandstone, it is extraordinarily colorful for a Canadian bank and features as well a multitude of lively ornament by the talented architectural sculptor Henry Beaumont.[25] Among the dour greystone houses that comprised the neighborhood, the first branch bank in the city's Upper Town was a conspicuous outrunner in what was soon to become Montreal's shopping core.[26]

When the Canadian Pacific Railway was completed in 1885, Canada's first transcontinental line stretched from Quebec City on the St. Lawrence estuary to Port Moody at the mouth of the Fraser River on the British Columbian coast. The eastern chartered banks went west with the railway. When the CPR reached Calgary in 1883, for example, the settlement consisted of half a dozen log buildings. Three years later the Bank of Montreal opened a branch in a rented frame store, and in another three was able to move into a new cream-colored sandstone building with three stories and an attic. Designed by Andrew Taylor, it was a simplified version of his West End Branch with a similar corner tower and pitched roof. Thus, within six years of the arrival of the railroad, this infant prairie community, outgrowth of a fort built in 1875 for the North-West Mounted Police, boasted a bank building which reflected the very latest architectural fashion in the East.[27]

The Bank of Montreal was the first eastern bank to open branches in British Columbia, beginning with Vancouver in 1887, which was barely a settlement when the CPR decided to take advantage of its fine harbor and extend the line westward from the original terminus of Port Moody. By 1892 Vancouver had a population of 15,000 and a Taylor-designed branch of the Bank of Montreal underway. Four stories, towered and gabled, this stone building was a dramatic improvement on the two-story frame structure which had served as the bank's first office.[28]

Bank of Montreal
1200 Government Street, Victoria, British Columbia
Francis Mawson Rattenbury

Founded: 1817
Chartered: 1822
Constructed: 1896–97 (not occupied by bank)

New cities like Calgary and Vancouver, which were created by the Canadian Pacific Railway, had to import architects to design prestigious bank buildings. Victoria, however, was an old community: first the Pacific coast headquarters of the Hudson's Bay Company, and then capital of the colony of Vancouver Island, and after union in 1886, of British Columbia. By the time the Bank of Montreal reached the city in 1891, professional architects were available. Indeed, in that year the British Columbia Institute of Architects was formed in Victoria.

The architect chosen by competition for the Victoria branch in 1896 was Francis Mawson Rattenbury, a Yorkshireman who, as a twenty-five-year-old newcomer to Victoria in 1894, had won an international competition for the British Columbia Parliament Buildings. He would thereafter become the Bank of Montreal's architect in British Columbia, designing branches in Rossland, Nelson, and New Westminster.

To contend with the long-established Bank of British Columbia, the provincial government's banker, the Bank of Montreal chose a design which deftly symbolized its own power and, whether intentionally or not, its close connection with the transcontinental railroad. Sited grandly, the towered, four-story bank is the focal point of a long vista down View Street. The main entrance is at the corner, but the most prominent architectural feature—a broad bay terminating in a steep neo-Gothic tower—fronts directly on Government Street, where it can dominate the prospect along View Street. The facing material above the rusticated granite base is the same pale grey Haddington Island stone used for Rattenbury's Parliament Buildings. The rugged granite is also used for the voussoirs of the round-arched ground-floor windows and corner entrance, creating visual and textural contrast with the bands of alternating rusticated and smooth ashlar Haddington Island stone used for the bulk of the building. The skilled handling of the masonry, including the fine foliated ornament enriching door and window areas, added considerably to the cost of the building and set it smartly apart from the Bank of British Columbia [25b], situated a block to the south. The architect of this bank, an Italianate palazzo erected in 1886, had relied heavily on molded cement and cast iron to create an impression of a solid stone exterior.[29] The *Canadian Architect and Builder* commented in 1899: "The first building which attracts attention as a very decided exception to prevailing mediocrity and excites feelings of interest and pleasure is the Bank of Montreal, which is an excellently handled little piece ."[30]

This "little piece" was composed of an eclectic mix of medieval Romanesque and Gothic elements, termed the Chateau style, which had originated in the United States for millionaires' mansions. The most celebrated example there was the Fifth Avenue house designed by William Morris Hunt for W. K. Vanderbilt, whose wealth was based on railroads. Similarly, in Montreal, where the head offices of the Bank of Montreal and the CPR were located, the Chateau style was used for city mansions built in the late eighties and the nineties for members of the clique who controlled the two closely connected corporations.[31]

In Canada, unlike the United States, the Chateau style was also used extensively in the commercial and public realm. Initially it became the corporate style of the CPR, which, after the completion of Bruce Price's Chateau Frontenac Hotel in Quebec City, used the mode for a series of spectacular hotels across the country intended to stimulate passenger traffic. "Since we can't export the scenery," said railway president William Van Horne, thinking in particular of the Rockies, "we shall have to import the tourists."[32] In the wake of the success of these romantic hotels, the style grew in influence until it was advocated and practiced as a Canadian national style, the only one acceptable for government buildings, and it remained an active architectural force until the Second World War.[33]

By 1903 it had become so firmly established as the style of the Canadian Pacific Railway, that Rattenbury employed it for his splendid Empress Hotel in Victoria, a CPR project completed in 1908. It was hailed as a hotel which would "make the Western gateway of the great transcontinental system a fitting companion to the historic pile [the Chateau Frontenac] on the heights of Quebec."[34] Although western Canadians have bitterly resented the dominating influence of the East,[35] the railroads, the banks, and other eastern enterprises were vital in tying the new nation together. Even Canadian historian Frank Underhill, for whom business was "an ogrish, evil force," felt compelled to observe in 1927: "The success of enterprises like the T. Eaton Company [department stores and mail-order catalogues], the Massey-Harris Company [farm equipment], the Bank of Montreal, and other such concerns organized and managed by Canadians, has done more to strengthen our national feeling than all the other speeches and posturing of our politicians since we first elected representative assemblies."[36] Eloquently represented by these Bank of Montreal western branches and as first clearly understood and practiced by the Canadian Pacific Railway's president, architecture, too, was a particularly effective means of unification.

·5·

AMERICAN AND CANADIAN BANKS

BEAUX-ARTS
CLASSICISM

As the colorful, picturesque styles of the Victorian era were reaching
an apogee in the eighties and nineties in both Canada and the United
States, the leading new architectural firm in New York—McKim, Mead &
White—was striving to reintroduce classical order and discipline into
architectural design. During their active period from 1879 to 1910, the
firm received over 785 commissions.[1] Surprisingly these included relatively few banks, although those they did design exerted enormous influence. Not only were their banks of outstanding quality, but many of the
leading American architects of the pre-Depression period who received
prestigious bank commissions had trained in the sought-after McKim office.[2] The firm's efforts were advanced by the World's Columbian Exposition held in Chicago in 1893, in which Charles McKim, who had studied at
the Ecole des Beaux-Arts in Paris, was deeply involved. The gleaming
white neoclassical buildings of the fair's Court of Honor, grouped majes-
tically around a lagoon, made an extraordinary impact on architects and
the general public alike, who could only compare the carefully planned
splendor of the fair with the chaotic lack of discipline characterizing most
North American cities. Andrew Taylor related his impressions at the annual meeting of the Province of Quebec Association of Architects in 1893:

> To pass from the noisy, dirty, half paved, half-baked chaotic city of Chicago, to
> the fair white city on the shores of Lake Michigan, with its lagoons and islands,
> pleasant winding walks, fountains, statuary and architecture, is like a transla-
> tion from Purgatory to Paradise.[3]

[26] *Bowery Savings Bank*
130 Bowery, New York, New York
McKim, Mead & White

Chartered: 1834
Constructed: 1893–95

The exhilarating sense of having passed from Purgatory to Paradise must have overwhelmed the customers of McKim, Mead & White's Bowery Savings Bank. Begun in 1893 just before the stock market crashed,[4] the project nevertheless continued and was finally completed in 1895, producing the "the first truly sumptuous bank in New York."[5] One of the first buildings to reflect the classicism and architectural civility of the Chicago fair, the Bowery Savings Bank was the harbinger of a new wave of porticoed banks that would spread across the continental United States and into rapidly developing Canada.

First opened in 1834, the Bowery Savings Bank had benefited from the prosperity of the post-Civil War period. Despite the serious financial panic that occurred in 1883, the bank made history the next year by granting the largest mortgage loan ever made by an American savings bank. This loan of $1.5 million financed the New York Produce Exchange, one of eminent architect George B. Post's finest buildings. This widely publicized transaction brought to the bank an aura of importance and prestige—and increased business. Whereas the institution's outstanding loans in 1883 were $7 million, the figure had risen to $10.5 million by 1885.

The exceptional prosperity of the nation in 1892,[6] coupled with the desperately crowded quarters of the existing bank, led the trustees to purchase property adjoining their site on the Bowery and to commission McKim, Mead & White to design a new building. The parcel of land surrounded but did not include a corner plot occupied by the Butchers and Drovers Bank.[7] Stanford White, the firm's brilliant ornamentalist and the partner in charge of the project, thus had a difficult L-shaped site to contend with. This he managed to exploit with an exceedingly skillful design incorporating entrances from the two principal streets. For the main entrance—through the constricted mid-block Bowery façade, which faced the dreary elevated railway tracks—White created a tall, templelike entry with two monumental Corinthian columns in antis, richly decorated pediment, and prominent attic. His majestic entrance gave access to a long corridor leading to a magnificent banking room, where a second entrance opened onto Grand Street. The Grand Street elevation was sufficiently broad to accommodate five bays: four windows and a central doorway. Here White placed a shallow pedimented portico with four Corinthian columns. On the less important but carefully detailed Elizabeth Street elevation, the rectangular windows, bracketed on the ground floor, are separated by Corinthian pilasters, a treatment carried over from the Grand Street front.

Impressive though the exterior is, the great glory of the Bowery Savings Bank is the banking room, which continues to inspire awe thanks to the careful restoration of the building undertaken by the bank in 1980. Although the pale, monochromatic exterior reflects an emerging taste for smooth, light-colored stone, White's interior has a lingering Victorian warmth and richness of color, the cumulative effect of painted and gilded surfaces, colored marbles and scagliola, and stained glass in the windows of the north and east walls and in the skylight above the deeply coffered, coved ceiling.[8] The effect is inviting rather than intimidating, an important quality for a building intended to attract and uplift the urban poor. The architect made good use of his long corridor leading from the Bowery entrance to the banking hall, thoughtfully filling the center with seating, segregated by sex, for weary depositors.[9]

Not surprisingly, the new building was good for business. Although most of the bank's customers were unused to such splendor, many of the struggling immigrants who moved on to better lives "trusted the Bowery so implicitly that they left their savings in its vaults." [10] Toward the end of 1895 there were more than 11,000 accounts and assets in excess of $60 million.[11] This experience undoubtedly prompted the bank to commission a second masterpiece, when they decided in 1923 to build their first uptown branch at Park Avenue and 42nd Street, to attract customer traffic from the newly built Grand Central Station.[12]

[27]   *Bank of Montreal Addition*
         119 St. James Street, Montreal, Quebec
     McKim, Mead & White and Andrew T. Taylor,
              Associate Architects

Founded: 1817
Chartered: 1822
Addition constructed: 1901–05

In 1900 McKim, Mead & White received the greatest Canadian bank commission to be carried out during the Edwardian period, the renovation and enlargement of the Bank of Montreal head office [10] on Place d'Armes. Construction began in 1901, supervised by Andrew Taylor, who served as associate architect with the firm. As architect to the bank and a nephew of the vice-president, Taylor had brought the eminent New York firm to the directors' attention.[13] The design has been attributed to McKim, who has also been cited as the partner in charge,[14] but Taylor's correspondence indicates that he worked primarily with Mead and that the two shared the fees equally.[15]

Two factors were critical in the development of the design: the site, which precluded lateral expansion on St. James Street, and the old bank's historic nature. The scheme ultimately retained the original building, linked it to a great addition at the rear, and added a new dome in Guastavino tile, a relatively recent vaulting technique. An attic story had been added to the bank in 1859 at the time the wooden dome was removed.[16] Augmented by four feet, this attic together with the rebuilt dome added mass, creating a more powerful main front than in the original architect John Wells's day, but one that was perfectly attuned to the expansive times.

In a superbly extravagant gesture, the old interior was transformed into a triumphal approach to the vast new banking hall, one of the largest spaces ever created by McKim, Mead & White. This huge basilica occupies the upper floor of the new addition.[17] For the grey Chelmsford granite façade of the addition, which overlooks Craig Street and could not be seen in relation to the old bank, the architects drew on the Renaissance palazzo tradition. However, its massive scale, smooth flat surfaces, and the restrained detailing distinguish it sharply from nineteenth-century versions. There are no public entrances from Craig Street: the elevation presents a defensive appearance. The new work is subtly related to the old by the device of using a bay module from Wells's Corinthian portico as the principal planning element. The broad Tuscan columns above the rusticated base (behind which the vaults lie) of the façade correspond exactly to the Corinthian columns located within in the banking hall, the module of both being based on Wells's scheme.

Whereas the interior of the Bowery Savings Bank [26] is warm and inviting, the remodelled Bank of Montreal interior is cool and intimidating. It is clear given the unprecedented vastness and grandeur of the banking hall and the use of the renowned old building merely as a vestibule, that it was still Canada's preeminent financial institution. No expense was spared. The columns of the approach from the old building and the thirty-two 31-foot columns which line the main banking room are of polished green Syenite granite from Vermont, with bases of Belgian black marble. The main walls of all the public spaces are of mauve-toned pink Tennessee marble. Gold was used extensively. The capitals of the columns are of solid bronze, plated with gold, and all the ornamentation of the intricate coffered ceiling of the banking hall is outlined in gold.

The project provoked bitter controversy, particularly among envious Canadian architects, since both talent and much of the material were imported. However, even Percy Nobbs, the director of the fledgling McGill School of Architecture in Montreal and no fan of McKim, Mead & White, believed it to be the firm's most perfect achievement. "[McKim] showed Canadians for the first time, on their own soil, what modern classic and planning in the grand manner really meant; also he gave us a much needed lesson on the cost of a first-class job!" [18]

Nobbs also poked fun at the pretentious religiosity of this interior. For satirical purposes he assumed the voice of a medieval gargoyle's ghost, a creature familiar with the Gothic cathedrals of Europe but totally ignorant of banks. As Nobbs begins his commentary in 1904, as the bank was nearing completion, the gargoyle's ghost has just vacated his perch on Notre Dame Church across the Place d'Armes from the bank:

> Opposite the church he had left was a great and spacious portico and in the centre a door, and devoutly preoccupied men were ascending the steps and entering in. Quoth the Gargoyle's ghost, "Is this also a temple of the Most High?" Being inquisitive though sceptical on the matter he followed the crowd. Now inside the door there were building operations in progress and the Gargoyle's ghost thought "how assiduous are these worshippers entering in with serious mien thus early in the morning a building not yet completed." By this time he knew they were worshippers indeed.
>
> As he passed the inner door a great glory struck his eyes. The floor was white and the ceiling was white and the walls were white, and before him was a row of great shining green granite columns. . . And it took the breath of the Gargoyle's ghost away from him and he hid behind a pillar. . . .
>
> Then noting that the worshippers stopped not, neither bowed down, he followed boldly into the great hall. . . .
>
> . . . an altar of green Italian serpentine inlaid with red Belgian marble ran from one end of the Temple to the other . . . and the ghost of the gargoyle wondered and said, "Although this temple is not dedicated to the praise of the Lord, he whom they worship here is a very great power and exactness and precision are the quality of his perfection. So the ghost of the gargoyle lingered till he was satisfied that it was here that the men of Montreal did their real worship and he concluded that the God must be very great to be worthy of so fine a temple . . . .

After pondering for a time, he decided that what the men of Montreal worshipped in the great hall behind the portico was the chief god of the land.[19]

Nobbs's colleague at McGill, Canadian political economist and humorist Stephen Leacock, also referred to this building in one of his satirical pieces on banks and bankers:

> So lofty the Hall, so dim the Light
> The Ceiling is almost out of Sight,
> So still, so calm it is, they say
> That at Times the Folk from across the Way,
> By accident wander in to pray.
> The Bank permits it, — in Fact is glad, —
> A thing like that is a splendid Ad.[20]

The unprecedented scale and splendor of these turn-of-the-century banks was typical of the work of firms such as McKim, Mead & White, which were heavily influenced by the prestigious Ecole des Beaux-Arts in Paris. Beaux-Arts training, whether acquired in Paris or in offices or universities in the United States, produced buildings that were well planned and constructed and beautiful according to traditional design criteria, all qualities guaranteed to appeal to clients in increasingly affluent and culturally ambitious North America.

[28]   ## *Bank of California*

400 California Street, San Francisco, California
Bliss & Faville

Chartered: 1864
Constructed: 1906–08

Two young Californians, Walter D. Bliss and William B. Faville, went East to learn, met in the McKim, Mead & White office, and proceeded to form a partnership in San Francisco in 1898. They were soon considered one of the leading firms in northern California and in 1905 were commissioned to design a new building for the West's preeminent Bank of California.

Organized in 1864, the bank had been the first joint-stock corporation in the state empowered to do commercial banking. Its original capital stock of $2 million had been paid up in gold coin, since gold-rich California long spurned paper money. The bank's guiding spirit, the financier William C. Ralston, was anxious to generate capital to develop Nevada's now famous Comstock Lode. D. O. Mills, the first president, had previously founded one of the oldest banks west of the Rockies, D. O. Mills & Company, Bankers, of Sacramento.[21] During the Civil War, the Bank of California was instrumental in financing the cultivation and export of wheat from California to Europe and the Atlantic states. The institution gave early financial support to irrigation and reclamation projects that ultimately made the San Joaquin-Sacramento Valley one of the world's great food producers. It helped many notable western enterprises to get a start: woolen mills, silk factories, canneries, shipyards, and real-estate developments.[22]

By 1867 the bank had moved into a sumptuous two-story Venetian palazzo on the present site. Designed by David Farquharson, a British architect attracted by the gold rush, it had long been one of the monuments of the Pacific Coast but was demolished in 1905 to make way for the new building. Additional land was purchased in 1905 to accommodate the new structure. When the San Francisco earthquake and fire occurred the next year, levelling every bank in the city, the Bank of California's site had already been razed, plans for the new building had been completed, and the granite already quarried and cut. The directors had only to wait for the ashes to cool before commencing construction. Within six weeks the building was underway and was occupied in 1908. As the first major structure to "rise from the ashes," the new Bank of California building symbolized the reestablishment of the city's financial district in its traditional location. The president said at the time: "The directors thought it their duty to put up the best bank building in the United States to show their absolute confidence and faith in San Francisco in spite of the disaster which has befallen." [23]

"The best bank building" was to be only one among many that were patterned on McKim, Mead & White's famous Knickerbocker Trust Company, then one of the most impressive buildings on Fifth Avenue. Contemporaneous with the Bank of Montreal project [27], it had been designed by Stanford White in 1901 and constructed between 1902 and 1904. White's design was for a thirteen-story skyscraper, but the financing for the upper floors fell through, leaving the Knickerbocker Trust with the four-story base, which, with the addition of a crowning balustrade, turned out to be a stunningly elegant white marble edifice, "which made its larger neighbors appear rather mean by comparison." [24]

While basing his design on a Roman temple, White had exploited the modern metal frame that was intended to carry the unexecuted superstructure. Colossal Corinthian columns and pilasters on the two street fronts soared from the podium to the ornate entablature, visually and literally supporting the flat roof. Between the columns and pilasters, a nonsupporting screen wall, composed of windows protected by grilles on the ground floor, gave the building a modernity unusual for the time. Glowingly reviewed by Montgomery Schuyler, the Knickerbocker Trust design spawned hundreds of derivatives throughout North America. [25]

Following White's lead, Bliss & Faville drew on a peripteral Roman temple prototype, similarly enlarging the scale for the Bank of California. Their building, however, is a more traditional interpretation, less open and transparent, even though it also is supported by a steel frame. Whereas White created a forward-looking equilibrium between openness and solid mass, Bliss & Faville favored mass, using more columns (both freestanding and engaged), broad piers framing the Sansome Street elevation, a solid parapet above the entablature, and long narrow windows set more deeply in the masonry façade behind the columns. These lofty windows shed light on the great banking hall within, but because they are covered by antiqued bronze grilles, they appear dark from the exterior.

While the monumental scale and lithic bulk of the grey California granite and the guarded windows speak to the passerby of the solidity and security of the bank, the marble-faced banking hall, 54 feet from floor to ornate coffered ceiling, relies on space even more than decor to create an impact. The interior expanses made possible by modern structural techniques, as found here and on an even grander scale in the Bank of Montreal addition [27], gave twentieth-century bank architects one of their most powerful and expressive tools. This aspect of the Bank of California has been intensified in a successful modern refurbishing commenced in

1965 in conjunction with the erection next door of the bank's twenty-one-story headquarters tower by the San Francisco firm of Anshen & Allen.[26] The entire project was remarkable at the time, for the sixties were marked by the wholesale destruction of similarly fine, historic buildings throughout North America.

◆ ◆ ◆

A major problem in late-nineteenth- and early-twentieth-century industrializing America was the organization or reorganization of banks to serve large-scale industry and transportation. In the thirty years following the conclusion of the Civil War, the United States became the greatest industrial nation in the world. Financing America's railroads and mighty industries, such as steel and oil, required capital on a scale hitherto unimagined. Yet American banks were typically small and unconnected, the majority, even in 1905, had capital of $25,000 to $300,000.[27] As it happened, no more than half a dozen firms and hardly twice as many men mastered this challenge before the First World War, for it took not only exceptional organizational ability but a "capacity to think in magnitudes which would have made dizzy . . . lesser contemporaries." [28] It also took ruthlessness in an era celebrated for such accomplished businessmen as Jay Gould and Jim Fisk, Commodore Vanderbilt and John D. Rockefeller.

The two bankers who dominated banking during this period of spectacular business and financial growth and consolidation were the private investment banker John Pierpont Morgan, the most powerful financier in the United States from the 1880s until his death in 1913, and the commercial banker James Stillman, president of National City Bank of New York from 1891 to 1908 and banker to Rockefeller. Both institutions, National City Bank and J. P. Morgan & Company, built new headquarters before the First World War, which reflected their dominating position on Wall Street, now the financial nerve center of North America.

[29]

National City Bank

Citibank
55 Wall Street, New York, New York
McKim, Mead & White

Chartered: 1812
Constructed: 1908

During his tenure, James Stillman, through the medium of investment banking, built a small local institution into the largest and strongest commercial bank in the country. By 1907 National City Bank was the prototype of the modern big business bank.[29] The institution had begun its corporate existence in 1812 in the building that had housed the New York branch of the first Bank of the United States, but Stillman had long had his eye on another historic and far grander edifice on Wall Street. This was Isaiah Rogers's monumental colonnaded Merchants' Exchange, which occupied a whole city block.[30] Designed in 1842, this three-story Greek Revival structure had served as the U. S. Custom House since 1863 but faced destruction with the removal of its federal occupant to Cass Gilbert's new Custom House, designed in 1899. That year Stillman made a deal with the

U. S. secretary of the treasury, purchased the property for $3,265,000, and in 1901 engaged McKim, Mead & White to make the building suitable for his bank.

After toying with the idea of a superimposed skyscraper, by 1904 Stillman and McKim had come up with a design which was simultaneously more respectful of the old building and more vainglorious. Four stories only were added, fronted by a Corinthian colonnade proportioned to Rogers's Ionic order below. By using stone removed from the lower part and matching Rockport granite, McKim ensured that the juncture between old and new work was almost impossible to detect. The interior was gutted and completely rebuilt. McKim transformed the rotunda into a magnificent 59-foot-high cruciform banking hall, dominated by a flood of light which streamed through a central oculus. Although Stillman's bank lacked the splendid processional way that had been created for the Bank of Montreal [27], this interior is one of the great spaces in New York.

The project ensured the survival of one of New York's threatened historic buildings, albeit in a modified state, and won the approval of the *Architectural Record,* which commented as the work neared completion:

> The day when the National City Bank shifted its scene of operations to the present larger and worthier edifice should be notable not only in the history of America's greatest banking institution, but should be equally remembered by New Yorkers and Americans as an occasion by which we have enriched our country by a monument worthy of our commercial importance.[31]

[30]   *J. P. Morgan & Company*

23 Wall Street, New York, New York
Trowbridge & Livingston

Founded: 1860
Constructed: 1913–14

Even before work had commenced on Stillman's monument, the prestige value of erecting low buildings for exclusive occupancy on the most expensive land in Manhattan had already been noted in the *Architectural Record,* which singled out three such new bank buildings in New York.[32] This was soon to be the path followed by J. P. Morgan, who built what is undoubtedly the most restrained bank building in relation to actual position of the entire period before the First World War.[33] Number 23 Wall Street, completed in 1914, the year in which Morgan died, is as icily reserved as the banker himself. The pale marble neoclassical building is a disdainful three stories high with a blind attic, yet it commands the corner of Wall and Broad streets. The main entrance occupies a narrow, diagonally placed façade at the junction of the two streets. Framed by a pair of severely simplified pilasters, it is otherwise unadorned except for handsome bronze grilles. Above the entrance, separated by an architrave, are three simply treated rectangular windows set in a friezelike band. Surmounting this is the most elaborate element of the exterior — the cornice — and above that is the recessed parapet of the attic. These features continue along the remaining two visible elevations, which angle back along the two streets and are pierced by tall rectangular windows on the ground floor, with the smaller frieze windows, grouped in pairs, above.

No grand Corinthian portico embellishes this building.[34] Instead, the broad, smooth marble surfaces are played off against the rectangular voids of the windows and the austerely elegant detail. The structure was designed by Trowbridge & Livingston, architects of Bankers Trust Company (1910–12)—an institution which was also controlled by Morgan; the architects' approach may have been suggested by McKim's severe New England Trust Company, in the heart of the Boston financial district.[35] Both the overall composition, including the diagonally cut off corner, and the simplified classical detailing are markedly similar. The corner entrance, however, was Morgan's idea.[36] The result is an exterior of great refinement and understatement, an apt architectural metaphor for the patriarch of American investment banks.

As the country's premier investment bank, there was no need for J. P. Morgan & Company to impress clients, and the interior was as quietly elegant as the most discriminating of gentlemen's clubs. It was designed with the help of a new type of professional, the bank specialist, in this instance Thomas Bruce Boyd. Morgan, who spent a great deal of time going over the plans, insisted on perpetuating the open character of the banking room, since he had been accustomed to see from his desk anyone who came in the front door or was in the outer office. As the great investment banker had informed the Pujo Committee investigating the money trusts at this time, commercial credit was based neither on money nor property, but upon character: "A man I do not trust could not get money from me on all the bonds of Christendom."[37] The desired unobstructed space gave rise to complicated engineering problems which were solved by modern methods of steel construction.

Less severe than the exterior, the banking room was still noticeably subdued. (Its original skylight was replaced by a glittering, ballroom-scale chandelier in the early 1960s.) The *Architectural Record* remarked in 1915 that the whole character of the building "seems intended to produce an atmosphere of serene reticence, contrasting with its florid and pretentious environment, even as the modest altitude of the building differentiates it from the surrounding skyscrapers."[38] Low-key though Morgan's bank is, the address and the building are known throughout the world. So much was it the symbol of American capitalism that an anarchist (or so it was thought) bombed the building in 1920, killing thirty-three people and injuring another four hundred. The scars can still be observed on the Wall Street elevation.

The rapid development which occurred in Canada in the early twentieth century thanks to the railroads coincided with the pinnacle of popularity of McKim, Mead & White. The influence on the Dominion of the New York firm and their followers was profound: the overwhelming dependency on British architectural styles was replaced by a desire to emulate the latest American architectural fashions, thus continuing a trend that had begun with the Richardsonian Romanesque and the Chateau styles in the 1880s. Writing in the 1930s, the Toronto architect Eric Arthur recalled the situation: "We once, and the writer was one of them, felt a reverence for McKim, Mead and White . . . little short of gods."[39]

Bank of Nova Scotia
254 Portage Avenue, Winnipeg, Manitoba
Darling & Pearson

Chartered: 1832
Constructed: 1908–10 (not occupied by bank)

A uniquely homogeneous collection of opulent Canadian bank buildings influenced by American Beaux-Arts classicism still stands in Winnipeg. First known as Fort Garry, a Hudson's Bay Company trading post about 60 miles north of the Minnesota border, it began as a collection of shacks situated in a vast prairie largely uninhabited except for the native Indians and the Métis, of mixed white and Indian blood. With the arrival of railroads in the 1880s giving it a strategic geographical location, Winnipeg was launched into a period of growth unequalled in Canadian urban history. By the end of the first decade of the new century the city had become the Canadian Chicago, the wholesale, administrative, and financial center of the West. By 1913 fourteen eastern banks maintained regional offices there, financing the grain trade, the erection of warehouses, and the distribution of goods to the western prairies.[40] Most of these institutions, competing fiercely to lend money, built imposing structures on Main Street, Winnipeg's "Bankers' Row." The most architecturally prestigious was the Bank of Montreal, designed by McKim, Mead & White (1909–12), which still occupies the crucial intersection of Portage and Main, the core of Winnipeg's commercial and financial district.

Among the banks venturing into Manitoba in these boom years was the Bank of Nova Scotia, which had operated as "a fairly sleepy local institution" in the Maritimes since its chartering in 1832.[41] The bank's first foray into Winnipeg in 1881 ended in failure in 1885. Four years later it reopened in rented quarters in an undistinguished office block on Main Street next door to the site of the grand neoclassical Canadian Bank of Commerce by Darling & Pearson (1900–01). In 1906, unable to afford the inflated real estate prices of Bankers' Row, the Bank of Nova Scotia bought land two blocks south and hired Darling & Pearson to design a building that would attract the local merchants.

The challenge was formidable. Although the greatest frontage was along Garry Street, the structure needed to dominate Portage Avenue, where the clients were. The architects employed the device of a rounded corner crowned by a dome, used in Willis Polk's celebrated Hibernia Bank Building, completed in San Francisco in 1892. This element helped to draw attention to the main entrance at the Portage and Garry junction and away from the narrow Portage Avenue front.[42] To provide the necessary grandeur, a colonnade of four colossal engaged Ionic columns framed by paired pilasters extends through three floors above the ground-floor base on the Garry Street elevation, leading the eye to the climax at the rounded corner. Here, two engaged columns rise to a curved entablature where the bank's name was once emblazoned,[43] and above which is the highly visible dome, the drum embellished with elaborate Baroque consoles and pierced by windows.

Not only is the dome noticeable; so too is the shining white facing material and unusually elaborate ornament. Rather than using traditional stone to sheathe the four-story steel-frame structure, Darling & Pearson chose an English-manufactured, semiglazed terra cotta, which was extremely durable. It was also easy to produce intricate ornamental detailing from this custom-made molded material, detailing which would have been prohibitively costly in stone and beyond the skills of local masons. While the lower portion of the base was constructed of grey granite quarried in British Columbia, the rest of the exterior was terra cotta — engaged fluted columns and pilasters, window surrounds, the parapet with its decorative wreaths, and, of course, the dome. The richly tasteful interior, enlarged and refurbished in 1930 but now destroyed, was executed in more traditional marble and plaster.

During the years between 1900 and the onset of the Great Depression, monumental banking headquarters arose all along Bankers' Row, by McKim, Mead & White and Carrère & Hastings of New York and by Darling & Pearson, who also designed a second, grander Canadian Bank of Commerce and the ten-story Union Bank, the West's first skyscraper.[44] Yet despite its location "below the salt," the Bank of Nova Scotia held its own among these splendid financial palaces, the only domed bank on the Canadian prairies, its elaborate terra cotta exterior unequalled in Winnipeg.[45]

By the end of the first decade of the twentieth century the Canadian West was well on its way to becoming one of the world's great granaries. During this decade about $800 million in new capital had been invested in manufacturing, the gross national product had increased by 64 per cent, and the population had grown by almost two million, well over a million being distributed throughout the three prairie provinces and British Columbia. In these years the Canadian economy was growing faster and the country's standard of living rising more rapidly than were those of its huge and envied neighbor, the United States.[46]

[32] *Canadian Bank of Commerce*

Canadian Imperial Bank of Commerce
415 Devonshire Road, Windsor, Ontario
Albert Kahn, Architect, Ernest Wilby, Associate

Chartered: 1867
Constructed: 1907

For all the western expansion in agriculture and resource exploitation, however, the heartland was still southern Ontario, especially those areas directly across the American border, with Toronto and the Grand Valley towns completing the core.[47] One of the fastest-growing industrial towns was Walkerville, today a part of Windsor, where an enterprising American from nearby Detroit, Hiram Walker, had opened a distillery in the 1850s. Walkerville was a paternalistic company town, the private domain of the Walker family until it was incorporated in 1890, whereupon the Walkers continued to influence the planning of the community through their extensive industrial and real estate holdings. In the 1880s Walkerville was still a very small place, but improved transportation — a ferry service to Detroit and construction of a railroad, both initiated by Walker — changed all that. The railway in particular attracted numerous industries, so that by the end of the first decade of the new century, the distillery town had been transformed into a flourishing industrial center. In 1904 the Ford Motor Company of Canada, successor to the Milner-Walker Wagon Works, was established just east of the Walker distillery, creating the industry that would make the area the "Auto Capital of the British Empire."[48]

The Walkers and Henry Ford, along with other Detroit industrialists, patronized the talented and versatile German-born architect Albert Kahn. One of the great pioneers of the early twentieth century, Kahn designed buildings to house industry, not only throughout North America, but worldwide.[49] Assisted by Kahn, Henry Ford would perfect that essential element of modern industry, the assembly line, in the Kahn-designed Highland Park plant from 1912 to 1915. Kahn was an accomplished traditionalist as well, who designed conservative mansions for Detroit's affluent industrialists.

Kahn began working for the Walker family in the 1890s, designing first the Hiram Walker main office building and then working with the Walker family to develop Walkerville into a garden city comparable to Bournville and Port Sunlight in England.[50] In 1904 Kahn completed plans for a stone and half-timbered Tudor manor house, "Willistead," for the new town's reigning family. Between 1901 and 1907 the architect designed row houses, residences, commercial blocks, and the local branch of the Canadian Bank of Commerce, located conveniently near Walkerville's railroad station and hotel.[51]

The Canadian Bank of Commerce had been founded in 1867 by a group of wealthy Toronto businessmen to fill a gap left by the failures of the Bank of Upper Canada and the Commercial Bank of the Midland District. Although heavily involved in the financing of international trade, the Commerce did not begin to establish a nationwide presence in Canada until the turn of the century, when it embarked on a period of rapid expansion.[52] By this time it was the Bank of Montreal's nearest competitor in the Dominion and felt secure enough to reverse its general policy of renting quarters and to begin constructing fine premises, many by Darling & Pearson. To give the branches a semblance of corporate identity, traditional classicism was maintained with individual variations.

Kahn's design is a particularly accomplished exercise in Beaux-Arts classicism, and is notable for the exquisite Roman and Grecian detailing executed in fine grey limestone. The handsomely proportioned rectangular structure is two stories high, fronted by a monumental tetrastyle Roman Ionic portico and crowned by a parapet rising above the entablature.[53] Kahn contrasted broad surfaces of beautifully laid limestone with the refined detailing of fluted columns and bracketed entrance surround, leaving the windows unmolded except for projecting sills and treating the secondary elevations with a calculated simplicity, separating the windows — single on the ground floor, paired above — by pilaster strips, repeating these in the parapet. Although the edifice bears a strong family resemblance to other pre-Depression Bank of Commerce buildings, Kahn's is one of the finest, and indeed a replica was completed in 1908 for the Bank of Commerce in Halifax, bastion of the Bank of Nova Scotia.[54]

·6·

AMERICAN AND CANADIAN BANKS

PRAIRIE STYLE

Despite the impact made by the classical grandeur on display at the World's Columbian Exposition in 1893, Chicago remained a center for progressive architectural design. Louis Sullivan had deviated from the official classical style in his Transportation Building for the Exposition, and until the end of his career he was committed to his self-imposed task of creating a fresh, original, and worthy American architecture. For this avant-garde architect, one of the founders of the Chicago School, the continued reworking of the past—in which McKim, Mead & White and their emulators excelled—was a betrayal of the needs and aspirations of the American people. It was not modern architecture. Sullivan compared the traditionalists to clerks at a notion counter, offering "Tudor for colleges and residences; Roman for banks and railway stations and libraries —or Greek, if you like: some customers prefer the Ionic to the Doric." [1] Sullivan did not dislike authentic Classical architecture, but to him the Roman temple was part of Roman, not American, life. Roman temple banks were particularly repellent. The banker who desired such a structure, Sullivan observed in his widely read *Kindergarten Chats,* should have to "wear a toga and sandals and conduct his business in the venerated Latin tongue." [2]

Sullivan's unswerving radical vision—and his drinking habits—cost him the important metropolitan commissions that had been his mainstay before 1900. After the turn of the century, it was to be in bank architecture that Sullivan's ideas were expressed. Between 1906 and 1919 a handful of Midwestern bankers risked hiring the difficult genius and were rewarded with buildings which "stand out like jewels" in tiny rural towns with names like Owatonna and Grinnell. [3]

33

National Farmers' Bank

Norwest Bank Owatonna
101 North Cedar Street, Owatonna, Minnesota
Louis Henry Sullivan

Chartered: 1873 (defunct)
Constructed: 1907–8

Perhaps the most famous Prairie School bank, Sullivan's seminal National Farmers' Bank at Owatonna, was the first to receive national publicity.[4] Indeed, the banker who chose Sullivan, Carl K. Bennett, wrote about it in the widely read art magazine *The Craftsman*.[5] Bennett was an uncommon individual, "a man who sought to live like a Renaissance prince in a world of Babbitts. . . . a shrewd idealist who believed that beauty was not only good for people but good for business as well."[6] A son of the bank's founder, Bennett had studied music at Harvard, had travelled in Europe, and knew at first hand the work of McKim, Mead & White and H. H. Richardson. He also knew he did not want a Roman temple for a bank.[7]

Sullivan had never designed a small-town bank before, but he and his working (although not official) partner George Grant Elmslie came up with a design which projected the image of strength and security Bennett wanted to attract new depositors. It was planned and equipped in the most modern manner to meet the real needs of its farmer customers and was, in addition, an astonishingly beautiful work of art, one that attracted enough business (as Bennett predicted it would) to cause the institution's assets to rise from $700,000 to $2,800,000 in the thirteen years following construction. Indeed the eminent architectural historian Henry-Russell Hitchcock, concerned in 1956 about a remodelling proposal, wrote to its owner: "Certainly no other town of its size has a commercial building of equal distinction."[8]

While dispensing with columns and pediments or any other overt historical references, Sullivan's basic boxlike shape and ordered, symmetrical arrangement is classical in essence, producing a structure of monumental dignity.[9] The simple, elemental form, and the broad expanses of finely laid masonry, and the two great semicircular windows that light the interior—all legacies of Richardson—provide the feeling of solid strength that Sullivan's client sought. Enlivening this powerful structure is the exquisite exterior ornament, inspired mainly by the natural forms so profoundly meaningful to the mystical, poetic Sullivan.[10] The ornamentation comprises arched stained glass windows, which produce a variegated bluish-green effect, and a wide band of polychromatic, but chiefly green, terra cotta, with an accompanying narrow band of predominantly blue glass mosaic. These bands enframe the south and west façades where the arched windows are placed. Luxuriant cartouches occupy the upper corners of these "frames." The reddish-brown tones of the richly textured tapestry brick walls and red sandstone base combine with the blues and greens of the terra cotta, the glass mosaic, and the stained glass to create a rich harmony of natural colors, a "color symphony" suggested to Sullivan by the surrounding landscape.

Nature similarly inspired the interior. "My whole Spring is wrapped up just now in the study of color and out of doors for the sake of your bank decorations," the architect wrote to Bennett in April 1908, "—which I wish to make out of doors-in-doors if I can. . . . There has never been in my entire career such an opportunity for a color tone poem as your interior plainly puts before me." [11] The interior which Sullivan and Elmslie, a gifted ornamentalist, created is a world apart from everyday Owatonna. Sullivan's biographer Morrison described it best: "The interior is a large square room, rich in decorative detail and glowing in color, although the total effect of light spaciousness absorbs the detail so that it is never obtrusive or over-brilliant. The room is amply lighted by the great arched windows on two sides and a skylight overhead, and there is a curious quality to the light — a greenish tinge, like sunlight passed through sea-water." [12]

The individual elements of the interior — terra cotta, stenciling, painted and gilded plasterwork, cashiers' grilles, electroliers, and specially designed furniture — were noteworthy examples of craftsmanship and, as Bennett observed, "astonishingly good for this machine-made age." [13] Also significant are the two large murals by Oskar Gross on the east and north walls analogous to the arched windows. [14] They represent dairy cows and harvesting, reflecting the source of the bank's and Owatonna's prosperity. [15]

Thanks to the integrity of Sullivan's vision, the overall effect of all this prairie splendor is not that of a personal monument to a prideful banker, although Bennett's sympathetic support was a crucial factor. It is rather a work of art for a democracy, designed for the people, a bank building that was, as the architect intended, both modern and American. "The greatest poet," Sullivan had proclaimed in 1899, "will be he who shall grasp and deify the commonplaces of our life." [16]

Sullivan was by no means the only Prairie School architect to design banks. Frank Lloyd Wright, Purcell and Elmslie, George W. Maher, and others have enlivened a fair number of small Midwest towns with their innovative buildings. In contrast to New England, where churches dominate the community, in the rural Midwest it is the banks which are situated on the most prominent corner on Main Street, while the churches are generally found on residential side streets. [17] Nine years after the completion of Sullivan's masterpiece in Owatonna, the Chicago architect Peter B. Wight wrote:

> The State of Minnesota is becoming famous for its new banks showing progressive tendencies in architectural design. They are to be found in the smaller cities, especially those where the support comes mainly from the surrounding rural districts. They have proved attractive to visitors, who have recognized in them works of art as well as utility; they have therefore exerted an educational influence in communities heretofore indifferent to architecture because of conventional and prosaic design. [18]

Wim de Wit, in his discussion of Prairie School banks, suggests several factors which help to explain the creation of these extraordinary bank buildings. [19] In the Midwest in the first two decades of the century, agriculture was more profitable than it had ever been. Many new banks were established with local farmers and businessmen as shareholders in a climate of general prosperity and great expectations. The striking modernity of these Midwestern banks reflected new attitudes which rural bankers had begun consciously to display in order to attract a broader range of customers — including women and children — and thus function as the financial heart of their communities. Many Prairie School banks accordingly provided a variety of public facilities: meeting rooms, waiting rooms, exhibition rooms, and in one case, a podium to show prize-winning cows.

34

Winona Savings Bank and Winona National Bank

Winona National and Savings Bank
204 Main Street, Winona, Minnesota
George Washington Maher

Chartered: 1874 and 1916
Constructed: 1914–16

Sullivan's bank in Owatonna [33] included a farmers' exchange room for conducting business or holding social functions. For farm wives and children who had accompanied father into town there was a waiting room with a convenient teller's wicket into the savings department. A more striking example of the bank-cum-community center, however, is the building for the joint Winona Savings Bank and Winona National Bank.[20] The architect, George W. Maher, had worked as a draftsman in Chicago in the 1880s—along with Wright and Elmslie—for J. L. Silsbee, architect of the Syracuse Savings Bank [18]. The Winona bank displays not the severe rectangular shapes of the Sullivan tradition, but rather the dynamic interplay of horizontals and verticals initiated by Wright in his Prairie houses.[21] Maher combined this radically new compositional method with the more overtly traditional concept of a heroically scaled, pylonlike centerpiece with columns in antis reminiscent of the old Bank of Louisville [6]. Since the building was intended to house a savings and a national bank, each institution could utilize one of Maher's low wings, with the common offices located in the dominating center section.

The unusual plan marked an expansionary move on the part of the Winona Savings Bank, controlled by the largest manufacturer in town, the J. R. Watkins Medical Company, maker of patent medicines, for whom Maher had already designed an administration and a manufacturing building.[22] By establishing a commercial affiliate, the Winona National Bank, the institution could offer customers a diversity of financial services under one roof and achieve a more rapid growth of earnings.[23]

The image of the up-to-date bank as a total service institution, the hub of community activity, is underlined by the civic pretensions of the Winona bank, which are eloquently expressed throughout Maher's design: the imposing portal with its 36-foot-high monolithic granite columns[24] (could this not be the town hall?), the luxurious banking floor with its green and white marble walls and Tiffany windows, and even more telling, the second floor, completely given over to public space. This floor included separate "institutional rooms" for men and women, reached by two marble stairways and provided with "tables and easy chairs, stationery, and every convenience that is found in fully equipped club rooms."[25] Between the two rooms was an exhibition area that ultimately came to be used in a personal way—to display the hunting trophies acquired by members of the King family, who mounted extensive safaris to Africa in the twenties. E. L. King, son-in-law of J. R. Watkins, was president of the bank from 1928 to 1949. The golden lion which serves as the bank's emblem reflects the King sporting passion.

In Canada there were no Prairie School bank architects corresponding to Sullivan or Wright; but there did appear at about the same time an ingenious, standardized "Prairie Type" bank building which became ubiquitous in western Canada, as characteristic of the small towns of Manitoba, Saskatchewan, and Alberta as the grain elevators.

The Canadian banking system with its branches did not encourage the same entrepreneurial and individualistic spirit that flourished in the United States. As the proliferating railroads opened up the Canadian West, the country's established banks rushed, like claim jumpers, to set up operations. Expansion in the twentieth century was phenomenal. By 1911 there were 1,846 more branches than in 1900, the bulk of the branches being opened in the four western provinces, where over a million new Canadians established themselves during these years.[26] Being the first to open at a new townsite along the railroad gave a bank a competitive edge, even though the premises might be no more than a tent or a shed with a hastily painted sign to indicate its function. Growth, however, depended on the erection of more substantial quarters to give prospective depositors that reassuring sense of solidity and permanence.

Two factors influenced the building of banks on the Canadian prairies: the scarcity of local materials and labor and the very real possibility that a newly created townsite might not survive. It was the ambitious Canadian Bank of Commerce that came up with the best solution to this challenge by developing a prefabricated laminated wood building that could be shipped in sections by rail.[27] A single bank branch occupied two standard boxcars, could be erected rapidly on site, and, if business did not materialize, could be dismantled and reassembled elsewhere.[28] Within a six-year span, seventy prefabricated Canadian Bank of Commerce branches appeared in the four western provinces, the majority being in Saskatchewan and Alberta, where they were often "the finest buildings in the small towns." [29]

Sectional or "knock-down" building systems that could be shipped by rail had already helped to house settlers in the American West, but these "ready-mades" were unsuited to the harsher Canadian climate.[30] In 1904, however, Edward Mahoney, an employee of the British Columbia Mills, Timber and Trading Company patented a sectional wall system of laminated wood which could withstand the Canadian winter. These were initially marketed in the form of one-story cottages aimed at the prairie settler market. Soon B. C. Mills produced a catalogue of house models which found a market not only in rural areas but in such thriving cities as Winnipeg and Vancouver. The Canadian Bank of Commerce, now a major presence in British Columbia after having acquired the Bank of British Columbia in 1900, adapted a house design for a branch which was erected in 1905 in the silver mining town of Cobalt, Ontario. This prefabricated building was so distinctive among the tarpaper shacks of Cobalt that the bank thereupon astutely commissioned the eminent firm of Darling & Pearson of Toronto to produce bank designs adaptable to the B. C. Mills system. Three models resulted: a modest one-and-a-half-story cottage with a hipped roof and front verandah similar to the Cobalt building, and two far more imposing two-story designs with front-gabled roofs, one featuring four fluted Ionic pilasters rising through two stories to the gable, which formed a pediment.[31] In the gable end of both two-story models, an elegant oeil-de-boeuf window lit the attic. The entrance door of the most elaborate design was surmounted by a broken pediment. In all the models, banking facilities, including the vault and manager's office, were located on the ground floor, while the floor above contained dormitory rooms to house staff. Fireplaces provided heat.

The management of the Bank of Commerce deliberately chose a conservative classical styling for the prefabs, just as they continued to exploit this same manner in the masonry branches that were being erected, such as the one in Walkerville. "The buildings erected by the bank are not the product of passing fashion. While modern in spirit and diverse in every legitimate respect, they are founded both in general design and in detail on those classical traditions which never fail to command respect." [32] Neither individualistic nor forward-looking in the manner of American Prairie School designs, the Canadian "Prairie Type" bank is nevertheless as typical, reflecting its own very different banking system and history and culture. Canadian writer Heather Robertson conveys the significance of these prefab banks in *Grass Roots,* her ode to the West:

> The bank is the grandest building in almost every prairie town, and its imposing presence lends an aura of permanence and stability to the shabbiest village. The Bank of Commerce is everywhere in the West, and all the Banks of Commerce look the same. . . . They make it hard to remember which town is which. Prairie towns all look alike: identical grain elevators, identical banks, identical railway stations, a main street that is called Main Street and a road along the tracks called Railway Avenue.[33]

[35]   *Canadian Bank of Commerce*
Canadian Imperial Bank of Commerce
Main Street, Innisfree, Alberta
Darling & Pearson

Chartered: 1867
Constructed: 1907

In the fall of 1905 Byron Edmund Walker, president of the Canadian Bank of Commerce, made a cross-Canada tour by train.[34] Upon stopping at the village of Delnorte, Alberta, he was impressed by a local view, comparing it to the Scottish town of Innisfree. The mayor of this largely Ukrainian settlement is said to have offered to change the name of his town if the bank would establish a branch, telling the townspeople before Walker's departure, so the story goes, that the name was now to be Innisfree in the banker's honor. In December of 1906 a branch duly opened in temporary quarters, a year later moving into a handsome prefabricated structure.[35] This well-preserved example of the most elaborate Darling & Pearson prefab design still functions as the Canadian Imperial Bank of Commerce branch in Innisfree. The deep-red, yellow, and white painted exterior is believed to perpetuate the original color scheme, while the original Canadian Bank of Commerce sign has been maintained above the main door, the branch having remained continuously open since its establishment.[36]

FEDERAL AND GREEK REVIVAL STYLES, UNITED STATES

PLATE 1.1 *Broad Street Façade, Bank of South Carolina, Charleston, South Carolina, 1797–98 (now Citizens and Southern National Bank of South Carolina, Trust Department). Architect unknown. Photograph by Len Jenshel.*

PLATE 1.2 *Detail, Interior Entrance, Bank of South Carolina, Charleston, South Carolina, 1797–98 (now Citizens and Southern National Bank of South Carolina, Trust Department). Architect unknown. Photograph by Len Jenshel.*

PLATE 2.1 *Main Street Façade,*
Nantucket Pacific Bank, Nan-
tucket, Massachusetts, 1818
(now Pacific National Bank of
Nantucket). Architect unknown.
Photograph by Serge Hambourg.

PLATE 3.1 *South Third Street Façade, First Bank of the United States, Philadelphia, Pennsylvania, 1795–97. Architect Samuel Blodget, Jr. Photograph by James Iska.*

PLATE 4.1 *Bank of Pennsylvania,*
Philadelphia, Pennsylvania,
1798–1800 (demolished). Archi-
tect Benjamin Henry Latrobe.
Watercolor by B. H. Latrobe
(1799), courtesy of Maryland
Historical Society.

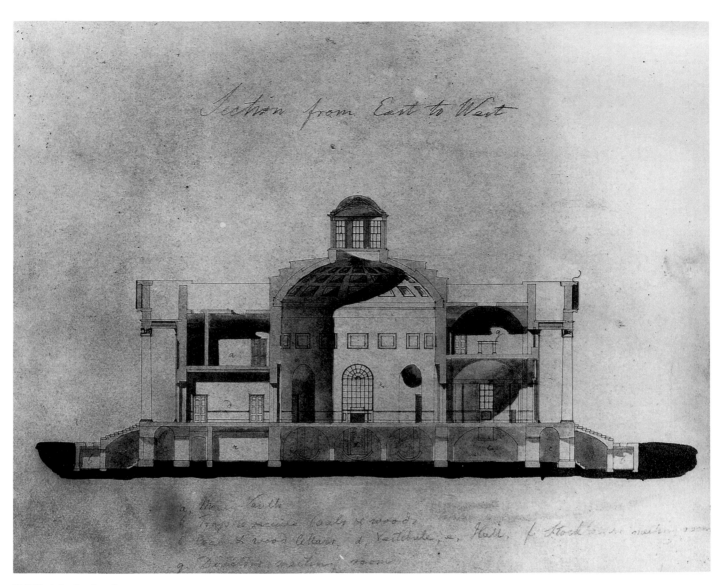

PLATE 4.2 *Section from East to West, Bank of Pennsylvania, Philadelphia, Pennsylvania, 1798–1800 (demolished). Architect Benjamin Henry Latrobe. Pen and ink rendering by B. H. Latrobe (c. 1798), courtesy of Historical Society of Pennsylvania.*

PLATE 5.1 *Chestnut Street Façade, Second Bank of the United States, Philadelphia, Pennsylvania, 1819–24. Architect William Strickland. Photograph by James Iska.*

PLATE 5.2 *Southeast Corner,*
Second Bank of the United States,
Philadelphia, Pennsylvania,
1819–24. Architect William Strick-
land. Photograph by James Iska.

PLATE 6.1 *West Main Street*
Façade, Bank of Louisville,
Louisville, Kentucky, 1835–37.
Architect James Harrison Dakin.
Photograph by John Pfahl.

PLATE 6.2 *Former Banking Hall,*
Bank of Louisville, Louisville,
Kentucky, 1835–37. Architect
James Harrison Dakin. Photograph
by John Pfahl.

LATE GEORGIAN, GREEK REVIVAL, AND VICTORIAN CLASSICAL STYLES, CANADA

PLATE 7.1 *Gibb House on St. James Street To right: Bank of Montreal, Montreal, Quebec, 1818–19 (demolished). Architect unknown. Watercolor by Charles C. Milbourne (1819), courtesy McCord Museum of Canadian History, Montreal.*

PLATE 8.1 *Adelaide Street Façade,*
Bank of Upper Canada, Toronto,
Ontario, 1825–27. Architect
William Warren Baldwin. Photo-
graph by Robert Bourdeau.

PLATE 9.1 *Wellington Street Façade Looking Toward Royal Bank Plaza and the CN Tower, Commercial Bank of the Midland District, Toronto, Ontario, 1843–45. Architect William Thomas. Photograph by Robert Bourdeau.*

PLATE 10.1 *St. James Street Façade, Bank of Montreal, Montreal, Quebec, 1845–47. Architect John Wells. Photograph by David Miller.*

98

PLATE 10.2 *Portico, St. James Street Façade, Bank of Montreal, Montreal, Quebec, 1845–47. Architect John Wells. Photograph by David Miller.*

PLATE 10.3 *Place d'Armes and St. James Street Façade, Bank of Montreal, Montreal, Quebec, 1845–47. Architect John Wells. Photograph by George Tice.*

MID- AND LATE-VICTORIAN STYLES, UNITED STATES

PLATE 11.1 *East Bay Street Façade,*
Farmers' and Exchange Bank,
Charleston, South Carolina, 1853–54.
Architect Jones & Lee. Photograph
by Len Jenshel.

PLATE 11.2 *Main Entrance, Farmers' and Exchange Bank, Charleston, South Carolina, 1853–54. Architect Jones & Lee. Photograph by Len Jenshel.*

PLATE 12.1 *Chestnut Street Façade, Farmers and*
Mechanics Bank, Philadelphia, Pennsylvania, 1854–55.
Architect John M. Gries. Photograph by James Iska.

PLATE 12.2 *Chestnut Street Façade from Alley past Second Bank of the United States, Farmers and Mechanics Bank, Philadelphia, Pennsylvania, 1854–55. Architect John M. Gries. Photograph by James Iska.*

PLATE 13.1 *Broadway (North)*
Façade and East Elevation, Bank of
Columbus, Columbus, Georgia, c.
1860. Architect unknown.
Photograph by Len Jenshel.

PLATE 13.2 *Capitals, Main Entrance, Bank of Columbus,*
Columbus, Georgia, c. 1860. Architect unknown.
Photograph by Len Jenshel.

PLATE 14.1 *Main Street Façade
and West Elevation, Southport
Savings Bank, Southport, Connecticut, 1863–65 (now People's
Bank, Southport Office). Adapted
from design by Henry Austin.
Photograph by Len Jenshel.*

PLATE 15.2 *Lion, Fourth Avenue Façade, Dollar Savings Bank, Pittsburgh, Pennsylvania, 1869–71 (now Dollar Bank). Architect Isaac H. Hobbs & Son. Photograph by George Tice.*

PLATE 15.1 *Fourth Avenue Façade, Dollar Savings Bank, Pittsburgh, Pennsylvania, 1869–71 (now Dollar Bank). Architect Isaac H. Hobbs & Son. Photograph by George Tice.*

PLATE 16.1 *State Street Façade,
Institution for Savings in Newbury-
port and its Vicinity, Newburyport,
Massachusetts, 1871. Architect
Rufus Sargent. Photograph by Serge
Hambourg.*

PLATE 16.2 *Diagonal View, State Street Façade,*
Institution for Savings in Newburyport and its Vicinity,
Newburyport, Massachusetts, 1871. Architect Rufus
Sargent. Photograph by Serge Hambourg.

PLATE 17.1 *Main Street Façade,
Wells, Fargo & Co., Columbia,
California, 1858. Architect
unknown. Photograph by Catherine Wagner.*

PLATE 17.2 *Interior, Wells, Fargo*
& Co., Columbia, California,
1858. Architect unknown.
Photograph by Catherine Wagner.

PLATE 17.3 *Original Gold Scales,
Wells, Fargo & Co., Columbia,
California, 1858. Architect
unknown. Photograph by Catherine Wagner.*

PLATE 18.1 *Salina Street Façade and Base of Sculpture in Clinton Square, Syracuse Savings Bank, Syracuse, New York, 1875–76. Architect Joseph Lyman Silsbee. Photograph by George Tice.*

PLATE 18.2 *Windows and Base of Tower, Syracuse*
Savings Bank, Syracuse, New York, 1875–76. Architect
Joseph Lyman Silsbee. Photograph by George Tice.

PLATE 19.1 *Public Square Façade, Looking Northwest,*
Society for Savings, Cleveland, Ohio, 1888–90 (now
Society National Bank). Architect Burnham & Root. Pho-
tograph by James Iska.

PLATE 19.2 *Lamp and Entrance, Corner of Ontario Street and Public Square, Society for Savings, Cleveland, Ohio, 1888–90 (now Society National Bank). Architect Burnham & Root. Photograph by Len Jenshel.*

PLATE 19.3 *Banking Hall, Society for Savings, Cleveland, Ohio, 1888–90 (now Society National Bank). Architect Burnham & Root. Photograph by Len Jenshel.*

PLATE 19.4 *Board Room, Society for Savings, Cleveland,
Ohio, 1888–90 (now Society National Bank). Architect
Burnham & Root. Photograph by Len Jenshel.*

PLATE 20.1 *Southeast View,*
Nassau Street Façade, Princeton
Bank, Princeton, New Jersey, 1896.
Architect William E. Stone.
Photograph by John Pfahl.

PLATE 20.2 *Chimney Detail, Nassau Street Façade,*
Princeton Bank, Princeton, New Jersey, 1896. Architect
William E. Stone. Photograph by John Pfahl.

MID- AND LATE-VICTORIAN STYLES, CANADA

PLATE 21.1 *Overall View Showing*
West and South Elevations,
Commercial Bank of the Midland
District, Kingston, Ontario,
1853–54. Architect William Hay.
Photograph by Robert Bourdeau.

PLATE 21.2 *Window and Balcony, William Street Façade, Commercial Bank of the Midland District, Kingston, Ontario, 1853–54. Architect William Hay. Photograph by Robert Bourdeau.*

PLATE 22.1 *St. James Street (North) Façade and West Elevation from opposite the Royal Bank Building, Molsons Bank, Montreal, Quebec, 1864–66 (now Bank of Montreal, International Service Center). Architect George William Richardson Browne. Photograph by Robert Bourdeau.*

PLATE 22.2 *Portico and Window Treatments, Main*
Entrance, Molsons Bank, Montreal, Quebec, 1864–66
(now Bank of Montreal, International Service Center).
Architect George William Richardson Browne. Photograph
by Robert Bourdeau.

PLATE 22.3 *Windows, West Elevation, Molsons Bank, Montreal, Quebec, 1864–66 (now Bank of Montreal, International Service Center). Architect George William Richardson Browne. Photograph by Robert Bourdeau.*

PLATE 23.1 *Main Façade,*
Northwest Corner of Front and
Yonge Streets and Surrounding
Skyscapers, Bank of Montreal, Tor-
onto, Ontario, 1885–86. Architect
Darling & Curry. Photograph by
David Duchow.

PLATE 23.2 *Main Façade,*
Northwest Corner of Front and
Yonge Streets, Bank of Montreal,
Toronto, Ontario, 1885–86.
Architect Darling & Curry.
Photograph by David Duchow.

PLATE 24.1 *Main Façade, Southwest Corner of St. Catherine Street and Mansfield, Bank of Montreal West End Branch, Montreal, Quebec, 1889 (now Guardian Trust). Architect Taylor & Gordon. Photograph by David Duchow.*

PLATE 25a.1 *Government Street Façade, Bank of*
Montreal, Victoria, British Columbia, 1896–97. Architect
Francis Mawson Rattenbury. Photograph by David Miller.

PLATE 25a.2 *Main Entrance, Bank of Montreal, Victoria,*
British Columbia, 1896– 97. Architect Francis Mawson
Rattenbury. Photograph by David Miller.

PLATE 25b.1 *Entrance, Corner of Fort and Government Streets, Bank of British Columbia, Victoria, British Columbia, 1886 (now Canadian Imperial Bank of Commerce). Architect Warren Haywood Williams. Photograph by David Miller.*

PLATE 25b.2 *Manager's Office,
Bank of British Columbia,
Victoria, British Columbia, 1886
(now Canadian Imperial Bank of
Commerce). Architect Warren
Haywood Williams. Photograph by
David Miller.*

BEAUX-ARTS CLASSICAL STYLE, UNITED STATES AND CANADA

PLATE 26.1 *Grand Street Façade
and Elizabeth Street Elevation,
Bowery Savings Bank, New York,
New York, 1893–95. Architect
McKim, Mead & White. Photograph
by Len Jenshel.*

PLATE 26.2 *Pediment, Grand Street Façade, Bowery Savings Bank, New York, New York, 1893–95. Architect McKim, Mead & White. Photograph by Len Jenshel.*

PLATE 26.3 *Banking Hall, Bowery*
Savings Bank, New York, New
York, 1893–95. Architect McKim,
Mead & White. Photograph by Len
Jenshel.

PLATE 26.4 *Check Writing Table, Banking Hall, Bowery Savings Bank, New York, New York, 1893–95. Architect McKim, Mead & White. Photograph by Len Jenshel.*

PLATE 27.1 *Craig Street Elevation, Bank of Montreal Addition, Montreal, Quebec, 1901–05. Architects McKim, Mead & White and Andrew T. Taylor, Associate Architects. Photograph by George Tice.*

PLATE 27.2 *Atrium, Bank of Montreal, Montreal,*
Quebec, 1901–05. Architects McKim, Mead & White and
Andrew T. Taylor, Associate Architects. Photograph by
David Miller.

PLATE 28a.1 *View down California Street, Bank of California, San Francisco, California, 1906 – 08. Architect Bliss & Faville. Photograph by Catherine Wagner.*

PLATE 28b.1 *Knickerbocker Trust, New York, New York, 1902–04. Architect McKim, Mead & White. Photograph from McKim, Mead & White Collection, courtesy the New-York Historical Society.*

PLATE 29.1 *National City Bank, New York, New York, 1908 (now Citibank). Architect McKim, Mead & White. Photographer unknown, courtesy Citicorp.*

PLATE 30.1 *Stock Exchange and Main Façade, J. P.
Morgan & Company, Corner of Wall and Broad Streets
Looking West, New York, New York, 1913–14. Architect
Trowbridge & Livingston. Photograph by George Tice.*

PLATE 30.2 *Wall Street, J. P. Morgan & Company, Trinity Church, Federal Hall, and Bankers Trust, New York, New York. Photograph by George Tice.*

PLATE A.1 *Façade, Dime Savings*
Bank of Brooklyn, Brooklyn, New
York, 1907, 1932. Architects
Mowbray & Uffinger; Halsey,
McCormick & Helmer. Photograph
by Serge Hambourg.

PLATE 31.1 *Main Façade,
Southwest Corner of Portage
Avenue and Garry Street, Bank of
Nova Scotia, Winnipeg, Manitoba,
1908–10. Architect Darling &
Pearson. Photograph by David
Duchow.*

PLATE 32.1 *View of Devonshire Road Façade and South Elevation from the grounds of the Customs House, Canadian Bank of Commerce, Windsor (Walkerville), Ontario, 1907 (now Canadian Imperial Bank of Commerce). Albert Kahn, Architect, Ernest Wilby, Associate. Photograph by Robert Bourdeau.*

PRAIRIE STYLE,
UNITED STATES AND CANADA

PLATE 33.1 *Bank and Town
Square, National Farmers' Bank,
Owatonna, Minnesota, 1907–08
(now Norwest Bank Owatonna).
Architect Louis Henry Sullivan.
Photograph by Serge Hambourg.*

PLATE 33.2 *North Cedar Street Façade, National
Farmers' Bank, Owatonna, Minnesota, 1907–08 (now
Norwest Bank Owatonna). Architect Louis Henry
Sullivan. Photograph by Serge Hambourg.*

PLATE 33.3 *Banking Hall from Balcony, National Farmers' Bank, Owatonna, Minnesota, 1907–08 (now Norwest Bank Owatonna). Architect Louis Henry Sullivan. Photograph by Serge Hambourg.*

PLATE 33.4 *Terra Cotta and Painted Detail, Interior,*
National Farmers' Bank, Owatonna, Minnesota, 1907–
08 (now Norwest Bank Owatonna). Architect Louis
Henry Sullivan. Photograph by Serge Hambourg.

PLATE 33.5 *Customers, Banking
Hull, National Farmers' Bank,
Owatonna, Minnesota, 1907–08
(now Norwest Bank Owatonna).
Architect Louis Henry Sullivan.
Photograph (1955) by John
Szarkowski, courtesy of the artist.*

PLATE 34.1 *Main Street Façade, Winona Savings Bank and Winona National Bank, Winona, Minnesota, 1914–16 (now Winona National and Savings Bank). Architect George Washington Maher. Photograph by Serge Hambourg.*

PLATE 34.2 *Balcony, Banking Hall, Winona Savings Bank and Winona National Bank, Winona, Minnesota, 1914–16 (now Winona National and Savings Bank). Architect George Washington Maher. Photograph by Serge Hambourg.*

155

PLATE 35.1 *Main Street Façade, Canadian Bank of Commerce, Innisfree, Alberta, 1907 (now Canadian Imperial Bank of Commerce). Architect Darling & Pearson. Photograph by David Duchow.*

ART DECO AND OTHER STYLES, UNITED STATES AND CANADA

PLATE 36.1 *Façade, Federal Reserve Bank of New York, New York, New York, 1921–24. Architect York & Sawyer. Photograph (1936) by Berenice Abbott, courtesy of the Canadian Centre for Architecture/Centre Canadien d'Architecture, Montreal.*

PLATE 36.2 *East Elevation from Nevelson Plaza, Federal*
Reserve Bank of New York, New York, New York,
1921– 24. Architect York & Sawyer. Photograph by
George Tice.

PLATE 36.3 *Window, Federal Reserve Bank of New York,*
New York, New York, 1921–24. Architect York & Sawyer.
Photograph by George Tice.

PLATE 37.1 *South LaSalle Street
Portico, Illinois Merchants Trust
Company, Chicago, Illinois,
1921–24 (now Continental Illi-
nois National Bank and Trust
Company of Chicago). Architect
Graham, Anderson, Probst &
White. Photograph by James Iska.*

PLATE 37.2 *LaSalle Street Façade, Looking toward Rookery, Illinois Merchants Trust Company, Chicago, Illinois, 1921–24 (now Continental Illinois National Bank and Trust Company of Chicago). Architect Graham, Anderson, Probst & White. Photograph by James Iska.*

PLATE 37.3 *Banking Hall, Illinois Merchants Trust*
Company, Chicago, Illinois, 1921–24 (now Continental
Illinois National Bank and Trust Company of Chicago).
Architect Graham, Anderson, Probst & White. Photograph
by James Iska.

PLATE 38.1 *Broadway Elevation, Looking toward Wall
Street, Irving Trust Company, New York, New York,
1929–31. Architect Voorhees, Gmelin & Walker.
Photograph by Catherine Wagner.*

PLATE 38.2 *Windows, Southeast Corner of Broadway and Wall Street, Irving Trust Company, New York, New York, 1929–31. Architect Voorhees, Gmelin & Walker. Photograph (c. 1950–60s) by Charles Pratt.*

PLATE 38.3 *Main Banking Room, Irving Trust Company,*
New York, New York, 1929–31. Architect Voorhees,
Gmelin & Walker. Photograph (c. 1932) by Fay Sturte-
vant Lincoln, courtesy of the Canadian Centre for
Architecture/Centre Canadien d'Architecture, Montreal.

PLATE 39.1 *King Street Façade, Canadian Bank of Commerce, Head Office, Toronto, Ontario, 1929–31 (now Canadian Imperial Bank of Commerce). Architects Darling & Pearson; York & Sawyer, Consulting Architects. Photograph by Edward Burtynsky.*

PLATE 39.2 *Window, Com-
merce Court Elevation,
Canadian Bank of Commerce,
Head Office, Toronto, Ontario,
1929–31 (now Canadian
Imperial Bank of Commerce).
Architects Darling & Pearson;
York & Sawyer, Consulting
Architects. Photograph by
Edward Burtynsky.*

PLATE 39.3 *Ceiling, Banking Hall, Canadian Bank of Commerce, Head Office, Toronto, Ontario, 1929–31 (now Canadian Imperial Bank of Commerce). Architects Darling & Pearson; York & Sawyer, Consulting Architects. Photograph by Edward Burtynsky.*

PLATE 40.1 *Hollis Street Façade,*
Bank of Nova Scotia, Halifax, Nova
Scotia, 1929–1931. Architects
John M. Lyle; Andrew R. Cobb, As-
sociate Architect. Photograph by
Serge Hambourg.

PLATE 40.2 *Banking Hall, Bank of Nova Scotia, Halifax, Nova Scotia, 1929–1931. Architects John M. Lyle; Andrew R. Cobb, Associate Architect. Photograph by Serge Hambourg.*

PLATE 40.3 *Exterior Details,*
Bank of Nova Scotia, Halifax, Nova
Scotia, 1929–1931. Architects
John M. Lyle; Andrew R. Cobb, As-
sociate Architect. Photographs by
Serge Hambourg (triptych).

PLATE 41.1 *Wellington Street Façade, Bank of Montreal,*
Ottawa, Ontario, 1929–32. Architect Barott & Blackader.
Photograph by Edward Burtynsky.

PLATE 41.2 *Ceiling and Interior Details, Banking Hall, Bank of Montreal, Ottawa, Ontario, 1929–32. Architect Barott & Blackader. Photograph by Edward Burtynsky.*

PLATE 42.1 *View down Market Street with Elevations of PSFS and City Hall, Philadelphia Saving Fund Society, Philadelphia, Pennsylvania, 1931–32 (now PSFS). Architect Howe & Lescaze. Photograph by David Miller.*

PLATE 42.2 *Street Level Shops,*
Corner of Twelfth and Market
Streets, Philadelphia Saving Fund
Society, Philadelphia, Pennsylva-
nia, 1931–32 (now PSFS).
Architect Howe & Lescaze. Photo-
graph by David Miller.

PLATE 42.3 *Escalator to Banking*
Hall, Market Street Entrance,
Philadelphia Saving Fund Society,
Philadelphia, Pennsylvania,
1931–32 (now PSFS). Architect
Howe & Lescaze. Photograph by
David Miller.

MODERN AND LATE MODERN STYLES,
UNITED STATES AND CANADA

PLATE 43.1 *Façade, Manufac-*
turers Trust Company, New York,
New York, 1953–54 (now
Manufacturers Hanover Trust
Company). Architect Skidmore,
Owings & Merrill. Photograph
(1968) by Yukio Futagawa.

PLATE 43.2 *Fifth Avenue Façade, Nighttime, Manufacturers Trust Company, New York, New York, 1953–54
(now Manufacturers Hanover Trust Company). Architect
Skidmore, Owings & Merrill. Photograph by James Iska.*

PLATE 44.1 *Chase Manhattan
Bank and Lower Manhattan at
Sunrise; Chase Manhattan Bank,
New York, New York, 1957–61.
Architect Skidmore, Owings &
Merrill. Photograph by John Pfahl.*

PLATE 44.2 *View from Royal Bank of Canada to Chase Manhattan Bank and Federal Reserve Bank; Chase Manhattan Bank, New York, New York, 1957–61. Architect Skidmore, Owings & Merrill. Photograph by Catherine Wagner.*

PLATE 44.3 *Dubuffet Sculpture on Chase Manhattan*
Plaza, Chase Manhattan Bank, New York, New York,
1957–61. Architect Skidmore, Owings & Merrill.
Photograph by John Pfahl.

PLATE 44.4 *Aerial View, Chase Manhattan Bank and
Federal Reserve Bank, New York, New York. Photograph
by Marilyn Bridges.*

PLATE 45.1 *Façade, Bank of*
Montreal, Don Mills, Ontario,
1957. Architect John B. Parkin As-
sociates. Photograph by James Iska.

PLATE 46.1 *Skyline, Overcast,*
Toronto-Dominion Centre,
Toronto, Ontario, 1964 – 69.
Architects Mies van der Robe, John
B. Parkin Associates, and Bregman
& Hamann. Photograph by George
Tice.

PLATE 46.2 *Skyline, Sunset,*
Toronto-Dominion Centre,
Toronto, Ontario, 1964–69.
Architects Mies van der Robe, John
B. Parkin Associates, and Bregman
& Hamann. Photograph by George
Tice.

PLATE 46.3 *Skyline, Twilight,
Toronto-Dominion Centre,
Toronto, Ontario, 1964–69.
Architects Mies van der Rohe, John
B. Parkin Associates, and Bregman
& Hamann. Photograph by George
Tice.*

PLATE 46.4 *Skyline, Night, Toronto-Dominion Centre, Toronto, Ontario, 1964–69. Architects Mies van der Rohe, John B. Parkin Associates, and Bregman & Hamann. Photograph by George Tice.*

PLATE 46.5 *View from Banking
Pavilion, Toronto-Dominion
Centre, Toronto, Ontario, 1964–
69. Architects Mies van der Rohe,
John B. Parkin Associates, and
Bregman & Hamann. Photograph
by George Tice.*

PLATE 46.6 *Marble Column, Banking Pavilion,*
Toronto-Dominion Centre, Toronto, Ontario, 1964–69.
Architects Mies van der Rohe, John B. Parkin Associates,
and Bregman & Hamann. Photograph by George Tice.

PLATE 47.1 *Plaza Elevation, First National Bank of Chicago, Chicago, Illinois, 1964–69. Architects C. F. Murphy Associates and Perkins & Will Partnership. Photograph by David Miller.*

PLATE 47.2 *Plaza, First National Bank of Chicago, Chicago, Illinois, 1964–69. Architects C. F. Murphy Associates and Perkins & Will Partnership. Photograph by David Miller.*

PLATE 47.3 *Banking Hall, First National Bank of Chicago, Chicago, Illinois, 1964–69. Architects C. F. Murphy Associates and Perkins & Will Partnership. Photograph by David Miller.*

PLATE 48.1 *Nicollet Mall Façade,*
Federal Reserve Bank of Minneapo-
lis, Minneapolis, Minnesota,
1970–73. Architect Gunnar Bir-
kerts & Associates. Photograph by
Edward Burtynsky.

PLATE 49.1 *View South from Pike Tower Roof, Rainier Bank Tower, Seattle, Washington, 1974–77 (now Security Pacific Tower). Architects Minoru Yamasaki; Naramore, Bain, Brady & Johanson. Photograph by Catherine Wagner.*

194

PLATE 49.2 *Pedestal, Rainier*
Bank Tower, Seattle, Washington,
1974–77 (now Security Pacific
Tower). Architects Minoru
Yamasaki; Naramore, Bain, Brady
& Johanson. Photograph by
Catherine Wagner.

PLATE 50.1 *Toronto Skyline,*
Royal Bank Plaza, Toronto,
Ontario, 1973–77. Architect
Webb, Zerafa, Menkes, Housden
Partnership. Photograph by
Edward Burtynsky.

PLATE 50.2 *Atrium, Royal Bank Plaza, Toronto,*
Ontario, 1973–77. Architect Webb, Zerafa, Menkes,
Housden Partnership. Photograph by Edward Burtynsky.

PLATE 51.1 *Façade from Corner
of Bank and Wellington Streets,
Bank of Canada, Ottawa, Ontario,
1937–38. Architects Marani,
Lawson & Morris and S. G.
Davenport/Bank of Canada Addi-
tion, Ottawa, Ontario, 1972–79.
Architects Arthur Erickson;
Marani, Rounthwaite & Dick.
Photograph by David Duchow.*

PLATE 51.2 *Wellington Street Façade, Bank of Canada, Ottawa, Ontario, 1937–38. Architects Marani, Lawson & Morris and S. G. Davenport/Bank of Canada Addition, Ottawa, Ontario, 1972–79. Architects Arthur Erickson; Marani, Rounthwaite & Dick. Photograph by David Duchow.*

PLATE 51.3 *Interior Junction of Old and New Buildings,*
Bank of Canada, Ottawa, Ontario, 1937–38. Architects
Marani, Lawson & Morris and S. G. Davenport/Bank of
Canada Addition, Ottawa, Ontario, 1972–79. Architects
Arthur Erickson; Marani, Rounthwaite & Dick. Photo-
graph by David Duchow.

POSTMODERN STYLES, UNITED STATES AND CANADA

PLATE 52.1 *East Cambridge Savings Bank, 1932. Architect Thomas M. James/East Cambridge Savings Bank Addition, East Cambridge, Massachusetts, 1976–78. Architect Charles G. Hilgenhurst & Associates. Photograph by John Pfahl.*

PLATE 52.2 *Interior, from Original Banking Hall to*
Addition, East Cambridge Savings Bank, 1932. Architect
Thomas M. James/East Cambridge Savings Bank
Addition, East Cambridge, Massachusetts, 1976–78.
Architect Charles G. Hilgenhurst & Associates. Photograph
by John Pfahl.

PLATE 52.3 *Interior from
Addition to Original Banking Hall,
East Cambridge Savings Bank,
1932. Architect Thomas M.
James/East Cambridge Savings
Bank Addition, East Cambridge,
Massachusetts, 1976–78. Architect
Charles G. Hilgenhurst & Asso-
ciates. Photograph by John Pfahl.*

PLATE 53.1 *Skyline, Looking South, RepublicBank Center, Houston, Texas, 1981–84 (now NCNB Center). Architect Johnson/Burgee. Photograph by Edward Burtynsky.*

204

PLATE 53.2 *Banking Hall, RepublicBank Center,*
Houston, Texas, 1981–84 (now NCNB Center). Architect
Johnson/Burgee. Photograph by Edward Burtynsky.

PLATE 54.1 *Banking Hall, M Bank Dallas, Momentum Place, Dallas, Texas, 1985–87 (now Bank One, Texas). Architect John Burgee Architects with Philip Johnson. Photograph by Edward Burtynsky*

PLATE 54.2 *View of Entrance across Banking Hall Bridge, M Bank Dallas, Momentum Place. Dallas, Texas, 1985–87 (now Bank One, Texas). Architect John Burgee Architects with Philip Johnson. Photograph by Edward Burtynsky.*

207

PLATE B.1 *Milam Street Façade,*
Daytime, Texas Commerce Motor
Bank, Houston, Texas, 1979–80.
Architects I. M. Pei & Partners; 3/D
International. Photograph by
Edward Burtynsky.

PLATE 55.1 *North Elevation, Norwest Center, Minneapolis, Minnesota, 1986–88. Architect Cesar Pelli & Associates. Photograph by Edward Burtynsky.*

PLATE 55.2 *Skyline, Norwest
Center, Minneapolis, Minnesota,
1986–88. Architect Cesar Pelli &
Associates. Photograph by Edward
Burtynsky.*

·7·

AMERICAN AND CANADIAN BANKS

TWENTIES
AND
THIRTIES

When the European banker Paul Warburg arrived in New York in 1902 to join the investment house of Kuhn, Loeb & Company, he was astonished at the individualism of the United States' banking system. Throughout much of the nineteenth century American commercial banking had developed in the absence of a central bank into a unique form comprising thousands of banking institutions, mainly without branches. Although the Treasury provided some central banking functions, during the severe financial crises in 1877, 1895, 1903, and 1907 the government had had to turn to the private banker J. P. Morgan to avert disaster. The Panic of 1907 was the last straw. In 1908 a National Monetary Commission was appointed to examine the prospects for a new central bank, while the House Banking and Currency Committee—the "Pujo hearings"— interviewed Morgan himself in 1912 during an investigation into big business and a presumed "money trust." Once again, Americans wrestled with the issue of whether it was right that any individual or small group should wield such overwhelming power in a republic that aspires to be a true democracy.

In 1913 President Woodrow Wilson signed the Federal Reserve Act creating a central banking system composed of regional Federal Reserve Banks and member commercial banks.[1] Twelve reserve banks, rather than one, were instituted—in the American anti-centralist tradition—to afford a more elastic currency for the nation while ensuring local control.[2] These banks were not designed to serve the general public but to provide banking services for the member banks: holding their cash reserves and lending to them, collecting and clearing checks and transferring funds, furnishing currency, and serving as the federal government's fiscal agency. In 1935 Congress approved a board of governors for the system with clear-cut, centralized decision-making authority. This caused the individual reserve banks to lose most of their independence, while the board in Washington evolved into the nation's chief monetary policy-maker and implementer. Through its ability to influence the country's credit supply and interest rates, the board, under its powerful chairman, attempts to ensure a stable economy. A broad supervisory and regulatory role also devolves on the board.[3]

[36]   *Federal Reserve Bank of New York*
33 Liberty Street, New York, New York
York & Sawyer

Federal Reserve Act enacted: 1913
Constructed: 1921–24

One regional bank has, nonetheless, been more equal than the others: the Federal Reserve Bank of New York, which handles foreign transactions for the U.S. Treasury and the entire Federal Reserve System. When the First World War caused London to abdicate for a time as the center for world finance, New York filled the gap, serving as the trade and financial capital and as a haven for foreign gold which poured into the United States for safekeeping. Political stability, willingness to buy and sell gold at a fixed price, and the convenience of centralized gold holdings, where payments could be made quickly and easily, would later keep international gold reserves in the United States.

Today in the gold vault of the New York Federal Reserve Bank, 80 feet below Nassau Street, lie tons of gold belonging to the United States, foreign nations, and international monetary organizations.[4] These gold bars represent the largest known accumulation in the world, about a third of the official monetary gold reserves of the noncommunist nations. In an age when money is transferred globally at the touch of a computer key, in the vault below Nassau Street gold bars are moved physically from one nation's compartment to another to settle debts.

The building housing this awesome treasure is the result of a competition held in 1919, which involved six of the most prominent architectural firms, including McKim, Mead & White[5] and Trowbridge & Livingston. The winner was York & Sawyer, a New York partnership that emerged as the leader in bank architecture after the First World War. The firm was responsible for some of the most splendid bank buildings commissioned in the United States and in Canada prior to the Crash of 1929. Not surprisingly, both principals had worked in the McKim, Mead & White office before the turn of the century, and the designing partner Sawyer had also studied at the Ecole des Beaux-Arts in Paris. Like McKim, Mead & White in their addition to the Bank of Montreal [27], Sawyer looked to the fifteenth-century Florentine palazzo, notably the semidefensive townhouses built to protect the Strozzi and Pitti families, wealthy merchants and bankers. His design draws inspiration as well from the late-thirteenth-century Palazzo Vecchio, Florence's strongly fortified town hall.[6]

While the Bank of Montreal addition, rising only two stories above street level, was a comfortable reinterpretation of the palazzo tradition, York & Sawyer expanded the palazzo to gargantuan scale. Their Federal Reserve

Bank is a fourteen-story steel-frame building which occupies an entire city block in the New York financial district. The architects' medieval and Renaissance borrowings in conjunction with the vast modern scale result in an exterior that forcefully expresses the actual functions of the building. This is no friendly fortress in the manner of Root's Society for Savings in Cleveland [19], but a federal stronghold, a bank for banks. The exterior walls of powerful rusticated stone, the arched and square-headed windows of the base guarded by stout wrought iron grilles, the cornice crenellations, and corner turret all contribute to the fortified image, while the midsection containing repetitive office windows indicates the less-romantic financial activities that also take place within, often around the clock. The less-forbidding set-back upper three floors, two of them recessed behind an open loggia, create an arcaded crown for the edifice and were designed to contain restaurants and recreational facilities for employees.[7]

Although the façade is sparingly ornamented, Sawyer combined Indiana and Ohio sandstone to achieve a polychromatic effect and add variety to what would otherwise have been an overwhelmingly grim exterior. The Florentine-inspired ironwork, which includes lanterns as well as window grilles, was executed by the Philadelphia craftsman Samuel Yellin and is an outstanding feature of the building. There are additional grilles and gates by Yellin displaying floral, animal, and geometric designs in the public lobby, a 30-foot-high chamber crowned by a vaulted ceiling. There is limited access to this heavily guarded structure: the principal entrance off Liberty Street, a single door for employees, and a gated garage entrance on Maiden Lane for armored trucks.

The First World War served as a catalyst for the United States economy and for the nation's banks. With Europe convulsed, trade with other nations increased dramatically, and the country shifted from importing capital to exporting it. North American banks thrived, a process which continued throughout the twenties while Europe lay in financial ruin. Unprecedented growth and profits and the anticipation of a perpetually bright future led countless banks to build ambitiously. The majority of architectural firms, like York & Sawyer, continued to work in a traditional idiom for both large and small bank buildings. Even in Chicago, home of the great pioneers of modern architecture, a new wave of classicism in office buildings appeared in the first decade of the century. This continued through the boom years of the twenties, a time of great prosperity for Chicago, the country's most important city after New York.

[37] *Illinois Merchants Trust Company*

Continental Illinois National Bank and Trust Company of Chicago
231 South LaSalle Street, Chicago, Illinois
Graham, Anderson, Probst & White

Merger: 1924
Constructed: 1921–24

One way that the commercial banks met the demands of the new century's industrial giants was to merge, creating strong banks with wider resources and capabilities. These mergers, however, were still localized and strictly governed and limited by the banking laws within each state. In 1919 three venerable Chicago banks decided to join: the Merchants Loan and Trust

Company, the Illinois Trust and Savings Bank, and the Corn Exchange National Bank. The result was one of the most important banking combinations of the time, the Illinois Merchants Trust Company. A new building to house the merged institution was begun on the block which confronted the Federal Reserve Bank across LaSalle Street. Completed in two phases (in 1923 and 1924), the edifice contains one of Chicago's great banking halls. The building is now known as the Continental Illinois Bank Building as a result of a second merger in 1928.

The structure was designed by the prestigious Chicago firm Graham, Anderson, Probst & White, inheritors of Burnham and Root's practice[8] and among the period's most accomplished classicists.[9] The firm designed such Chicago landmarks as the Wrigley Building, the Chicago Union Station, the Civic Opera House, and the Merchandise Mart, as well as other major buildings from New York to Los Angeles.

Faced with Indiana limestone, the exterior of the twenty-one-story bank[10] is nearly indistinguishable from other office buildings built according to a classical formula that was widely used at the time: a tall rectangular block composed of a base, a shaft of identical office floors, and a terminating crown topped off by a strongly projecting cornice. This formula had been initiated by Sullivan as an elegant solution to the compositional problem posed by the new skyscraper, and it had been enthusiastically adopted by traditionalist architects.

To ensure that this new building would be clearly recognizable as a bank, the architects affixed a five-story, hexastyle Ionic portico on the LaSalle Street elevation, which faces the similarly grand portico of the Federal Reserve Bank, completed in 1922.[11] The impressive portico of the Illinois Merchants Trust is matched on the interior by one of the most grandly conceived banking halls in the country: 167 feet wide and 200 feet long, rising 53 feet from the French Hauteville marble floor to the central skylight. Located on the building's second floor and approached by two grand staircases, the huge banking chamber consists of a great central area surrounded by a colonnade comprising twenty-eight Ionic columns of light Cunard pink marble and flanked by two full-length wings which have 30-foot-high plaster coffered ceilings and brass-railed balconies at the third-floor level. Tall windows and a skylight provided illumination for this vast interior.[12]

Also contributing to the impact of the banking room is the frieze of colorful murals by Jules Guerin above the colonnade,[13] referring to the countries encompassed by the bank's international ambitions: the figure representing Switzerland holds a clock, for example. The backgrounds of the murals are also significant, for immortalized here are the principal buildings of the 1893 Chicago World's Fair, reminder of the city's splendid achievement.[14] Interspersed between the murals and completing the iconographic scheme are eight quotations on finance, specially chosen by C. W. Barron, owner of *The Wall Street Journal* and founder of *Barron's* magazine. One choice observation: "America has a system of banking which surpasses in strength and excellence any other banking system in the world. — Sir Edward H. Holden."[15]

The effect produced by this most famous surviving Chicago banking chamber is singularly appropriate for the nation's rail hub, since the vast room, with its slick marbles and pastel colors, might almost be mistaken for the concourse of one of the great Beaux-Arts railway stations of the time. The themes of the murals also support such a transportation theme.[16]

As an interesting historic footnote, the east half of the new bank's site was occupied until the time of the bank's construction by the Grand Pacific Hotel, where the General Time Convention had been held in 1883 to develop a uniform time system to facilitate railroad operations. This scheme, comprising four equal time zones, is still in use today.

In 1928 the Illinois Merchants Trust joined with the Continental and Commercial National Bank and Trust Company to form the Continental Illinois Bank and Trust Company.[17] This billion-dollar bank made Chicago finally independent of eastern capital and one of the world's major financial centers. At the time of this merger, two floors were added, and several private dining rooms were constructed on the topmost twenty-third floor. Two of the dining rooms contain sixteenth-century oak panelling transported from a Tudor house in England, as well as parquet floors, leaded glass windows with stained-glass medallions, sculptured plaster ceilings, and sixteenth- and seventeenth-century paintings and furnishings.[18] Perhaps only Louis Sullivan could have found words sufficient to describe the bizarre effect of arriving by elevator at these century-old rooms that presently inhabit the top of a steel-frame skyscraper in Midwestern America.

Two events in the early 1920s signified dramatically to North American architects that Europe was breaking with the tenacious revivalist tradition. The first was the highly publicized international competition for the Chicago Tribune tower of 1922, which attracted a number of advanced European designs; the second was the innovative Paris Exposition des Arts Décoratives et Industrielles Modernes in 1925. The immediate result in America was the advent of a widely popular style, now called Art Deco or Modernistic, which strove for a contemporary look while welcoming ornament and influences ranging from European Cubism and Expressionism to American Indian art. It was a gentler modernism than what would come to be known as the International Style.

The earliest skyscraper in the Art Deco style in North America was the Barclay-Vesey Building, which opened in 1926 at 140 West Street in lower Manhattan.[19] The architect was Ralph Walker, a young Easterner employed by the New York firm of McKenzie, Voorhees, and Gmelin. The building, which contained offices and a switching center for the New York Telephone Company, emerged during the design process as an irregular, stepped structure, shorn of historical detailing, its ultimate form having been determined by zoning, economic, and functional imperatives. Praised by the critics, the work made Walker's name, winning him recognition as a proponent and designer of Art Deco skyscrapers and as a prominent member of a new generation of New York architects that included his friends Raymond Hood and Ely Jacques Kahn.

Walker and his colleagues felt strongly that contemporary design should involve more than the expression of function, structure, and material propounded by the more extreme modernists. Walker despaired: "The whole tendency in modern architecture, and this is especially true in Germany, has been to treat these humanly inhabited buildings with a lack of the humanities and to think of them in terms of the stark nakedness of silos and grain elevators."[20] "The human mind," he later wrote, "as it is part of a civilized community is not interested in stark simplicity."[21] Instead, Walker and his friends exulted in the poetry and glamour as well as the modernity of the twentieth-century skyscraper and sought all manner of means to express it. Made a partner in 1926 (the firm became

Voorhees, Gmelin & Walker) Walker crowned the decade with one of the great bank commissions of the extravagant twenties, the Irving Trust Building, built on a magnificent site — Number One Wall Street, at the corner of Broadway just opposite the graveyard of historic Trinity Church.

[38]   *Irving Trust Company*
1 Wall Street, New York, New York
Voorhees, Gmelin & Walker

Chartered: 1851
Merger: 1926
Constructed: 1929–31

The Irving Trust Company, which had originated in 1851 as the New York Exchange Bank, was by 1928 one of New York's leading banks, with over two thousand employees and assets of nearly a billion dollars. Before the Depression the institution could well afford the cost of the plot of land which, according to Walker, was the most expensive on record. Still, it was necessary to build tall in order to be economical, and the building ultimately rose to fifty-one stories. Although the Crash occurred while work was in progress, its impact was not immediately felt, and like a number of other bank clients of the time, the Irving Trust Company chose the optimistic route, seeing their building through to completion in 1931.[22]

Like the Barclay-Vesey Building, the Irving Trust is stepped — a twentieth-century change in skyscraper design compelled by a 1916 zoning law passed to prevent New York streets from becoming dark canyons. The bank building is a compact vertical unity which rises in a series of narrow setbacks beginning at the twentieth floor, making a gradual transition from the base to the tower. Walker's inspiration for the extraordinary rippling effect of the façades was, he said, the current notion that the exterior of a modern building was in the nature of a curtain wall covering the structure.[23] The stone sheathing was thus handled like folds of drapery, enhancing the soaring height of the structure. Moreover, without resorting to traditional means, Walker's Modernistic "linenfold" wall treatment and tall, narrow ground floor openings project a Gothic quality that accords well with Trinity Church. Indeed Walker was quite satisfied that his building did relate well to the old church.[24]

The interior of this great skyscraper is one of the richest and most original of the time. Two areas are especially noteworthy: the reception room, unlike any banking chamber ever designed, and the observation lounge (now somewhat modified) in the tower for the bank's officers, which has great windows providing spectacular views over Wall Street and New York harbor.

A Futurist-inspired ceiling mural by Kimon Nicolaides in the elevator lobby, entitled *The Only Reason for Wealth is the Attainment of Beauty,* succinctly expresses Walker's philosophy. While the designers of traditional bank interiors relied on such elements as monumental columns, Walker followed a wholly abstract route for the reception room, utilizing a scheme of mosaic work for the walls and ceiling that produces an extraordinary impact. The dazzling color scheme was coordinated by Hildreth Meière, the artist who executed the elevator lobby ceiling mural. The floor is red terrazzo; the marble dado is a shade of deep burgundy; walls and ceiling are covered in glittering mosaic that gradually changes from red tesserae set in blue grout to orange set in black. An integral linear pattern in shaded gold appears to play over the mosaic, catching the light. Here, as on the exterior, surfaces are broken, adding further to the theatrical quality. This astonishing room, the very first the bank's clients enter, suggests the set of one of the German Expressionist films that were known in the United States throughout the twenties. Walker in fact went to Berlin with his associate Perry Coke Smith to supervise the making of the mosaic components, which are responsible for so much of the total effect.[25]

The officers' lounge at the top of the tower was also ingeniously conceived. The undulating walls were covered with a fabric whose pattern was inspired by an American Indian war bonnet and executed in colors of grey, buff, and dark red. The faceted ceiling was studded with seashells. In keeping with the inclusive nature of Art Deco design, Walker was happy to use all kinds of materials—old and new, natural and manmade— anything that would achieve his objective to "please and entertain the mind," providing "mental relief and pleasure."[26] While there are many equally magnificent banks and banking interiors dating from the affluent twenties, that of the Irving Trust is unique.

[39]   *Canadian Bank of Commerce*

Canadian Imperial Bank of Commerce
25 King Street West, Toronto, Ontario
Darling & Pearson; York & Sawyer,
Consulting Architects

Chartered: 1867
Constructed: 1929–31

Canadians also constructed some extraordinarily lavish skyscraper banks in the twenties, although these buildings were more conservative than Ralph Walker's. Notwithstanding an improvement in architectural education in Canada since the establishment of university schools such as McGill's in 1896, Americans continued to receive some of the choicest commissions, notably York & Sawyer. This firm designed the new head offices for the Royal Bank of Canada in Montreal and for the Canadian Bank of Commerce in Toronto. Between 1898 and 1911 the Bank of Commerce had increased its branches outside Ontario from one in Winnipeg to 149 from coast to coast.[27] With this infrastructure in place, the bank became a key player in the spectacular transformation of Canada during the twenties from a predominantly agricultural country to a modern industrial nation.

Located originally in the building occupied by the Bank of Upper Canada before its collapse, the Bank of Commerce had constructed its first new head office between 1889 and 1890 in the Toronto financial district.[28] This had been a tall building for the time—seven and a half stories— dwarfing the three- and four-story buildings that surrounded it. Although extensively renovated by Darling & Pearson, the old building was finally demolished in 1928 to make way for the thirty-four-story skyscraper that was advertised as the tallest building in the British Empire. The structure was clearly meant to eclipse the twenty-three-story Montreal head office of the rival Royal Bank, which had also enjoyed brief renown as the country's tallest structure. The Canadian Bank of Commerce even engaged the same architects.[29] Their mighty tower and the twenty-three-story building for the *Toronto Star* were the first of a new generation of skyscrapers in Toronto.

York & Sawyer's two Canadian banks share a family resemblance—a tower set on a high, broad base. This was a method of skyscraper design used by American classicists as an alternative to the rectangular tripartite block represented by the Continental Illinois Bank [37]. In the classically detailed Royal Bank in Montreal, base, shaft, and crowning pavilion are strongly demarcated in a traditional manner, whereas the Bank of Commerce displays a complex setback scheme not found in North American skyscrapers designed before the mid-twenties.[30] York & Sawyer used setbacks in the seven-story base, which was occupied exclusively by the bank, as well as in the shaft, where, starting at the twenty-third floor, gradually narrowing setbacks, together with continuous piers, visually intensify the structure's verticality.[31]

The stylistic treatment of the limestone exterior reflects the influence of York & Sawyer's uptown branch for the Bowery Savings Bank at Park Avenue and Forty-second Street, completed in 1923 and detailed in a free Byzantine and Romanesque manner. The entrance bays of the two buildings are remarkably similar: the main entrance of the Toronto edifice is an elaborate version of the great recessed archway surrounding the entrance of the smaller New York bank. The chief feature of both, however, is their banking halls. The Bowery's—one of New York's great interior spaces—is executed in a style that complements the exterior. For the Bank of Commerce hall the architects eschewed Byzantine-Romanesque in favor of a Roman classicism of unparalleled opulence: higher and wider and only slightly shorter than McKim, Mead & White's precedent-setting banking hall for the Bank of Montreal head office [27]; even higher than Continental Illinois' vast space [37]. Although modelled on a favorite Beaux-Arts source, the Baths of Caracalla in Rome, this great chamber is no cool, awe-inspiring sanctum but a warm, gloriously inviting public space —still the most exhilarating banking room in the country.[32] The walls here and in other banking areas on the main floor are of a deep plum-colored limestone quarried near Washington, D.C., while the coffered, vaulted ceiling is painted a rich blue, with surrounding moldings finished in gold and connecting bands of buff. The marble of the counters (now unfortunately removed) was selected to tone in with the wall surfaces, while the floor is of monochrome travertine, discretely banded with marble mosaics.

While ingratiating magnificence best describes the interior decor, the small-scale exterior ornament is less formal. The archivolt of the entrance door is adorned with a band of interlace containing bears, squirrels, roosters, bees, and beehives—symbols of thrift and industry; the tympanum displays Mercury, patron deity of bankers, flanked by seated female figures representing Industry and Commerce in front of a background displaying a grain elevator, the new building, and a flight of Canada geese. Other street-level carvings depict major Canadian industries such as grain growing, logging, fishing, water transportation, fur trading, and mining. Those who ascended to the observation promenade on the thirty-second floor—a tourist attraction for nearly half a century—were rewarded not only by the vista but by a close-up view of four giant heads, each 24 feet high including 10-foot beards which cascade down the piers. Symbolizing Courage, Observation, Foresight, and Enterprise, they were designed to be visible from the ground 450 feet below. The *Toronto Star* suggested during the building's construction that "the heads are intended to symbolize the eternal vigilance of the financier looking all ways out over the country."[33]

After the Bank of Commerce merged with the Imperial Bank of Canada in 1961 to form the Canadian Imperial Bank of Commerce, the enlarged institution took part in a new wave of bank tower building in the Toronto financial district beginning in the 1960s and continuing through the 1980s. However, unlike the Toronto-Dominion Bank and the Bank of Montreal, the Commerce did not demolish their existing Toronto office. Rather, they restored and renovated the historic structure at great expense, using it as the centerpiece of a new complex, Commerce Court, built between 1968 and 1972. Once again looking over their shoulder at a new Royal Bank head office in Montreal, housed in I. M. Pei's Place Ville Marie, the Commerce chose the same architect.[34] Pei's Toronto design involved the creation of a quiet fountain court behind the old skyscraper. Around the court are arranged a five- and a fourteen-story office block, both clad in complementary limestone, and a fifty-seven-story silvery glass-and-stainless-steel tower. Pei so designed the court to leave clear views of other historic bank buildings in the area: the Greek Revival Commercial Bank of the Midland District [9], the Traders' Bank Building of 1905–6, and the Dominion Bank Building of 1913–14.

[40] *Bank of Nova Scotia*

Hollis and Prince Streets, Halifax, Nova Scotia
John M. Lyle; Andrew R. Cobb, Associate Architect

Chartered: 1832
Constructed: 1929–31

The Canadian Bank of Commerce saw their building through to completion despite the onset of the Great Depression, as did two others, the Bank of Montreal in Ottawa [41] and the Bank of Nova Scotia, which proudly opened a new six-story office in Halifax in 1931. The Bank of Nova Scotia had been a regional bank lacking important branches until mergers between 1910 and 1923 gave it the national presence it needed to survive in Canada. In 1929 a site in Toronto was purchased for the bank's effective head office, which had moved to Toronto from Halifax at the turn of the century. In addition, a new building for the symbolic head office in Halifax was also commissioned for a prime site facing Province House, the fine Anglo-Palladian edifice built between 1811 and 1818 as the provincial parliament building. Both banks were designed in 1929 by the Toronto architect John Lyle.[35] The deteriorating economic situation, however, caused the postponement of the Toronto project, which would not be resumed until after the Second World War.[36]

John MacIntosh Lyle had come to Canada with his family from Ireland at the age of six. After study in Paris at the Ecole des Beaux-Arts and subsequent work in New York under John Galen Howard and as a renderer with Carrère & Hastings and Warren & Wetmore, he returned to Toronto in 1906 to become one of Canada's leading classicists.[37] Following Frank Darling's death in 1923, Lyle assumed the position of preeminent Canadian bank architect. He had begun designing banks soon after opening his Toronto office, working not only for the Bank of Nova Scotia, but for the Imperial Bank, the Bank of Toronto, the Bank of Commerce, the Sterling Bank, the Bank of Ottawa, the Metropolitan Bank, and the Dominion Bank. Lyle's bank buildings, like those of his predecessors Andrew Taylor and Darling & Pearson, can be seen from the Atlantic provinces to British Columbia.

Despite the presence of able architects in the Dominion, prestigious bank commissions continued to go to American firms: first R. A. Waite of Buffalo in the late nineteenth century, then McKim, Mead & White, followed by Carrère & Hastings and York & Sawyer. By 1926 all these firms had designed head offices, a fact which understandably rankled Canadian architects. Lyle was a leading challenger of American architectural hegemony, seeking to create a distinctly Canadian expression. The lavish Halifax bank commission was his most fully realized effort toward this goal.

Although Lyle stated that he had been "anxious to strike a modern note" in his design, he was acutely conscious of historic Province House across the way and referred to its classic tripartite composition in his own design.[38] He used a rusticated two-story base to contain the banking hall and fluted pilaster strips to tie the four office floors to the base and frieze of his otherwise spare, flat-roofed block. While Lyle dispensed with the columns and pediments which are notable features of Province House, the centers of his street elevations break forward in a Palladian manner.

Lyle correctly foresaw that if the extreme modernist viewpoint were adopted, there would be "no national or distinctive architecture, all architecture would look alike." [39] Yet his own solution to the perplexing problem of creating a modern nationalistic architecture was neither original nor imaginative in the manner of Sullivan or Ralph Walker, but highly conventional. Although his forms are flattened and simplified in keeping with current Art Deco or Modernistic fashion, Lyle not only remained firmly within the classical tradition but relied heavily on figurative ornament to express Canadian themes.

As soon as Lyle received the Halifax commission he sent an employee to the Royal Ontario Museum in Toronto to make color drawings of Indian forms. A bank publication notes: "At first his staff wasn't interested. However, his research began to change their minds, and soon they were mining the rich source of inspiration lying dormant in the plants, animals and ocean life of the Maritimes." [40] The Bank of Nova Scotia's façade alone contains eighty-six different Canadian motifs, carved on the Bedford limestone jambs, spandrels, cornices, and capitals, and incorporated into the bronze doors and window grilles.[41] A relief on the Prince Street elevation depicts ships; another, the smelting industry at Sydney. The sculptor was Ira Lake, who had worked on the war memorial arch that Lyle had designed earlier for the Royal Military College in Kingston. Despite the cautiously modern flattening and conventionalizing, every element is clearly readable — important to Lyle, since ornament is the carrier of so much of his "Canadian" content.

The interior of the bank is a veritable Noah's Ark of native animals. And not only are there Canada geese, dolphins and dories, but seashells, pine cones, sheaves of wheat, and Canadian coins. The crest of the bank, executed in metal, is embedded in the banking hall floor. A major item among the profusion of ornament is a colorful mosaic above the entrance which celebrates the Halifax-born Samuel Cunard's *Britannia,* the paddle steamer that inaugurated the first regular mail service across the Atlantic in 1840.

Lyle was able to extend his range in the interior, designing everything from the boardroom carpet with its seashell motif to the extravagant bronze and metal cheque desks with their metal lamps. For Lyle, who did not lack affluent clients, the Bank of Nova Scotia's decision to proceed with the Halifax building provided one of the last opportunities in Canada to work in a traditional, handcrafted manner using the full gamut of architectural arts. Commissions for total works of art of this type and magnitude were killed by the Depression and another World War. Later, advanced modernist ideology would demand very different forms of expression.

[41]   *Bank of Montreal*
144 Wellington Street, Ottawa, Ontario
Barott & Blackader

Founded: 1817
Chartered: 1822
Constructed: 1929–32

In 1929, the same year that the Halifax branch was designed, the Bank of Montreal, still banker to the Dominion government, initiated their most noteworthy building project since the McKim, Mead & White head office enlargement of the turn of the century [27]. Not only was the bank outgrowing their existing Ottawa premises, dating from the early 1870s, but both the Bank of Nova Scotia and the Bank of Commerce had constructed impressive new buildings nearby,[42] and it was important that the Bank of Montreal brush up their Ottawa image. Stung by the strong criticism resulting from their patronage of McKim, Mead & White, the Bank of Montreal limited this important competition to Canadian architects. On the building's completion in 1932, the bank made much of the fact that only Canadian architects, contractors, methods, and products had been used.[43]

This was not entirely true. The competition was won by a distinguished Montreal firm, Barott & Blackader, whose principal, Ernest I. Barott, was an American-born and -trained architect. Barott had worked for McKim, Mead & White before emigrating to Canada, where his skill in Beaux-Arts design rapidly won him such enviable clients as the Canadian Pacific Railroad, the Hudson's Bay Company, the Bank of British North America, and the Bank of Montreal. He kept in close touch with the latest developments in New York, knew Ralph Walker, and was concurrently working on one of Canada's first Art Deco skyscrapers, the Aldred Building in Montreal, which was strongly influenced by Walker's Barclay-Vesey Building.

Barott's winning design is extremely skillful. The site lay along three streets: Wellington, where the principal government buildings were located; Sparks, Ottawa's main shopping street; and sloping O'Connor, which linked the two. The design called for a monumental one-story block set on a basement with grand entrances opening onto both Wellington and Sparks. Since there was a 12-foot drop between the two streets, the Sparks Street entrance opened into the basement, where a wide marble staircase led up to the banking hall on the same level as Wellington Street. The slightly projecting central block contains the banking chamber, lit by tall windows on the flanks, while two lower end pavilions contain the entrance vestibules, offices, and a conference room. The basement houses the safety deposit department and vault.

The exterior was described at the time as "a modern interpretation of Greek design," a traditional temple bank in Modernistic guise: the balanced, classical massing cubistic, the ornament stripped and flat.[44] The extreme severity of the limestone and granite façades is offset by the exquisitely disposed openings, splendid exterior metalwork in bronze and iron, and a program of relief sculpture. The exterior ornament is more restrained and abstract than Lyle's Halifax façades [40], which gives the Bank of Montreal a more modern look. The major elements are the incised lettering on the street facades, the fluted pilasters of the end pavilions, and eight allegorical relief panels—the result of a collaborative effort between Barott and the New York sculptor Emil Siebern. Not surprisingly, the panels depict the development of Canada and the Bank of Montreal's prominent role therein, with both the Montreal head office [10] and the new Ottawa building making an appearance. The sculpture and the architectural detailing alike are meant to recall the austere forms of archaic Greece, and they harmonize perfectly with Barott's severe, contained classical composition.

In the interior Barott, like Lyle, added color and rich materials, using both luxurious marbles and manmade Benedict Stone, with sleek custom-designed furnishings to achieve an understated, up-to-date splendor that reflected his client's enduring position. Indeed no bank of the time could have asked for a more perfect balance between modernity and tradition than Barott provided with his elegant, sophisticated design. The work won the Royal Architectural Institute of Canada Gold Medal for 1932.

[42]   *Philadelphia Saving Fund Society*
PSFS
1212 Market Street, Philadelphia, Pennsylvania
Howe & Lescaze

Chartered: 1819
Constructed: 1931–32

Occasionally, American banks have represented the stylistic avant-garde, as did Latrobe's Bank of Pennsylvania [4], the second Bank of the United States by Strickland [5], and Sullivan's Midwestern banks. Between 1931 and 1932 a thirty-two-story tower was erected for the venerable Philadelphia Saving Fund Society that was not only the most radical bank building of its time, but the most advanced skyscraper in the world.[45] The structure's unprecedented complex massing was determined by functional considerations rather than the visual preferences that governed the gothicized massing of the Irving Trust [38]. The architectural historian William Jordy writes: "Any list of the most significant American buildings embodying what has come to be popularly termed the 'functional phase' of modern architecture, which began to appear at the very end of the 1920's in the United States, would surely include—and probably at the top—PSFS (thus neon letters announce it to downtown Philadelphia)."[46]

This daring venture notwithstanding, PSFS is one of the three oldest mutual savings banks in the country, its doors having first opened in 1816. The institution had a tradition of fine architecture, including its two historic headquarters on Walnut Street: a Greek Revival building of 1839–40, designed by Thomas U. Walter, and a larger Italianate bank dating from the late 1860s by Addison Hutton, with sympathetic later additions by Frank Furness.[47]

The new PSFS building, by Howe & Lescaze, comprises a base or podium from which rises an asymmetrically positioned twenty-seven-story office tower. Externally, the component elements are clearly differentiated. The base was designed to contain shops at ground level to attract traffic to the bank. Cantilevered over this area is the elevated banking chamber, reached by an interior escalator and lit by a broad expanse of glass. This fenestration, like the shop windows below, curves without interruption around the corner. The banking hall is surmounted by three more floors which accommodate bank offices and act as a transition between the base and the rental office tower. A cantilevering over Market Street of the upper floors expresses the beginning of this tower, shaped and placed off-center to permanently ensure light and air to the interior. The narrow spine at the rear — set at right angles to the tower, giving the slab its T shape — contains elevators, fire stairs, and vertical utilities. At roof level the architects provided an executive suite and terrace, an observation platform, and cooling towers for the air conditioning, masked with a hinged billboard emblazoned with their now-famous red neon sign announcing PSFS to all Philadelphia.[48]

PSFS was the second skyscraper in the United States to be completely air-conditioned. The decision to embark on this expensive undertaking was made after the building was underway and despite the onset of the Depression. The bank was aware that their competitors, the Fidelity-Philadelphia Trust and the Girard Trust, were completing buildings with rental space that did not offer this modern convenience.

Not only the shape but the sheathing of the steel-frame structure indicates the internal arrangements. Polished charcoal-grey granite is used for the podium exclusive of the two upper transitional floors, which are faced in sand-colored limestone, a material that is also used for the columns of the office tower. The spandrels of the tower are a grey brick, the windows aluminum; black brick is used for the service spine. Apart from the beauty derived from high-quality materials and meticulous craftsmanship, neither the exterior nor the interior was ornamented in the traditional sense. The banking hall, a vast open space made possible by bridging trusses that support the structural columns of the office tower, contains flanking rows of piers. These marble-clad uprights, while providing the barest hint of classical banking rooms, were left completely plain. Elsewhere in the room sumptuous but subdued traditional materials were used — marbles and granite, played off against satin-finished stainless steel and large areas of glass. Surfaces were sleek and streamlined.

The early International Style manner that PSFS displays involved a radically new set of design criteria. Modern building technology now permitted architects to exploit volume (the raised, cantilevered open banking room with its transparent window walls made possible by the steel frame and trusses), so that mass need no longer be a dominating factor. Asymmetrical compositions generated by functional considerations replaced the symmetry of Beaux-Arts composition; and traditional ornament, which smacked of the past, was shunned.[49]

The critic Paul Goldberger has remarked: "The act of commissioning such a structure in conservative Philadelphia in 1929 must go down as one of the great leaps of architectural faith on the part of any major client in the twentieth century."[50] The effective client was the elderly president of PSFS, James M. Willcox. Extraordinarily well-educated, Willcox was a great respecter of tradition. He also respected his architect, George Howe, who after designing a series of orthodox branch banks for PSFS, daringly left a successful Main Line partnership in order to embrace modernism.[51] Howe shortly took on a partner, William Lescaze, a European committed to the modern movement, and with Willcox they evolved the radical final design for PSFS during 1930. Willcox trusted the Groton- and Harvard-educated Howe and moreover was concerned that the building be "ultra-practical" and as his monument (he retired in 1934) remain for decades competitive with other office buildings. Willcox's faith and his continual testing of the architects' ideas did indeed result in a monument, one that was proclaimed the Building of the Century by the American Institute of Architects at their centennial in 1969.[52]

·8·

AMERICAN AND CANADIAN BANKS

MODERNISM
AND
LATE MODERNISM

The Depression combined with the Second World War seriously cur-
tailed building in the United States: it was not until the end of the
1940s that construction began to pick up again. Yet if architectural offices
were idle during those trying years—and many, of course, closed—
Americans continued to learn about European modernism. In 1932 the
newly founded Museum of Modern Art opened its first exhibition devoted
to international modern architecture. An accompanying catalogue and a
book by the exhibition's curators, the renowned architectural historian
Henry-Russell Hitchcock and architect Philip Johnson, isolated the principles which they believed defined the International Style, as they named it.
Museum director Alfred H. Barr, Jr., in his introduction to the book, sum-
marized these principles: "emphasis upon volume—space enclosed by
thin planes or surfaces as opposed to the suggestion of mass and solidity;
regularity as opposed to symmetry or other kinds of obvious balance; and,
lastly, dependence upon the intrinsic elegance of materials, technical
perfection, and fine proportions, as opposed to applied ornament." [1] One
of the few American firms invited to exhibit was Howe & Lescaze, and
their Philadelphia Saving Fund building [42] represented the key work by
American architects in the show.[2]

The political turmoil in Europe also brought to the United States some
master practitioners of this new style: in 1937 Walter Gropius was called to
Harvard University as chairman of the Department of Architecture, and
Ludwig Mies van der Rohe arrived in America, soon to be head of the
architectural school at the Illinois Institute of Technology (then the Ar-
mour Institute) in Chicago. The impact of these men was extraordinary:

"In little more than a decade, every architectural school of consequence was at least professedly 'modern.' " [3]

Concurrent with the dramatic departures in the architectural realm were changes in banking brought about by the historical events of the thirties and forties. The Great Depression, beyond halting the growth of those banks that managed to withstand the calamity, provoked far-reaching changes which would shape expansion after the war and over which legislative battles are still being fought. The stock market crash and the vast number of bank failures led to an abundance of government regulations intended to protect the public and make banks safe and stable. The major pieces of reform legislation were the Banking Act of 1933, also known as the Glass-Steagall Act, and the Banking Act of 1935. Among their provisions were the creation of federal deposit insurance, the separation of investment from commercial banking, the prevention of speculative uses of bank credit, the banning of demand-deposit interest, and the setting of a ceiling on time-deposit rates. These two acts also affected the Federal Reserve System: creating the Federal Open Market Committee, which has the power to control credit fluctuations by the open-market purchase and sale of government securities, and reorganizing the Federal Reserve Board into the present Board of Governors. Provisions in the Securities Exchange Act of 1934 empowered the Board to set margin requirements regulating the amount of credit that banks and brokers may extend for the purchase of listed securites.

Heavily regulated and seeking fresh areas of growth after the war, commercial banks began to promote a new image — openness and accessibility. With GIs returning home in droves and starting families, consumer banking became increasingly attractive. Many formerly commerce-and-industry-oriented institutions began to exploit this profitable new market, a significant source both of deposits and of credit demand.

[43]   *Manufacturers Trust Company*
Manufacturers Hanover Trust Company
Fifth Avenue and Forty-third Street, New York, New York
Skidmore, Owings & Merrill

Chartered: 1905
Constructed: 1953–54

In 1952 a highly visible metal-and-glass slab was completed on Park Avenue, its modern materials and form markedly disrupting the pattern of the surrounding blocks. The building's glass-skinned tower, radically confined to a mere quarter of the site, appeared to hover weightlessly above a podium set on slender stilts, or pilotis. Beneath the podium was an open public plaza — the first in the area. The structure, Lever House, was one of the earliest glazed curtain-walled skyscrapers and represented the opening of a new period in skyscraper design not only for New York but ultimately for the world. In the use of metal and glass and in the inclusion of a plaza it established a new standard for office buildings after the war. The American designer, Gordon Bunshaft, a partner in the firm of Skidmore, Owings & Merrill, made his name with this building. His next significant commission would be a small glass branch bank in New York for Manufacturers Trust Company, in which he brilliantly used the glass curtain wall and disruption of the street block to promote new desiderata in commercial banking.

Bunshaft's "all-glass display case for banking" for Manufacturers Trust Company[4] was like no other bank building in history. As the architect has remarked, it "broke the masonry-fortress psychology of branch banking up to then. From then on banks all across the country became friendly."[5] This Fifth Avenue branch announces itself to prospective customers in two ways: through transparency—the open, glowing interior is clearly visible from the street—and by dislocation of the street block.[6] Surrounded by skyscrapers reflecting Manhattan's high land costs, the bank is a mere four stories high with a rooftop penthouse. Rectangular in shape, the structure has a visible framework of eight interior concrete-covered steel columns and beams, which support reinforced concrete decks that cantilever on two sides. The glass skin, which in 1954 featured the largest sheets of glass ever placed in a building (9 feet 6 inches x 22 feet x 1/2 inch), is a true curtain, each aluminum panel mullion hanging from the cantilever edge above, with the glass free to "ride" in its surround as expansion and contraction take place. Such a structure required enormous precision in construction: the builder's superintendent described it "more like jewelry than building."[7]

Although Bunshaft had exploited an arresting asymmetry in composing Lever House, placing his tower at one end of the stilted podium, the bank's Fifth Avenue façade displays a classic symmetry that evokes traditional bank architecture. There are nevertheless strong diagonal and corner accents in the interior: the shiny escalator to the mezzanine and the beautiful stainless steel and polished bronze vault dramatically displayed at sidewalk level—an ingenious means of assuring depositors that this glass bank is perfectly safe. Great care was taken to make the interior conspicuous at all times to imply accessibility. Light colors and specially designed luminous ceilings minimize reflection from the glass, permitting a clear view from the inside and outside.

The eye is attracted, too, by the 70-foot-long golden screen in bronzed sheet metal which divides the public and work spaces of the second-floor banking room.[8] This commissioned abstract mural by Harry Bertoia and other specially chosen paintings and sculpture started a tradition in Skidmore, Owings & Merrill banks; indeed artwork became a notable feature of the "SOM style" in their more luxurious interiors.[9] The plan of the building makes clear the market being targeted by this carefully orchestrated effort in public relations: while regular and commercial accounts were to be serviced on the second floor with its stylish Bertoia mural, the street-level banking room was planned to handle payroll checks and installment loans.

The new glass bank had an immediate effect. Not only did Skidmore, Owings & Merrill design subsequent branch banks in this pattern in New York and elsewhere, but architects all over North America produced their own variations. Even the pioneer of the glass pavilion, Mies van der Rohe, would design a one-story glass bank branch in the following decade for the head office complex of the Toronto-Dominion Bank [46].

Chase Manhattan Bank

1 Chase Manhattan Plaza, New York, New York
Skidmore, Owings & Merrill

Merger: 1955
Constructed: 1957–61

A year after the opening of the Manufacturers Trust building (during which the branch's business tripled), the nation's third-largest bank, Chase National Bank of New York, which served large business and financial institutions, took a decisive step into consumer banking by merging with the historic Bank of The Manhattan Company (founded by Aaron Burr in 1799) with its fifty-six New York branches.[10] In that same year the merged Chase Manhattan Bank called on the firm that had done the Manufacturers Trust bank — Skidmore, Owings & Merrill — to design a new skyscraper head office. The result would be another International Style paradigm, not only for bank head offices but for corporate headquarters worldwide.

This was a bold move by Chase's management, for the International Style had gained a mere toehold in New York. The early monuments, the United Nations Secretariat (1947–50) and Lever House (1951–52), were but a few years old, while Mies's Seagram Building (1955–58) had not been completed. Yet Chase, led by the new chairman, John J. McCloy, not only rejected plans by another firm for a more conventional skyscraper but also decided to stay in the financial district.[11] This was the most critical decision of all, since the future configuration of Manhattan depended on it. At the time the alternatives were being weighed, many firms, including bank customers, were deserting Wall Street for Park Avenue. Chase's decision to remain would ensure the survival of the city's historic financial core. McCloy later recalled:

> It was not an easy decision. Downtown was the hearthstone of the city. It was here where the Old Federal Building was first set up, where Washington took his oath of office, in which the Bill of Rights was adopted, . . . The tip of Manhattan had a great tradition and it had real beauty, at the confluence of two rivers. It seemed to me that it had some significance not only to the city but to the nation to keep in existence this area, where, in and out of those narrow streets for a period of a century, the progress of the country had been financed.[12]

With the help of real estate developer William Zeckendorf, Chase put together two blocks divided by Cedar Street, for which Skidmore, Owings & Merrill submitted two proposals. It was Executive Vice-President David Rockefeller who urged the Chase board to choose the most modern and dramatic approach — Bunshaft's simple rectangular shaft rising from an open plaza. Rockefeller has said that once the decision was made to remain downtown, he felt the bank should proceed in a "way that people would recognize as a decisive move on our part, which would change the climate and preserve Lower Manhattan."[13] This proposal required the city to close and deed to Chase the part of Cedar Street separating the two blocks and to grant variances from the setbacks normally required for tall buildings.

When it was completed in 1961, Chase's $96-million, sixty-story tower was a remarkable sight. Henry-Russell Hitchcock found it exalting:

Up among the serrated spires of the 'teens and the 'twenties has appeared the top of a plain rectangular slab, realistic where they are fantastic, yet almost transparent thanks to the extent of the fenestration. Even from a great distance the sturdy steel skeleton, expressed in the external piers, and even the storeyed interior . . . are clearly visible, while the older skyscrapers appear solid and without structural articulation owing to their massive brick and stone cladding.[14]

The new building did indeed revitalize the financial district: its plaza, embellished with a sunken stone garden by Isamu Noguchi and a large sculpture entitled *Group of Four* by Jean Dubuffet, initiated a chain of plazas in the area. Yet as Christopher Woodward noted at the beginning of the reactive seventies, the mammoth curtain-walled slab dislocated not just a street or a block but the entire built form of Lower Manhattan, including the historic view from the Staten Island Ferry.[15] For an ambitious bank to dominate the entire environment of Wall Street was, of course, a splendid feat of architectural one-upmanship, despite the honest civic-mindedness of its inception. Other North American business executives hurried to engage Skidmore, Owings & Merrill and their often far less able followers to design new corporate headquarters in emulation of Chase Manhattan's austere, abstract appearance, which was suitable for any type of office. Its duplication *ad nauseum* throughout the world has led to a current disenchantment not unlike that of the 1850s when Wall Street's Greek Revival temples in grey granite were referred to as "grim temples."

Another aspect of Chase's new headquarters drew attention: the art collection. The program developed out of a need to add warmth and color to the unadorned interior, with David Rockefeller and Gordon Bunshaft playing key roles. Bunshaft felt that a modern building should have modern art and that experts should choose it. A selection committee was formed with Rockefeller, who was on the board of the Museum of Modern Art, as chairman.[16] The other members were Bunshaft; McCloy; Alfred H. Barr, Jr., first director of the Museum of Modern Art, and Dorothy Miller, its senior curator of painting and sculpture; James Johnson Sweeney, former director of the Guggenheim Museum; Robert B. Hale, curator of American painting and sculpture at the Metropolitan Museum; and Perry Rathbone, director of the Museum of Fine Arts in Boston.[17] In addition to contemporary art, American folk art, which also suited the plain interiors, became a component of the collection, the rationale being that both connoted the bank's rich role in American history. Works of art from other countries were also acquired, many chosen by Rockefeller on his frequent trips abroad and reflecting the global interests and ambitions of Chase.

The headquarter's immense influence was a result not only of its own initial impact but of the organizational structure of Skidmore, Owings & Merrill, which did the most to spread the postwar International Style throughout North America. Founded in Chicago in the thirties by three Midwesterners, Louis Skidmore, Nathaniel A. Owings, and John O. Merrill, the firm was committed both to modern design and to capitalizing on a trend that had been growing in the United States — the large architectural office. The McKim, Mead & White office had been among the largest early in the century with as many as a hundred employees. That number was still considered large in 1950, but by 1958 Skidmore, Owings & Merrill, beneficiary of air travel, was a national enterprise with over a thousand employees and major offices in Chicago, New York, San Francisco, and Portland, Oregon.[18]

Modelling their firm on a large business enterprise, the principals developed a team approach, providing their clients with a total package comprising every aspect of architectural, engineering, planning, interior, and environmental design, as well as project management services. Skidmore, Owings & Merrill's "leave it all to us" approach has been highly successful in an age when producing a large building is an incredibly complex and expensive undertaking. Their own commissions in addition to those of countless imitators made the International Style glass and steel slab the emblem of business everywhere, as democratic a vernacular as the Greek Revival temple of the Republic's early years.

[45] *Bank of Montreal and Bank of Nova Scotia*
877 and 885 Lawrence Avenue East, Don Mills, Ontario
John B. Parkin Associates

Constructed: 1957

The influence of American architecture and architects accelerated in Canada after the Second World War. In 1957, three years after Manufacturers Trust's glass bank opened, the Bank of Montreal and the Bank of Nova Scotia carried out an unprecedented collaborative venture, erecting glass-walled branches side by side in Don Mills, a pivotal planned postwar development, which forms part of Greater Toronto. Hailed at the time as drive-in banks, a genre that had existed in the United States since the late 1930s and in Canada since 1950, they were in fact branches designed with ample parking areas in the rear but which still required customers to do their banking inside.[19]

The nearly identical one-story buildings—the earliest International Style glass banks in the Dominion—were designed by the Toronto firm of John B. Parkin Associates, the largest architectural firm in Canada during the later 1950s and 1960s and one which boasted an integrated practice similar to that of Skidmore, Owings & Merrill. The partner in charge of design at the time was John C. Parkin (no relation to John B. Parkin), who had studied under Gropius at Harvard during the 1940s. His two glass boxes follow the pattern of the Miesian pavilion, recalling Philip Johnson's celebrated Glass House of 1951. This was a more appropriate response to a suburban environment than Bunshaft's four-story Manufacturers Trust [43].[20] The intent, however, was exactly that of the New York building. An advertisement placed in the *Toronto Daily Star* began with the words: "Who ever heard of a glass bank!" The text continued: "Not just an architect's wild dream! And Canada's First Bank—the Bank of Montreal—has brought this latest development in banking architecture to Toronto, in the new premises of its Don Mills branch, which opens today." The bank's management felt obliged to add: "In case you're wondering, security has not been sacrificed in giving Don Mills B of M glass walls. Every precautionary device to safeguard customers' interests has been installed, including a steel-and-reinforced-concrete vault."[21] The only opaque walls were those of the small service cores which protected the vaults.

By late 1962 both the Royal Bank and the Canadian Bank of Commerce occupied International Style curtain-wall skyscrapers in Montreal, the former inhabiting part of I. M. Pei's cruciform Place Ville Marie, the latter erecting its own glass-and-steel slab designed by Peter Dickenson of Toronto with the Montreal firm of Ross, Fish, Duschenes & Barrett acting as supervising architects. Like Chase Manhattan Plaza [44], these pioneer Canadian towers served as the galvanizers of postwar urban redevelopment, although unlike Chase, both were built uptown on Dorchester Boulevard, beginning the fragmentation of Montreal's historic financial district.

[46] *Toronto-Dominion Centre*

55 King Street West, Toronto, Ontario
Mies van der Rohe, John B. Parkin Associates,
and Bregman & Hamann

Merger: 1955
Constructed: 1964–69

In contrast to Montreal, the erection in 1965–67 of the first International Style bank tower in Toronto anchored for the foreseeable future what was now the financial heart not only of Toronto but of Canada. A century and a half earlier, the building of the Commercial Bank of the Midland District [9] had signalled the establishment of Toronto's financial hub on the northern fringe of the emerging wholesale district, near the early banks' principal customers.[22] Today the soaring headquarters of four of the country's five leading banks can be found vying for attention a block to the north, while nearby rise the gold towers of the Royal Bank [50].[23]

These, the city's fourth generation of bank office towers, were initiated by the International Style Toronto-Dominion Centre, designed by Ludwig Mies van der Rohe. When the principal component of the Centre, the Toronto-Dominion Bank Tower, was completed in 1967, this fifty-six-story glass and steel edifice could be seen 19 miles away from the west and 30 miles from the north. It was the beacon marking the new center of Canada's powerful banking industry, despite the existence of titular head offices elsewhere.

The Toronto-Dominion Centre is located in a congested area in the midst of such establishments as the Toronto Stock Exchange. By 1969 it comprised the bank tower, an independent single-story banking hall, and the forty-six-story Royal Trust Tower, all standing on the most expensive four-acre plaza in Canada.[24] Below the plaza is a three-story substructure containing a public shopping concourse and two levels of parking.

This historic Canadian effort in large-scale urban redevelopment began with the merger in 1955 of the Bank of Toronto, established in 1856, and the Dominion Bank, incorporated in 1871. For Allen T. Lambert, who became the organization's president in 1960, a new office headquarters was a top priority.[25] According to Robert W. Collier, who has studied large-scale development in Canadian cities, Lambert was approached early on by the director of the City of Toronto Planning Board, who urged him to consider a larger project than a head office building—namely, a complex in the midst of the financial district that would testify to Toronto's postwar growth and industrial success.[26] Another early character in the story was the omnipresent William Zeckendorf, who had put together the Chase Manhattan land parcels and was also the developer of Montreal's landmark Place Ville Marie. Zeckendorf's grandiose schemes usually staggered the imagination of local officials, but in this case "the client felt the Zeckendorf treatment was too tame for the desired image." [27] In fact, the bank's management was unhappy with a proposed cluster of towers to be designed by I. M. Pei, which, straddling both sides of Bay Street, would not have furnished the smallest of the Big Five banks with a distinctive architectural identity.[28] It particularly galled Lambert that John Lyle's handsome building for the Bank of Nova Scotia, the country's fourth-largest bank, caused it to be mistaken by the public for the largest.[29]

In 1961 Toronto-Dominion agreed to a proposal by Cemp Investments for a joint venture leading to a mammoth development intended to rejuvenate the downtown core. Predictably Lambert first approached Gordon Bunshaft at Skidmore, Owings & Merrill, but the developers were unhappy with both aesthetic and technical aspects of Bunshaft's proposal for the bank tower, which involved flaring piers and a ground-level banking hall. Such a scheme, Lambert believed, diminished the presence of the banking function.[30]

Cemp Investments, the bank's partner, was until 1987 the private investment company owned by the trusts created for the heirs of Canadian industrialist Samuel Bronfman, founder of Distillers Corporation-Seagrams Limited. On the advice of his daughter, Phyllis Lambert (no relation to Allen Lambert), Bronfman had commissioned Mies van der Rohe to design the magnificent Seagram Building on Park Avenue, completed in 1958. Not surprisingly, it was Mies who was brought in as chief designer for the Toronto-Dominion Centre, and the project became the last great work in which he actively participated before his death in 1969. Since Mies was not licensed to practice in Ontario, his Canadian associates, the John B. Parkin office and Bregman & Hamann, prepared the contract drawings and supervised construction. Mies, who is cited as consultant, designed the buildings and prepared the preliminary drawings in collaboration with his own staff.[31]

Although Allen Lambert had hoped to preserve the existing Bank of Toronto head office, designed by Carrère & Hastings and completed in 1913, Mies felt this sumptuous colonnaded marble temple could not be accommodated within his pristine modernist scheme. Thus Mies's own version of a classic temple—a single-story, 150-foot-square, clear span, steel and glass pavilion—serves as the head office's flagship branch and, as architectural historian William Dendy remarks, "a ghostly reminder of lost splendour." [32] The isolated banking pavilion, Mies's contribution to the growing repertoire of glass bank branches, gives prominence to the banking function that Lambert desired, while providing the freer, more flexible space that Mies felt was functionally appropriate but which was unrealizable within an office building.[33]

The utilization by the master of his own two primal paradigms, the high-rise slab and the low pavilion, for a bank complex was not original; for Skidmore, Owings & Merrill had already designed a complex for the First City National Bank of Houston, completed in 1961, which involved an office tower and a low banking pavilion.[34] Mies's intention in architecture, however, was not to be original but rather to achieve the greater perfection—through the refinement of the details—of forms he had already developed. He was the great classicist of International Style modernism: like the enduring temples of ancient Greece, Mies's buildings of the fifties and sixties differ from one another only slightly. Thus his low element, the Toronto-Dominion banking pavilion, resembles (without the overhanging roof) his contemporaneous National Gallery for Berlin (1962–68); while the two towers, although much larger, are similar to the Seagram Building.

To many critics this late work of Mies personifies a once fresh and vital style that had become "codified and listless." [35] Yet it was for Canada a highly visible example of the work of one of the founders of modern architecture, as important in its way as was McKim, Mead & White's work on the Bank of Montreal head office [27] at the turn of the century. Like theirs, it is a first-class job. The pure geometric forms of the towers and pavilion are sheathed in a beautiful skin which celebrates the austere, standardized materials and methods of modern structural technology. This skin is an exquisitely proportioned and balanced grid composed of matte-black painted steel verticals and horizontals, which are welded together, and bronze-grey tinted glass set in an extruded aluminum glazing frame with a matte-black baked finish. Arranged on the grey granite plaza like freestanding sculpture, Mies's meticulous black towers have an elegance that is unsurpassed by subsequent coarser rivals in the immediate neighborhood.

The Toronto-Dominion Centre was the most important new commercial complex of Toronto's postwar construction boom. Within a few years its influence had extended not only to two other corners of King and Bay streets but elsewhere in the city and thence across the country. Its beauty notwithstanding, the complex's deficient response to urban problems led both to imperfect backlash legislation aimed at curbing the destruction of Toronto's historic core, which it had precipitated, and to attempts to humanize the uninviting plaza on which Mies's monumental buildings stand. One result is that Saskatchewan ceramicist Joe Fafard's group of seven larger-than-life bronze cows now recline peacefully on a patch of grass west of the IBM Tower.

[47] *First National Bank of Chicago*

1 First National Plaza, Chicago, Illinois
C. F. Murphy Associates and Perkins & Will Partnership

Chartered: 1863
Constructed: 1964–69

During 1964, before construction of the Toronto-Dominion Centre had even begun, the management of a major Chicago bank approved a design for a new skyscraper that challenged Miesian dogma on the master's home territory. The First National Bank of Chicago, chartered in 1863, was another American wholesale bank that, like Chase Manhattan, had recast its role after the Second World War, moving into the consumer and international fields. Under bank chairman Homer Livingston and Gaylord Freeman, who was president, vice-chairman, and then chairman and chief executive officer, First National Bank introduced low-cost, no-minimum-balance checking accounts and computerized teller transactions, moved into the new field of bank credit cards, and by 1974 had become the fourth-largest U. S. bank in number of overseas installations. The building program the bank embarked on in 1964 would provide an appropriate headquarters for a great international institution.

Asked by Livingston to talk to several architects about the proposed project, Freeman relates that he saw

> . . . all the local Chicago firms and most of the nationally known ones, including Yamasaki whom I admired, I. M. Pei, the associates of Saarinen, Philip Johnson (who said he wouldn't be interested in doing a bank), Charles Luckman, Pereira, and Chicago's own Mies van der Rohe, to whom I made the mistake of saying that I didn't want the last of the chaste, square, glass buildings but preferred to have the first of a new and stronger style. As you can imagine, some of my conversations were quite brief![36]

In the end chairman Livingston decided to use two local firms, Perkins & Will and C. F. Murphy Associates (predecessor of Murphy, Jahn). A fascinating series of notes and sketches kept by C. William Brubacker, now vice-chairman of Perkins & Will, records the collaborative process between the two firms and the bank's management in designing the building.[37]

The result, completed in 1969, was the highly visible sixty-story tower that tapers upward in a sweeping curve from the heart of Chicago's Loop.[38] This graceful form, together with the contemporaneous but more rigid-looking X-braced John Hancock Building by Skidmore, Owings & Merrill, represented a decisive break with the Miesian rectangular box. It also provided the bank with the widest possible floors near street level for public banking activities and narrower upper floors to house offices and tenants. Although a Lever House configuration—a tower on a podium—might have accommodated such a program, the gigantic tapered tower of the First National Bank is, significantly for its locale, a further development of the American skyscraper pioneered by the Chicago School before the turn of the century and brought to perfection by Mies after the Second World War.

The unprecedented form of the First National Bank announced that this was not just another corporate headquarters. The splayed base with its tall windows proclaims not only a particularized function but hints at the existence of a vast banking chamber. This interior space, however, is handled in a very different manner from that of the great Beaux-Arts banking halls, for example the hall of the nearby Continental Illinois Bank [37]. Since archaic Illinois banking laws did not permit branch banking, and therefore all transactions had to take place on a single block, the huge uninterrupted space that the architects provided by means of a truss could not be used solely for symbolic purposes. Thus the public banking area includes a hovering mezzanine supported by columns and free of the perimeters. Reached by escalators, it is filled with additional tellers' counters.

In addition to its unorthodox form, the First National Bank of Chicago displays natural stone cladding: a warm-toned, speckled Texas granite dubbed "bankers' grey" by the architects. In conjunction with the bronze insulated glass and metal components of the curtain wall, the dignified grey stone covering furnishes this modern skyscraper with the appearance of solidity that has distinguished bank buildings since their historic beginnings. The building continues to enjoy nearly full occupancy and is looked upon as "a benchmark of quality and success for Loop office buildings." [39]

One contributor to this success is the lively multilevel plaza, which provides more than an acre of inviting open area in the middle of Chicago's high-rise business district. In contrast to inhospitable early plazas, the First National Bank Plaza is colorful and friendly, enhanced by trees, shrubbery, flower beds, sunny places to sit, a fountain, scheduled entertainment, and a 70-foot-long mosaic wall titled "The Four Seasons," by Marc Chagall.[40] Much of the credit for the liveliness of this urban open space belongs to Mrs. Freeman. While accompanying her husband on business trips, she made a study of existing plazas to determine ways to accomplish the bank's goal of dispelling the dullness of the downtown core and providing a refreshing spot for lunch-time and after-work crowds.[41] Such a gathering place was, of course, a means of attracting customers, as were the shops on the ground level of the Philadelphia Saving Fund Society [42]. From the plaza, indeed from any vantage point, the tapering granite-clad curtain walls of the bank tower create a powerful presence, evoking the Egyptian pylon, one might even say an updated version of the battered end walls that gave strength to the façade of the Greek Revival Bank of Louisville [6], tiny in comparison. In Chicago the immense scale even challenges the pyramids — a suitable gesture in the birthplace of the modern steel-frame skyscraper.

Just as the architecture of the First National Bank comments on the infinitely repeatable International Style tower pioneered by Chase Manhattan [44], so too was their art collection intended to be different from that of the New York bank. While acknowledging that David Rockefeller had led the way with Chase's distinguished collection, chairman Freeman, while favoring architectural innovation, believed that a bank's art collection should not be avant-garde: "People who save money are conservative and hence would like conservative art." [42] The noted former art dealer, curator, and critic Katharine Kuh was engaged to buy the art works.[43] With her primary goal being to enrich the lives and widen the horizons of all the bank's employees, she installed the greatest works in the bank's huge public spaces: "We do not lock them up or hide them away in the executives' offices." [44]

[48]   *Federal Reserve Bank of Minneapolis*

250 Marquette Avenue, Minneapolis, Minnesota
Gunnar Birkerts & Associates

Federal Reserve Act enacted: 1913
Constructed: 1970–73

Alternatives to the sheer tower soaring straight up from an open plaza continued to be explored during the late sixties and seventies. Two striking examples of visual form as well as feats of modern engineering are the Federal Reserve Bank in Minneapolis, completed in 1973, and the Rainier Bank Tower in Seattle [49], which opened in 1977. The Minneapolis bank was the first completely new building in the Federal Reserve system since the initial round of construction had created banks "securely sealed behind inscrutable Renaissance façades." [45] The challenge facing the Michigan-based firm of Gunnar Birkerts & Associates was to project a fortress-like image without resorting to such traditional techniques as rusticated masonry, wrought iron grilles, turrets, and machicolation. Birkerts's design involves a breathtaking structural scheme, worked out by engineers Skilling, Helle, Christiansen, Robertson, whereby the visible eleven-story administrative portion is suspended like a bridge over a 2-1/2-acre plaza. Beneath the plaza is hidden the "secure" portion of the bank: two levels for security operations and vaults plus one for parking and ramps.

There was no prototype for this structure, which consists of two granite-clad concrete towers, designed as huge H-columns to resist wind loads on the long façades and to support the hammocklike suspension frame — catenaries composed of cable and welded steel plate. These clearly visible catenaries are the primary supporting members for the office floors and are braced against unsymmetrical loads by a 28-foot-deep truss at the roof. The innovative system provides unobstructed office floors of 60 by 275 feet—almost the width of the site. No occupied floors ever before spanned such a distance. Since the elevators occupy a freestanding tower, the floors are uninterrupted by columns or service risers. Moreover this glass-enclosed administrative area, which needs to be accessible to few other than employees, perches out of reach 20 feet above the plaza. Only a single entrance off Marquette Avenue provides pedestrian access. Because the secure area beneath the plaza was designed to slope upward to the building and then drop off sharply to the level of Marquette Avenue, the pedestrian and truck entrances are through a rampartlike, 20-foot-high wall beneath the plaza level. The novel suspension system also allows for uninterrupted space below the plaza to accommodate the intricate vault and truck-ramp arrangement. Although obviously an expensive undertaking, the structure was designed to carry an additional six stories using an arch system that transfers loads to the concrete end towers.

As abstract form, the vast building is stunning and eloquent, a successful union of architecture and engineering. But the bank's very success, practically and aesthetically, nullifies the public plaza concept that is also an important feature of the design. Located on a prominent site in the Gateway Renewal Area, which links the downtown core to the Mississippi riverfront, the plaza was advertised as a setting for outdoor concerts and other public gatherings. Yet detached as the bank is from the plaza, designed to discourage if not repel would-be attackers, the building can hardly be said to serve as an appropriate backdrop for festive human activities. Visually stunning, urbanistically the Minneapolis Federal Reserve Bank is a failure.

[49]   *Rainier Bank Tower*

Security Pacific Tower
1200 Fourth Avenue, Seattle, Washington
Minoru Yamasaki; Naramore, Bain, Brady & Johanson

Chartered: 1889
Constructed: 1974– 77

Another engineering tour de force, the Rainier Bank Tower, designed by Minoru Yamasaki, architect of New York's World Trade Center (1966–76), deals somewhat more successfully with the problem of urban responsibility, an increasingly urgent issue as more and more formula skyscrapers invaded North American cities. The complex which Yamasaki designed (with Naramore, Bain, Brady, & Johanson of Seattle as project architects) for downtown Seattle involved two clients: the land owner, the University of Washington, and the National Bank of Commerce, which changed its name to Rainier National Bank in 1974, just as construction began.[46]

Yamasaki, who was born in Seattle, "wanted to use as much of the site as possible to further the creation of a 'green downtown,' to introduce landscaping and open space where it is too often lacking." [47] The inventive architect's solution was to place his thirty-two-story, aluminum-clad steel-frame office tower on top of a 121-foot pedestal constructed of thick poured-in-place concrete and embedded in "an unimaginable amount of concrete below grade." [48] The tower's perimeter acts as a Vierendeel truss, transferring wind load to the pedestal. Although it appears to be precariously balanced, the engineers claim, according to Yamasaki, that it is one of the most earthquake-resistant structures ever built, a necessity in the area.

By lifting the bulk of the building high off the ground, the architect reduced the impact at street level and permitted views of the surrounding neighborhood. The design also gave the bank a distinctive presence on the Seattle skyline, while the considerable area left free by the narrowing pedestal could include pleasant landscaped terraces and several levels for shops and restaurants. The actual banking facility is located in the shopping-mall area, with a roof terrace to set off the office tower and provide splendid views of nearby older buildings.

Despite an arresting form and urbanistic awareness, the Rainier Bank Tower is less successful as modern bank architecture than either the First National Bank of Chicago [47] or the Minneapolis Federal Reserve Bank [48]. The vision of a mighty tower supported by a delicate, narrowing curvilinear base is disturbing, recalling Barnett Newman's daringly balanced sculpture *Broken Obelisk* (1963–67). Might not this skyscraper topple, destroying the bank? Unresolved, too, is the radically reduced scale at ground level, for here Yamasaki becomes dainty, using, for example, minute tiles to face the pedestal. Architectural critic Paul Goldberger earlier disapproved of Yamasaki's sheathing the mammoth 110-story World Trade Center towers with a delicate tracery coating, calling it "so obviously false that the entire project seems disingenuous." [49] The Rainier Bank Tower is in fact a good example of various dilemmas facing architects in the late twentieth century as they struggle to integrate buildings of unprecedented size and scale into the human environment.

A Canadian banker recalled the tremendous impact that the Toronto-Dominion Bank Tower [46] made upon the closely knit banking and business fraternity when it opened in 1967. Although conservative by American standards, it seemed in his words "avant-garde, stunning, and sexy." [50] The chief executives of three of Canada's five major banks were clearly impressed but not amused, for in the late 1960s and early 1970s soaring new towers were built in Toronto by the Canadian Imperial Bank of Commerce (1968–72), the Bank of Montreal (1972–75), and the Royal Bank of Canada [50] (1973–77). The first two of these institutions hired famous American International Style architects—I. M. Pei and Edward Durell Stone.

Moreover, the Bank of Nova Scotia, the original thorn in the side of Toronto-Dominion's Allan Lambert, commenced the most megalomaniacal bank complex of all, when it announced in 1984 the projected $400-million Scotia Plaza. The project involved density concessions considerably in excess of those allowed by the Central Area Plan approved by the Toronto City Council in 1976. This trend-setting, comprehensive plan to control development was mainly a response to the new high-density bank towers. Campeau Corporation, the developers of Scotia Plaza, gained approval for a sixty-eight-story office tower nearly twice as large as the official limit by using various techniques such as bonuses for preservation of historical buildings (including the old Lyle bank), for amenities (day-care centers and a site for subsidized housing), and for density transfers (from a waterfront property). In 1984 Richard Thomson, Lambert's successor at the Toronto-Dominion Bank, went on a "personal mission to Toronto City Hall, trying to convince politicians to stop the $400-million Scotia Plaza development." [51] He was unsuccessful.

[50]   *Royal Bank Plaza*
200 Bay Street, Toronto, Ontario
Webb, Zerafa, Menkes, Housden Partnership

Chartered: 1869
Constructed: 1973–77

Scotia Plaza, which features an eleven-story glass atrium linking the old Lyle headquarters to the new red-brown granite-faced office tower, is the tallest and most ambitious of the competing bank projects, but the most visually spectacular is the Royal Bank Plaza. Completed in 1976, this was the first of the new Toronto headquarters of a Big Five bank to be designed by a Canadian firm — Webb, Zerafa, Menkes, Housden Partnership, which subsequently received the commission to design Scotia Plaza. The firm was formed following the death in 1961 of the principals' employer, Toronto-based Peter Dickinson, architect of the Canadian Imperial Bank of Commerce tower in Montreal. Although none of Dickinson's major uncompleted projects came their way, by the mid-eighties the firm had opened offices in Toronto, Montreal, Vancouver, Calgary, and five U.S. cities. Their twin-towered edifice for the Royal Bank is golden (what better color for a bank?), incorporating 2500 ounces of gold coating on the inside panes of double glazing set within the stainless steel mullions of the curtain walls. The bank is dazzling on the Toronto skyline as the sun glitters on its faceted golden skin.

The Royal Bank, chartered in 1869 as the Merchants Bank of Halifax, changed its name in 1901. Four years later it moved its head office to Montreal and by the 1920s this aggressive bank together with the Bank of Montreal controlled upward of 40 per cent of Canada's banking assets.[52] Today it is the largest bank in Canada and one of the largest in North America in assets and deposits. Although the head office is still located in Montreal in Place Ville Marie, the bank established a presence in Toronto shortly after the turn of the century with the erection of a building on King Street East designed by Carrère & Hastings. The growing organization moved twice more in Toronto before planning the Royal Bank Plaza in the early 1970s, by which time all large sites had been taken in the central banking district at King and Bay. Thus slightly outside of "bankers' Valhalla," as William Dendy describes it, the Royal advertised its presence with a structure dramatically different from the cool slabs that Mies, Pei, and Stone had designed for its rivals.[53]

The large site lies — strategically for pedestrian traffic — between Union Station and the subway and the intersection of King and Bay a block to the north. A sufficiency of land allowed for the erection of two triangular towers, forty-one and twenty-six stories tall, set at opposite corners of the site and joined by a banking-hall atrium, which diagonally connects the busy corner of Wellington and Bay with Front Street opposite Union Station. Abundant traffic, especially during the cold Canadian winter, is thus ensured. The lower two levels are given over to an underground shopping mall leading to the subway, Union Station, the Royal York Hotel, and much of the downtown core.

The glitter of the exterior is not merely a result of the golden glass but also a function of the serrated aluminum curtain walls, which break up the surface of the buildings like facets cut in a gem. It is an exterior beloved by Torontonians, by now bored with the height race, a warming vision on grey winter days. Unfortunately, thc atrium — containing the two banking floors joined by an escalator — might have been a triumphal space but is merely dull, a sad letdown of expectations raised by the exterior. Not surprisingly, the pioneers of atrium banking halls were Skidmore, Owings & Merrill. In 1967 they had designed the first, for the Illinois National Bank in Springfield, which has at its center a five-story skylighted rectangular atrium surrounded by open balconies on all sides. A pool with two splashing fountains and columns of hanging ivy enliven the ensemble.[54] Unlike the Royal Bank's atrium, it is a congenial place for customers, bank personnel, and tenants.

[51]   *Bank of Canada Addition*
         234 Wellington Street, Ottawa, Ontario
         Arthur Erickson; Marani, Rounthwaite & Dick

Bank of Canada Act enacted: 1934
Addition constructed: 1972–79

Reflective glass — although not gold-tinted — has also been used with great effect for the Bank of Canada addition in Ottawa, completed in 1979 and designed by the country's most famous architect, Arthur Erickson. A native of Vancouver, Erickson is the first Canadian-born designer to be widely known internationally, the first to counter the historic directional flow of architects moving between Canada and her powerful neighbor.

The Bank of Canada had been created by legislation passed in 1934 to serve as the country's central bank. At first privately owned, it became wholly owned by the government in 1938. It issues the country's paper currency, acts as fiscal agent and banker for the federal government, sets the bank rate, and implements and helps to formulate the country's monetary policy. Unlike the older Federal Reserve System in the United States, it was organized as a centralized institution from its inception. It is appropriately housed in a solemn silver-grey granite building on Wellington Street not far from Barott's Bank of Montreal [41]. The latter, as a result of the Bank of Canada Act, lost its historic role as banker for the government, which it had enjoyed since 1863.

The dignified Modernistic classical structure designed for the Bank of Canada by the Toronto firm of Marani, Lawson & Morris, completed in 1938, was far too small by the early 1960s; indeed many bank personnel were then occupying supposedly temporary buildings constructed during the Second World War. In early 1964 the decision to build was announced and the architects chosen: Marani, Morris & Allan, successors to the original firm. Their unexciting plans, however, were ultimately superseded by a design by Erickson, whose appointment as consultant architect was announced in 1971, during the prime ministership of the dashing Pierre Elliott Trudeau. Erickson would work with Marani, Rounthwaite & Dick, as the firm was now called.[55]

With the exception of Darling & Curry's festive Bank of Montreal in Toronto [23] and perhaps the glittering Royal Bank Plaza [50], Canadian banks have traditionally been a remarkably sober group of buildings. Erickson's design brought a refreshing, sophisticated wit to Canadian bank architecture, without sacrificing either dignity or beauty. His plan consisted of two twelve-story office towers of green-tinted reflective glass, slightly set back and flanking the original building on the east and west. The towers are linked at the rear by a full-height glass atrium, which also contains the back portion of the old bank. On Wellington, which has the Houses of Parliament and other federal edifices, the old bank's unaltered façade and two-thirds of the side elevations stand free, framed like a sacred object by the glass towers and atrium. Reflected by the glass are the Chateau-style Confederation building opposite — a government office block — and other neighbors, as well as portions of the old bank. The "complex relationship between the bank and the government is mirrored, literally, in the architecture."[56]

Providing the main point of public entry and visible to the inner offices, the atrium is a vast greenhouse filled with pools and luxuriant planting, for which the old bank's rear façade serves as a stately backdrop. Flying bridges pass through the atrium at various levels connecting the upper floors of the old and new blocks. Erickson's fastidious choice of materials contributes significantly to the sensuous elegance of this interior oasis, or Garden Court as it is called, and indeed to the entire addition. The paving employed throughout the complex at street level is a beautiful blue-green English slate that ties in with the green-tinted glass and oxidized copper used extensively in the new work. This copper, which was artificially aged by a process developed in Japan, is also an important means of relating this unusual federal building to the many historic copper-roofed structures in the capital.

Since the railroad first linked the nation's disparate parts, eastern Canada has imposed its bank architecture on the West. It is fitting that in this, the country's federal bank, the trend was finally reversed. Erickson's new Bank of Canada, while respecting, indeed enshrining, the self-contained old bank, introduces into the harsher eastern context some of the hospitable, nature-embracing qualities of modern British Columbian architecture.

·9·

AMERICAN BANKS

POSTMODERNISM

By the 1970s the negative aspects of postwar modernism were widely recognized. Neither slabs and pavilions nor sculpted towers set off by plazas constituted the ideal human environment their creators envisioned. Accordingly, thoughtful architects began looking for ways to enrich and humanize the language of architecture. Above all, they sought to reintegrate the past, which had been so forcefully rejected by the orthodox modernists and so much evidence of which had been tragically destroyed—in large part by well-meaning urban renewal schemes. The architect Charles Jencks dates the symbolic death of modern architecture to July 15, 1972, when several blocks of high-rise public housing in St. Louis, designed in 1951 by Minoru Yamasaki following the most progressive International Style ideas, were deliberately blown up by the authorities after continuous vandalism by inhabitants.[1]

The term Postmodernism, defined by Jencks, has been used since the mid-seventies to describe a contemporary hybrid style that strives for a greater balance between the present and the past. Armed with a more sympathetic attitude toward historical architecture, practitioners of Postmodernism, while often facile, can also be extraordinarily successful when dealing with older buildings.

East Cambridge Savings Bank Addition

292 Cambridge Street, East Cambridge, Massachusetts
Charles G. Hilgenhurst & Associates

Chartered: 1854
Addition constructed: 1976–78

By the mid-1970s, the East Cambridge Savings Bank had outgrown its small 1932 building and had engaged the Boston firm of Charles G. Hilgenhurst & Associates to design an addition. The gracious Depression-era structure was, like the original Bank of Canada, a symmetrical self-contained rectangular block, seemingly not amenable to enlargement. Designed by Boston bank specialist Thomas M. James, the old building is in the simplified proto-modern idiom that prevailed in the 1930s, the finely proportioned façade pierced by three tall semicircular-arched openings that contain the central entrance and three windows. The bulk of the building, containing the banking hall, was faced in a Maine granite called Swenson's Pink, while a full-height brick wing at the rear was divided into two floors to contain the board room, work space, and washrooms.[2]

East Cambridge in the 1930s was a working-class neighborhood. The handsome bank, which features elaborate exterior and interior carving, bronze-work, Numidian marble interior walls, and a splendid Adam-Pompeian-type painted ceiling,[3] is reported to have provided considerable local employment and perhaps to have been a statement of the bank's continuing health during hard times. The overall style is a Byzantine-Romanesque mix, undoubtedly influenced by York & Sawyer's popular work.

Adding to this well-loved community landmark was a challenge met with exceptional grace by architects Warren Schwartz and Robert Silver of the Hilgenhurst firm.[4] Their inspired design solution of 1976, which doubled the space, involved reusing one of the granite bays from the west side of the old building that would be covered by the new construction and rotating it 90 degrees until it aligned with the bank's symmetrical main front. The reassembled section became the frame for the street entrance to the new wing and of course matched the façade of the old building perfectly. It was linked to the existing building by means of a curving transparent glass and acrylic wall, whose steel ribs repeat exactly the shape of the building's arched openings. Elsewhere brick walls enclose the addition on the inconspicuous new western side and rear.

The architects made only minor changes to the old banking hall, carefully refurbishing the floor and walls and changing the teller counter from a U-shape to an L to facilitate internal access to the addition. Prefaced by an invitingly open double-height reception area, the addition accommodates staff offices and mortgage facilities. The feeling here is subtly thirties modern, providing contrasting bright, clean-surfaced open space, which nevertheless accords neatly and meaningfully with the thirties traditionalism of the old bank.[5]

Thanks to the recycling of the side wall bay and the sensitive geometry of Schwartz and Silver's design, the visual aesthetics between old and new are superbly harmonious. "The effect is delightful," wrote Robert Campbell in the *Boston Globe* in 1978. "The new front seems to have popped out of the old building like a jack-in-the-box on a curving spring. It's part of the original yet doesn't compete with it. It's a kind of outrigger to the old bank."[6] The two architects, who categorize Postmodernism as "cynical and cartooned" and do not consider either themselves or their bank addition as Postmodern, think of the relocated bay as an artifact.[7] In fact it is the integrity of their design, with its intense respect for both the old and the new in architecture, which elevates it above Postmodernism as it is widely practiced today. What they achieved is a new entity that transcends the sum of its parts, an expanded building more beautiful and less formidable than the original gem, a conspicuous improvement to a rather rundown urban neighborhood, and a practical, pleasant work place. A pioneer and model for current contextualism, the project was an eye-opener for many architects. Schwartz and Silver's design won for Hilgenhurst the Harleston Parker Medal for 1979 awarded by the Boston Society of Architects for the most beautiful building of the year in the Greater Boston area.

[53]   *RepublicBank Center*

NCNB Center
700 Louisiana Street, Houston, Texas
Johnson/Burgee Architects

Founded: 1876 (RepublicBank Houston defunct)
Constructed: 1981–84

Downtown Houston rises dazzling like Oz from the flat Texas landscape, as much a period piece in its own way as historic Charleston. The city's central business district was totally transformed during the oil-rich 1970s with the building of a series of skyscrapers designed by the most prestigious architectural firms in North America. To compete on the crowded Houston skyline with one's ablest peers and indeed with oneself was the task facing Philip Johnson and his partner John Burgee when they were commissioned in 1981 to design a new building for RepublicBank Houston (formerly Houston National Bank), then the city's fifth-largest bank.

Johnson/Burgee[8] had already designed the best-known building in Houston's business center, Pennzoil Place, a 1976 monument of abstract formal beauty comprising twin black towers with angled tops. Paul Goldberger has written about Pennzoil Place: "A city had not seen so recognizable a skyscraper top since the Empire State Building's."[9] In 1983 RepublicBank moved into a building that had a profile even more arresting, for the fifty-six-story tower has two major setbacks creating the illusion of three gables, each stepped in a Dutch Renaissance manner — like the old Princeton Bank [20]. Moreover, the huge building is clad in Napoleon red granite nearly as bright as the red brick that helped the little Princeton Bank stand out from its Nassau Street neighbors.

Three years after Pennzoil Place was completed, Johnson, proselytizer and respected practitioner of the International Style, put aside his old robes and assumed the mantle of high priest of Postmodernism. Johnson and Burgee's mannered AT&T building in New York, with its historicizing "Chippendale" crown, is one of the most famous skyscrapers of the late twentieth century. "The building so startled the editors of the *New York Times* that they put a rendering of it on the front page when the design was made public in 1978."[10] The partners' far more flamboyant RepublicBank Center initiated the skyscraper bank into the Postmodern era.

Speaking about RepublicBank Center in 1983, the Houston bank's chairman and chief executive officer Ronald Brown uttered some familiar phrases: "We recognized as we started on this process that we had an opportunity to be involved in the making of a significant architectural statement . . . We wanted something distinctive."[11] The bank (or the developer Gerald D. Hines), in fact, appears to have urged Johnson into his new mode, for the architects' original proposal, sympathetic to their neighboring Pennzoil Place, was rejected.[12] Armed with Postmodernism's catholic approach, however, the ceaselessly inventive Johnson (who had obviously warmed up to the idea of designing a bank since his conversation with Gaylord Freeman in 1964) together with Burgee could look to history to provide their clients with a distinctive image. The RepublicBank Center is fraught with historical references, much as so many twenties skyscrapers were, but it is marked by a disingenuousness these earlier towers lack. Other differences, including record-breaking scale, stem from new materials and construction techniques. Indeed the romantic skyscrapers of the twenties form part of the Postmodernists' repository of historical motifs.

RepublicBank Center has not only a dramatic red tower, but also an attached low-rise banking hall, also faced in red granite, with a stepped gabled roof to match that of the office tower. Both components are roofed in lead-coated copper, a material used as well on the finials which embellish the gable-end steps. The low element gives the banking function a well-defined presence and also serves to conceal an existing Western Union switching facility that could not economically be moved. This hidden structure actually occupies one quarter of the ground level. While the style of the banking hall, like that of the tower, is expressly intended to recall Dutch guildhalls — Northern Renaissance Europe's most flamboyant mercantile architecture — the exterior elevations of the banking hall and of the lower tower floors are more like a palazzo.[13] The latter is as evocative of historical bank architecture of nineteenth- and early-twentieth-century America as of fifteenth-century Italy. The classicizing elements in this unabashedly eclectic ensemble, which also includes borrowings from French eighteenth-century architect Claude-Nicolas Ledoux,[14] enable Johnson and Burgee to give the lower floors an impregnable look and to create a colossal 75-foot arched entrance to the banking hall opening onto Louisiana Street, the site's most important boundary street. Moreover, the overscaled entrance is nicely placed on axis with the gap between the two Pennzoil Towers across the way.

Unrestrained eclecticism and colossal scale are continued in the interior. To reduce the impact of the space lost to the Western Union building, the architects divided the ground level plan into quarters by means of two great axial corridors that intersect in the center and link the four street entrances, banking hall, and office tower elevator lobbies. A four-faced Seth Thomas clock, dating from 1913 and purchased specially by developer Hines, marks the crossing.

The major axis is the ribbed, barrel-vaulted corridor or arcade running east-west between the Louisiana and Smith Street entrances, which the architects meant to resemble the nave of a Romanesque church. Paved and flanked in granite, filled at the ends in a churchly manner with glass, this awesome 80-foot-high space is spanned at three levels by pedestrian bridges with wrought-iron railings. The ironwork, which is also used to define the officers' area in the banking hall, is based on the work of the Austrian Art Nouveau architect Josef Hoffman. Copies of Hoffman's striking chair designs appear in the bank offices, among the elements conceived by Gensler & Associates of Houston, who served as interior architects.[15] Johnson and Burgee, however, were responsible for the bulk of the ground-level architectural design, including the spectacular upper reaches of the 125-foot-high banking hall.[16] This area is a great network of white dry-wall-enclosed trusses and row upon row of skylights which rise in steps conforming to the exterior roof. Further complexity is produced by the screen walls that define the main corridor, which has white upper sections consisting of rows of superimposed segmental arches.

In a video presentation prepared for the bank, Johnson makes much of the granite cladding and of the revival of the master craftsman, as if he had emerged from a masonry building tradition rather than from the modern glass and steel aesthetic of Mies. The red stone, quarried in Sweden, cut and fabricated in Italy, and finally hand set in Texas, is used in three different finishes: flamed, honed, and bush-hammered. While it does contribute significantly to the building's visual drama and costly appearance, its nonstructural use and the obvious revival of picturesque eclecticism would horrify Johnson's mentor Mies. Indeed the apostate Johnson has said that "he no longer believes in principles or overblown philosophy."[17]

The overpowering aura of this instantly famous Texas bank and office tower was clearly not devised to increase consumer banking but rather to impress the corporate customers that were RepublicBank's main clients and to attract tenants for the office tower. As Ada Louise Huxtable, former architecture critic of the *New York Times,* notes: "The developer [Hines] . . . has found that rental response relates directly to a building's recognition factor on the skyline. Identity and novelty give a builder a different product and a competitive edge." "But," she adds, "what is being sold is rarely architecture; it is a gimmick with a designer label."[18]

[54]   *Momentum Place*

Bank One, Texas
1717 Main Street, Dallas, Texas
John Burgee Architects with Philip Johnson

Chartered: 1917 (MBank Dallas defunct)
Constructed: 1985–87

In his seventies when he and Burgee designed RepublicBank Center, Philip Johnson, the perennial trend-spotter and -setter, both here and in their next Texas bank, Momentum Place in Dallas,[19] perfectly captured the prevailing ethos described in the *New York Times* in early 1988 following the 1987 stock market collapse as "not just any old greed, but postmodern greed, nouveau greed, state-of-the-art greed."[20] Indeed the focus of Johnson and Burgee's mind-boggling five-story open banking hall in Momentum Place, headquarters for MBank Dallas and MCorp (the holding company), is "a state-of-the-art capital markets trading floor."[21] Located below street level, the 11,000-square-foot floor is visible from a marble pedestrian bridge that extends from the main entrance across its width and from five levels of tiered balconies that jut into the barrel-vaulted atrium banking hall finished in marble and cherry wood. In the space-age trading "pit" can be seen long rows of slate laminate desks fitted out with high-tech tools: built-in micro computers, multifunction keyboards, video monitors, intercoms, and phone lines. Nearby are electronic news tickers, a 34-foot LED inventory board, and six international clocks.

MBank represents the first time in the United States that a bank trading floor has served as the focal point in a building design, the purpose being to advertise the latest center of attraction in commercial banking: capital markets functions, including trading and funding, securities sales, and investment banking. As James B. Gardner, chairman and chief executive officer of MBank Dallas and MCorp group chairman, has remarked: "Through sight and sound, some of the mystery of banking is put on display. The activity and vitality of the new trading floor will invigorate the bank and create excitement for both retail and commercial customers who know they are doing business with a bank that is on the leading edge of industry." [22]

Yet while the new furniture was still being uncrated in the fall of 1987 MCorp—one of the five biggest bank holding companies in Texas in 1984, when the headquarters was being designed—was in trouble. The oil industry's difficulties, South American debt losses, the collapse of the stock market, and overcompetition in the capital markets combined to make Momentum Place as the architectural symbol of a particular banking institution instantly obsolete. RepublicBank's position at the time was similarly dismal.[23]

[55] *Norwest Center*

Sixth Street and Marquette Avenue, Minneapolis, Minnesota
Cesar Pelli & Associates

Chartered: 1883
Constructed: 1986–88

While mega-scale seems a nearly unavoidable response to today's economic and technical realities, less overweening attitudes on the part of clients and architects can produce high-rise buildings of more judicious character than those on display in Texas. Cesar Pelli's new fifty-seven-story home for Norwest Corporation in Minneapolis represents a serious attempt to revive an old-fashioned concept: architectural civility. Pelli, former dean of the Yale School of Architecture, has expressed his current position in this way: "We should not judge a building by how beautiful it is in isolation, but instead by how much better or worse that particular place—a city, a campus, a neighborhood or landscape—has become by its addition." [24] Norwest Corporation, a holding company originally built around the Northwestern National Bank of Minneapolis and a pioneer in group banking, concurred.

In fact, the building is the second designed by Pelli for Norwest Center; the first was a sixty-six-story tower that was to have been jointly erected by Norwest Corporation and Oxford Properties. Intended to fill an entire block, the scheme was abandoned early in 1985 mainly because of a perceived decline in demand for downtown office space. Later that same year Norwest chose another developer, Gerald T. Hines, to work with them in developing the eastern portion of the site, which had been occupied by the fire-damaged Northwestern National Bank building. Pelli was again engaged as architect and elected to design an entirely new building for this altered set of circumstances.

Before embarking on the design process, Pelli took long walks through Minneapolis looking for "the essence of what the city is." [25] The architect and his team took note of beloved buildings, architectural and atmospheric coloration, and the city's special personality. What was absorbed in this way were, in Pelli's words, "impressions of some qualities that one is in sympathy with. These, one tries to strengthen. Occasionally, there are qualities that one wishes to make better than they are." [26] Foremost among the latter would be the enhancement of the city's skyline.

Like those of other major urban centers, the skyline of Minneapolis changed dramatically during the seventies and eighties with the addition of a number of high-rise buldings. The most distinguished is Johnson and Burgee's breathtakingly beautiful IDS tower, an abstract form sheathed in dark reflective glass that relates stylistically to their slightly later Pennzoil Place in Houston. More than 50 per cent higher than the next tallest building (the Foshay Tower of 1929) when it was completed in 1973, the IDS Center initiated a new level of height in Minneapolis. By the early eighties other tall buildings had, as Pelli puts it, "popped up here and there. But for some reason, they popped up a bit farther apart than . . . in most cities, so they are not seen as a grouping of buildings, but rather as vertical elements with spaces in between." [27] From two critical perspectives—the east and the west—a gap was apparent between IDS Center and the nearby City Center by Skidmore, Owings & Merrill. Plugging that space with an appropriately designed building would, Pelli felt, give the heart of the city "more focus and a sense of concentration." [28]

In creating their highly visible plug, Pelli and his design team built a city model and six basic building forms out of wood. These forms with their varying silhouettes met the given requirements but represented six different responses. Drawings exploring alternatives in greater detail also figured in the process. As a part of determining the most appropriate shape, the top or crown was very important. Lloyd P. Johnson, chairman, president, and chief executive officer of Norwest Corporation, recalls a series of "hats" that Pelli could whip on and off a drawing of the proposed structure.[29] As the design process neared completion, the opportunity arose to stretch the 772-1/2-foot tower by a couple of feet so that it would rise above IDS to become the tallest building in Minneapolis. Pelli and the building committee felt this was not in keeping with the real spirit of the city. "Minneapolitans," Pelli had observed, "are very proud of their city, but it's a pride that is never boastful or extravagant." Topping IDS would have been, in his words, "gauche." [30]

The shape of the completed Norwest Center is in total contrast to the Minimalist formalism of the IDS tower. Pelli's arresting yet courteous newcomer is stepped in a way that recalls the glamorous, urbane skyscrapers of the twenties and thirties. The narrowing setback configuration is most reminiscent of the RCA Building in Rockefeller Center, that renowned example of corporate urbanism in the thirties, but it also alludes to a venerable Minneapolis skyscraper, the Dain (formerly Rand) Tower of 1929 by Holabird & Root. Clearly this is not simply another example of what one writer so aptly terms "caricature historicism," as practiced at RepublicBank, Houston [53]. Cynicism and gratuitousness play no part in Pelli's conception. As his stylistic allusions suggest, this architect loves and respects the skyscraper as a building type of the modern era: its amazing technics, its urban character, its authentic historic tradition. While Postmodernism can lead to staggering architectural license, it can provide a disciplined architect with the freedom he needs to tackle the real challenges of the latest generation of skyscrapers.

Like Johnson and Burgee in Texas, Pelli employs some traditional materials on his exterior, but the primary facing, rosy-beige Kasota stone, is quarried in Minnesota and harmonizes with the tonality of the city's older stone and brick buildings. Smaller amounts of white marble were used to bring out the rosiness and to visually heighten the building's vertical thrust. These traditional finishes are not used as structure-concealing veneer but read as thin applied strips. Glass, a favorite material of Pelli's, is an equal — even dominant — partner, the blue color chosen to complement that of IDS Center and other modern neighbors. The resultant skin is light and vitreous as befits a modern engineering marvel.

The treatment of the lower three floors, constituting the base, was equally carefully planned to counteract an incipient loss of urban liveliness at street level. No boring blank walls front the sidewalks; instead, windows were placed all around for the enjoyment of pedestrians. Since the building replaces the half-century-old bank that served as Norwest headquarters until a disastrous fire in 1982, it was important to continue to express the banking functions that would take place within the new building. This was done by creating a soaring rotunda on Sixth Street, a space flooded with natural light, intended as a "people place" connecting with the Minneapolis skyway system (enclosed pedestrian bridges which link downtown buildings) and as a dignified lobby for the banking areas. Here — serving as elements of continuity with the past — are 10-foot-tall chandeliers, bronze railings, and plaster medallions salvaged from the old bank building after the fire.

While the references in RepublicBank may suggest the history of banking to the architectural intelligentsia, Pelli's accessible imagery celebrates the modern architectural tradition and is true to his tall building type. Moreover, he looks to the appealing, universally known skyscrapers of the twenties and thirties, not only for their cultural resonance, but for their lessons in urbanity, which is perhaps the overriding architectural challenge of our time. The fact that in this major recent bank commission feasibility, accommodation, and civic sensibility won out over raw competitiveness and unrestrained opulence suggests a more hopeful prospect for the future.

·10·

CONCLUSION

The United States

Commercial banking on this continent is just over two hundred years old, instituted to further the Revolution and soon used to facilitate American enterprise. Although banks themselves are businesses, when they began constructing their own buildings—usually as soon as means were available—they did not resemble the utilitarian structures occupied by other businesses.

There were certain physical requirements that needed to be met in the earliest bank buildings: they had to be resistant to fire and theft to protect the funds and other valuables deposited within. Consequently they were constructed of permanent materials—brick or stone—a fortunate occurrence, since some of them not only survive but continue to serve their original purpose, notably the Bank of South Carolina [1] and the Nantucket Pacific Bank [2].

The interior planning of these first banks called for a number of rooms of varying size. The plans for two of Latrobe's banks show an entrance vestibule, a banking room, a vault, a room for the directors to meet, offices, and in one a room for the stockholders.[1] In some early banks the second floor served as an apartment for the manager. All these space requirements could have been met in a straightforward manner, but the earliest banks were extraordinary buildings, often designed by the greatest of America's rare professional architects, such as Latrobe, Bulfinch, and Strickland. These banks resembled the grandest houses and public buildings in the new nation, in part because they were chartered by the state or federal government, which gave them a status beyond that of other businesses. Latrobe's Bank of Pennsylvania [4] was, for example, the state bank, and the nearby first and second Banks of the United States [3,5] were the banks of the federal government.

But there was more to it than that, for the mansionlike Bank of South Carolina and the Nantucket Pacific Bank were ordinary commercial banks, albeit chartered by their respective states. Robert Morris, America's earliest banker, financier of the Revolution, and founder of the first commercial bank (the Bank of North America) admits how precarious American banking was initially. The revolutionary government was broke when he started his bank. Not having Europe's long accumulation of accessible capital to finance either war or enterprise, Americans "had to invent, improvise, covenant, and pretend. If they were to form a bank at all, they had to do it by 'clubbing together' their scanty funds and gain all the adventitious credit they could from public association and corporate charter." [2] These words of Morris's reveal the other essential aspect of banking—psychology. To succeed, the pioneer banks had to convince people that they were solvent, stable institutions when in fact they were the very opposite. To do this bankers did what people have always done when they wanted to display either real or pretended wealth, they built themselves a fine house, modified very slightly for banking purposes but inspired by the finest American houses they knew.

Latrobe was the first architect to see how a European structural technique little known in America could meet both the physical and the psychological requisites of banking. This technique—masonry vaulting —was not only immensely strong and fireproof but it could also produce the awe-inspiring domed interior spaces found in sacred buildings and palaces in the Old World and, exceptionally, in Soane's work at the Bank of England. In the United States in 1800 there was no building that could match Latrobe's Bank of Pennsylvania [4] in architectural sophistication or beauty. His masterpiece has long been recognized as the first structure in America in which masonry vaulting was used to achieve architectural effect and which featured a Greek order, but what has been missed is that it was also the first fully developed example of specialized bank architecture—as original as the New World enterprise that inspired it.

At this point national sentiment diverted bank architecture from the path pioneered by Latrobe. With the winning by his pupil Strickland of the competition for the second Bank of the United States [5], the most important bank of the time, the fashion for Greek temples was launched. As James Fenimore Cooper's character reminds us, however, two decades later even breweries were housed in temples. Yet the appeal of this classical form for banks, referred to as "temples of mammon" at least as early as 1857, has endured for over a century and a half, in spite of all the changes that have occurred in banking and in bank architecture. It is still the temple on Main Street that constitutes the popular image of what a bank looks like, so much so that when a Wisconsin bank was temporarily obliged to locate a branch in a mobile home in 1969, they commissioned a local sign company to devise a painted temple-front to place before the trailer. [3]

The early banks were profitable businesses and soon had rivals, creating the need for distinctive structures to compete for customers or to attract a particular clientele. Here, too, Latrobe was a precursor. His Neoclassical Bank of Pennsylvania [4] was in direct competition with the older Federal-style Bank of the United States [5]. Latrobe's next bank, the Philadelphia

Bank, was established for a different group of customers and was therefore given a novel neo-Gothic treatment.

Despite the longevity of the Greek Revival in the United States, the nineteenth century was characterized by rapidly changing fashions in architecture, providing banks with the means to distinguish themselves radically from their competitors or to outdo rivals by updating or replacing an old building. The Moorish Revival Farmers' and Exchange Bank [11] and the Dutch Revival Princeton Bank [20] demonstrate the visual effectiveness of this ploy: the former, the home of an ambitious new institution; the latter, an eye-catching new building for a long-established local bank. The Postmodernists, most notably Johnson and Burgee at RepublicBank Houston [53], have revived this attention-getting eclectic approach on a scale hitherto unimagined.

From the beginning fine materials such as marble were used for display purposes. Eighteenth- and early-nineteenth-century architecture was restrained by late-Georgian taste and Republican virtue, but Victorians enjoyed elaboration. Such delectable banks as the Dollar Savings Bank [15], the Institution for Savings in Newburyport [16], and the Bowery Savings Bank [26] are among the happy survivors of the mid- and late-nineteenth-century's love of extravagance, all three intended to entice the multitudinous savers needed to enable a savings bank to thrive. Moreover, by the 1850s it was possible to create opulent façades from economical cast iron. The Bank of Columbus [13] is a relatively subdued and elegant example of the use of cast iron.

During the last quarter of the nineteenth century, with the advent of the elevator and advances in metal framing, height became another means by which banks could advertise themselves and surpass competitors. Moreover, additional stories meant surplus office space which could be rented out. The Syracuse Savings Bank [18] and the Society for Savings [19] are good examples of early tall buildings. These two have remarkable styles which also made them distinctive, but by the early 1920s the ubiquitous classicizing structures which many big metropolitan banks occupied were indistinguishable from other tall office buildings. Thus, to identify the Illinois Merchants Trust [37] as a bank, the architects attached a commanding Grecian portico to the principal façade.

The first break with tradition was already evident in a number of small-town banks designed by the Prairie School architects and constructed as early as the first decade of the new century. Loathing temple banks as outdated and un-American, Sullivan spurned overt historical references in his National Farmers' Bank [33], using shape, axiality, and organic ornament to evoke the quasi-religious aura that temple banks had so long and so successfully supplied. Some of the Prairie School banks also display an original means of attracting customers, for they were designed as virtual community centers. One of the best examples is the Winona Savings Bank and Winona National Bank in Minnesota [34].

The most radical bank building since Latrobe's Bank of Pennsylvania [4], Howe & Lescaze's Philadelphia Saving Fund Society [42], did not appear until the twentieth century. Like Latrobe's monument, the design of PSFS incorporated the functions as well as the psychology of banking into a totally unprecedented work. An example of the early phase of the International Style, this harbinger was denied progeny by historical events — the Depression and the war. After the war, the protective regulating role assumed by the federal government, assisted by modern alarm and sprinkler systems, conjoined with the more standardized postwar International Style to produce revolutionary changes in bank design. The paradigms were Bunshaft's glass-walled Manufacturers Trust [43] and the soaring glass-and-steel Chase Manhattan tower [44]. With these seminal New York banks, the secure image of the fortress, allusions to past styles, and elaborate ornament disappeared from bank architecture altogether for a quarter of a century, as powerfully expressive tools that had traditionally served the banking industry were excised from the architectural repertoire.

Since the proliferating postwar International Style buildings looked alike, the psychological side of banking had to be covered by means other than architectural. In the case of Manufacturers Trust, a secure-looking safe prominently displayed in the window was one such measure, while the museum-quality art collection at Chase, projecting both assets and status, was another. A few banks of this period, the First National Bank of Chicago [47] and the Minneapolis Federal Reserve Bank [48], successfully evoke the venerable banking qualities of strength, security, and prodigious assets by abstract means. In the former, granite cladding, which was structurally unnecessary and added significantly to the expense, was used for expressive purposes. High-quality materials of all types, incremental advances in style, and notable architects continued to serve the image needs of banks through the eighties, although during the first half of the decade Johnson and Burgee had already opened a new phase in bank architecture by flaunting old methods in their RepublicBank Houston [53].

Location has always been important to banks—for accessibility as well as for reasons of prestige. Beginning with Philadelphia's Chestnut Street, Bankers' Rows have evolved into remarkable architectural milieus as a city's leading and aspiring banks jockeyed for position. Today many of these areas have been designated historic districts, or individual bank buildings have been listed on the National Register of Historic Sites. The first and second Banks of the United States [3, 5] and the Bank of Louisville [6] are National Historic Sites. Even today, when electronic banking has dispensed with the need for physical proximity, location continues to be important for image requirements. Renaming the location after the bank situated there is a current preoccupation—thus, Chase Manhattan Plaza in New York and First National Plaza in Chicago. In smaller cities and towns the busiest corner location on Main Street—which attracts traffic from two directions—will long have been the site of a bank, although nowadays a prominent spot in a shopping mall is often preferable as a prime branch location and is certainly desirable for automatic teller machine installations.

Canada

When Canadians erected their first banks, these structures, like their American predecessors, were exceptional buildings. British North America's initial chartered banks were founded by local elites and empowered at an early stage to establish branches in other towns and provinces. To compete provincially, interprovincially, and later nationally, branch banks had at least to match the well-housed local bank and usually included living quarters for the branch manager, who was a person of high rank in the community. A substantial colonial mansion (or clublike edifice) of brick or stone adapted for banking purposes and dressed in sober classical garb imported from Britain was so suited to Canada's small, conservative cities and towns that it was widely used by many banks throughout the century. Competition was fierce, but it took place within a more stable and regulated banking environment, largely untouched by the democratic chaos unleashed during the Jacksonian era in the United States. A well-built bank in a good location was desirable, but exotic styles and extreme individuality in design were not helpful advertising devices in Canada during the nineteenth century, as they were in the United States. Too, the hard limestones of eastern Canada and the severe climate did not permit architectural excess. Only with the construction of railroads was it feasible to import softer stones from the United States, as can be seen with Molsons Bank [22], constructed of Ohio sandstone.

The American Greek Revival temple, expressing independence, was highly inappropriate in loyal British North America and so did not supplant the semidomestic bank. The remarkable temple built for the Bank of Montreal [10] in 1846 was based on an Imperial Roman prototype suitable for a proud capital city (as Montreal was) and indicative of the position and power of this, the oldest Canadian bank. The wooden dome, however, was purely symbolic: it did not crown a vaulted banking hall, which would have been beyond local building skills. For branches elsewhere throughout the rest of the century, the Bank of Montreal continued to use the house or club mode. A brief flirtation with nonclassical styles occurred in the 1880s and 1890s, resulting in such eye-catching structures as the Bank of Montreal West End Branch [24] and the Bank of Montreal in Victoria, [25a], but classicism returned with a vengeance after 1900. In contrast to the nineteenth century, British influence was waning, and styles as well as architects were imported from the United States. Indeed Canadian bankers have been among the best customers of the prestigious American firms since McKim, Mead & White expanded the Bank of Montreal head office at the turn of the century.

Despite the growing admiration for American accomplishments, a trend that began in the late nineteenth century, early skyscraper banks did not appear in Canada until the first decade of the twentieth century — and then only sporadically — when a handful of Canadian cities began to grow dramatically as a result of the completion of the transcontinental railroad in 1885.[4] Pride in this heroic national achievement was expressed by such unabashed splendor as that displayed by the new Bank of Montreal Toronto office [23], the first truly exuberant bank in the history of Canadian bank architecture. This spirited work, which was begun in the year the railway was completed and was, appropriately, designed by a Canadian firm, is surely the closest in originality and expressiveness of design to the masterly banks of Latrobe, Sullivan, and Howe & Lescaze.

The gloriously opulent architecture of the Edwardian era followed by the sleeker classicism of the 1920s perfectly suited the self-assured, expansionary mood of Canadian banks striving to create or maintain a national presence once the Dominion was linked by rail. For reasons of prestige, many of the biggest banks followed the lead of the *grande dame* of Canadian banks, the Bank of Montreal [23,27], and erected extravagant but comparatively low major branches for their sole use, at least until the end of the 1920s. Imposing examples can still be seen in Montreal, Ottawa [41], and Winnipeg [31]. Height and locale did conjoin in Toronto to produce some splendid classical skyscrapers in the 1910s and 1920s [39], as well as the current spectacle at the crossing of King and Bay streets, where four of the Big Five Canadian banks confront one another in their post-1965 towers [46].

Throughout the history of Canadian bank architecture there has been greater uniformity in bank design than in the United States, not only because of conservative attitudes and the long-lived popularity of classicism, but also because of the branch system, which ultimately forced banks to expand nationally in order to survive. While tents or shacks may have served temporarily in gold rush territory or on the prairies, the designs of permanent branches from coast to coast were approved by head offices in Toronto or Montreal and were the work of a favored few architects. Presaged by Andrew Taylor's similar branches in Montreal [24] and Calgary, in the early twentieth century leading banks consciously sought a degree of similarity in the design of new branches as a competitive measure enabling potential customers to recognize their bank. The prefabricated wooden branches of the Canadian Bank of Commerce [35] are an extreme example of this standardization and also of the loyalty to classicism. This uniformity has more recently been extended to the skylines of cities where, from Halifax to Vancouver, the black Miesian towers of Toronto-Dominion banks are recognizable from miles away.

The Future

If, as the state-of-the-art trading floor of MBank Dallas [54] and the pervasive automatic teller machine indicate, modern technology is affecting massive changes in banking both globally and on a personal level, it would still appear that the institution and its significant architecture will be with us for some time to come. Banks' head offices — as RepublicBank Center [53], Momentum Place [54], and Norwest Center [55] all indicate in their different ways — are still intended as show pieces as much as their earliest ancestors in Philadelphia or Montreal, with the most celebrated architects called upon to design them. If wall installations, telephone-booth-size kiosks, and credit cards have made the erection of small branch banks less necessary, money continues as a circulating medium — people still like the feel of it in their pockets. Hence the 1980s has witnessed such noted (and very different) architectural firms as those of Stanley Tigerman and I. M. Pei [B.1] designing drive-ins.

Banks have traditionally been powerful, privileged corporations, housed in "palaces" from the start. David Pearce in *The Great Houses of London* defines the palace as "not just a big house . . . nor even necessarily the residence of an aristocrat [but] . . . as a house designed for ceremony, a house of parade, self-consciously formal. It is lifted above the ordinary by its scale, drama and, perhaps, beauty." [5] The constant aspect of bank architecture in both the United States and Canada, despite changing stylistic fashions and differing cultural preferences, has been the "house of parade," the building "lifted above the ordinary," whether it be a brick Federal-style bank in the old whaling port of Nantucket or a black glass-and-steel tower designed by Mies van der Rohe for modern Toronto.

While inevitable change will alter both the banking and architecture of these generally friendly neighbors in unknown ways, it is reasonable to assume that American and Canadian bankers will continue to use fine architecture to project, if not physical safety, the other qualities that play an enduring role in their institutions' existence and survival: stability, security, and sound judgment. As one candid bank president recently put it: "We're only solvent as long as people think we are." [6]

GLOSSARY OF
ARCHITECTURAL TERMS

acroterion In classical architecture, a pedestal for a sculpture or ornament (or the sculpture or ornament itself) at the peak and corners of a **pediment.**

anthemion motif Ornament based on the honeysuckle flower and leaves, common in Greek and Roman architecture.

architrave In classical architecture, the lowest of the main divisions of the **entablature,** which is the assembly of horizontal members **(architrave, frieze,** and **cornice)** carried by the columns.

archivolt The group of moldings that follow the shape of an arched opening. Also, the underside of an arch.

Art Deco The prevailing modernism in America of the late twenties and thirties. Also called Moderne and Modernistic.

ashlar Squared, hewn stone laid in horizontal courses with fine joints, as opposed to rubble or unhewn stone straight from the quarry.

atrium Originally the main or central room of an ancient Roman house, open to the sky at the center. Now used to refer to large glass-covered interior spaces in modern buildings.

attic In a classical building, a story built above the wall **cornice.** Also refers to that part of the **entablature** above the cornice used to hide the roof or to make the structure more impressive.

barrel vault The simplest form of masonry **vault,** having a continuous semicylindrical roof unbroken by cross vaults. Also called a tunnel vault.

basilica The large town halls of the Romans, typically oblong with a high central space lit by a clerestory and lower aisles all around, and with apses or exedrae for the seats of the judges. Early Christian churches evolved from this Roman building type.

battered Inclined from the vertical. A battered wall recedes as it rises.

Beaux-Arts Used to refer to the generally classical architecture of the late nineteenth and early twentieth centuries designed by architects who trained at the Ecole des Beaux-Arts in Paris or at schools or offices in the United States that were influenced by the Ecole's teaching.

belt course A horizontal band of masonry extending across the façade of a building. Also called a **stringcourse.**

blind arch An arch in which the opening is permanently closed by wall construction.

bracketed cornice A projecting ornamental molding along the top of a building carried on supporting pieces, which are often merely decorative and frequently resemble scrolls.

bull's-eye window A round or oval window. Also called an **oculus** or **oeil-de-boeuf.**

cartouche An ornamental panel or tablet in the form of a scroll or of an elaborately framed oval or circle, often bearing an inscription.

catenary The curve formed by a flexible cord or cable hung between two points of support.

cladding A synonym for a curtain wall (an exterior wall having no structural function). Also refers to a protective surfacing covering a structural material.

classical Pertaining to the architecture of ancient Greece and Rome. The architecture on which the Italian Renaissance and subsequent styles such as the Baroque and Classical Revival were based.

coffered ceiling A ceiling with deeply recessed square or octagonal ornamental panels.

Composite order A rule of composition in classical architecture developed by the Romans which combines the acanthus leaves of the **Corinthian order** with the volutes of the **Ionic** and other details also elaborated.

console An ornamental bracket in the form of an S-shaped scroll, projecting from a wall to support a cornice, a door or window head.

corbel A block or bracket projecting from the face of a wall that supports a **cornice** or beam.

Corinthian order A rule of composition in classical architecture developed by the Athenian Greeks and distinguishable by the capitals of the columns, which are bell-shaped with volutes and two rows of acanthus leaves. It was subsequently much used by the Romans, who admired its ornateness.

coved A concave interior corner or molding, especially at the transition from wall to ceiling. A coved ceiling has such a cove at the wall lines or elsewhere.

crenellation A fortified parapet with alternating solid parts and openings. Also called a battlement.

dado Ornamental panelling applied to the lower walls of a room, above the baseboard.

Doric order A rule of composition in classical architecture developed by the Dorian Greeks and distinguishable by the simple cushion capitals of the columns and a **frieze** composed of alternating triglyphs (slightly raised blocks of three vertical bands separated by V-shaped grooves) and metopes (plain or sculptured panels).

Dutch Revival An architectural style (also called Dutch Renaissance or "Pont Street Dutch" in England) influenced by the Renaissance architecture of the Low Countries that began in London in the late 1870s and appeared in North America in the1880s. In the United States it was also inspired by that country's Dutch colonial heritage.

electrolier A chandelier for electric lamps.

elevation The external faces of a building; also a drawing made in projection on a vertical plane to show any one face.

entablature In classical architecture, the assembly of horizontal members (**architrave, frieze,** and **cornice**) carried by the columns. The proportions and detailing are different for each of the classical orders. An entablature may also be used to crown a wall without columns.

fanlight A semicircular window over a door, with radiating glazing bars in the form of an open fan.

Federal The American adaptation of the delicate **Neoclassicism** associated with the Adam brothers in Great Britain. It prevailed from circa 1790 to 1830.

fenestration The design and disposition of the windows and other exterior openings of a building.

finial An ornament that terminates the point of a spire, gable, pinnacle, etc.

Flemish bond A type of brickwork in which the headers and stretchers are laid alternately in the same course.

frieze The middle division of a classical **entablature,** between the architrave and the cornice. It may be decorated or plain. Also refers to the decorated band along the upper part of an interior wall, immediately below the **cornice.**

Georgian An architectural style derived from classical, Renaissance, and Baroque forms that prevailed in Great Britain and the North American colonies during the eighteenth century.

Gothic Revival An architectural style that flourished in the nineteenth century in Europe and North America that aimed to revive the spirit and forms of Gothic architecture.

Greek Revival An architectural style, based on the use of Greek forms, that flourished, mainly in Britain and the United States, in the early nineteenth century.

Guastavino tile Thin, flat tiles set in extremely tenacious mortar used to create vaulted spaces, a fireproof Spanish structural system introduced to the United States in the 1880s by Raphael Guastavino.

hexastyle A building **portico** having six frontal columns.

High Victorian A phase of the **Gothic Revival** style that occurred in the 1850s and 1860s in England and North America and is marked by the use of colored building materials (polychromy).

hipped roof A roof which slopes upward from all four sides of a building.

Imperial Roman Refers to architecture dating from the period of the Roman

Empire (27 B.C.–A.D. 476). To this period belong such major monuments as the Colosseum, the great baths, and the Pantheon, structures which depended on arches and vaults—all products of Roman engineering skills.

impost The member, usually a projecting, bracketlike molding, on which the end of an arch rests.

in antis Said of a **portico** which is recessed into a building or of the columns in such a portico. These columns, standing between pilasters (antae) placed at the ends of the portico, range with the front wall.

interlace An ornament composed of elaborately intertwined bands or stalks, sometimes including fantastic images.

Ionic order A rule of composition in classical architecture developed by the Ionian Greeks and distinguishable by the capitals of the columns, which consist of large spiral-like scrolls or volutes.

Italianate An architectural style that was fashionable in England and the United States in the 1840s and 1850s, inspired by Italian Renaissance domestic architecture.

keep, donjon The massive inner tower or stronghold of a medieval castle.

keystone lintel A horizontal bridging over an opening ornamented with a central wedge-shaped block or **voussoir.**

lithic Pertaining to or consisting of stone.

machicolation An overhanging parapet on a castle wall or tower, with floor openings through which boiling oil, missiles, etc. could be dropped on attackers.

mansard A roof having a double slope on all four sides, the lower slope being longer and steeper.

mullion A vertical upright dividing a window or other opening into two or more lights, each of which may be further subdivided into panes.

neo-Baroque Refers to architectural styles in which Baroque motifs and forms are imitated.

Neoclassicism An architectural style that prevailed in Europe and America in the late eighteenth and early nineteenth centuries. Classically "incorrect" motifs were rejected in favor of those more archaeologically correct.

octastyle A building **portico** having eight frontal columns.

oculus An opening at the crown of a dome. Any small round or oval window.

oeil-de-boeuf A round or oval window. Also called an **oculus** or **bull's-eye.**

Palladian Refers to an architectural style derived from the buildings and publications of Italian Renaissance architect Andrea Palladio (1508–80). Introduced to England by Inigo Jones (1573–1652) in 1615 and revived as a Jones-Palladio revival early in the eighteenth century. From England the style spread to the American colonies in the 1760s.

parapet A low, solid, protective wall or railing along the edge of a roof or balcony. In an exterior wall, the part entirely above the roof.

pediment A triangular gable surmounting the façade of a building in a classical style. Also, any similar triangular crowning element used over doors, windows, and niches.

peripteral Refers to a building, such as a temple, surrounded by a single row of columns.

pilaster A shallow pier or rectangular column projecting slightly from a wall, often with a capital and base.

pilotis The free-standing columns, posts, or piles which support a building, raising it above ground level.

podium A continuous pedestal or base to a building.

portico A porch, open or partly enclosed, forming the entrance and center-piece of the façade of a building, often with detached or attached columns and a **pediment.**

Postmodernism A term used since the mid-1970s to refer to recent architecture that goes counter to orthodox modernism by means of an inclusive, eclectic approach.

Prairie School An early-twentieth-century reformist architectural movement, centered in the Midwest, which rejected historical styles and is marked by long, horizontal forms.

Queen Anne An architectural style used mainly for houses that was fashionable in England and North America in the 1870s and 1880s. Misnamed after Queen Anne, it was an eclectic style that blended Tudor Gothic, English Renaissance, and, in the United States, Colonial elements.

Richardsonian Romanesque The massive Romanesque Revival architectural style as practiced by the American architect Henry Hobson Richardson (1838–1886) and his followers.

Roman Republican Refers to architecture dating from the period of the Roman Republic (510–60 B.C.).

rusticated quoins Dressed stones at the corners of buildings having strongly recessed joints and smooth or roughly textured faces, used to create an appearance of impregnability.

scagliola Material composed of cement or plaster and marble chips or pigments to imitate marble.

Second Empire An elaborate architectural style named after the French Second Empire of Napoleon III, which was fashionable in North America in the 1860s and 1870s. Its characteristic feature is the **mansard** roof.

spandrel The triangular space between the exterior curve of an arch and the rectangular framework surrounding it; the space between adjacent arches in an arcade; also, in a multistory building, a wall panel filling the space between the top of a window in one story and the sill of the window in the story above.

stringcourse A horizontal band of masonry extending across the façade of a building. Also called a **belt course.**

surround An encircling border or decoration.

Tuscan order A rule of composition in classical architecture supposedly developed by the Etruscans. Simpler and more massive than the **Doric order,** it has a plain frieze.

tympanum The triangular or segmental space enclosed by a **pediment** or arch.

vaulting Vaulting work or vaults collectively. A vault is an arched roof or ceiling constructed of stone or brick, although it may be imitated in wood or plaster.

Victorian Gothic A term used to distinguish **Gothic Revival** architecture as it developed beginning in the late 1830s from the picturesque, unscholarly Gothic of the late Georgian period.

Vierendeel truss A truss or girder (named after a Belgian engineering professor) which has no diagonals so that it can be used in walls which require openings for windows or doors. Also called an open-frame girder.

voussoir One of a series of wedge-shaped stones or bricks that form an arch.

NOTES

1. *American Banks — Federal Period through the Greek Revival*

[1] In eighteenth-century America, the word "bank" was used in three different senses. It was used for corporate institutions, such as the Bank of England, of which there were none in North America until the Bank of North America began operating. It was also used for an issue of bills of credit by a colonial government or for an association of private persons who issued their own bills of credit. The latter two were methods of providing a circulating medium, of which there was a great scarcity in colonial times. During colonial times, many banking functions were performed by merchants who had access to British capital through their trading connections. See Bray Hammond, *Banks and Politics in America from the Revolution to the Civil War* (Princeton: Princeton University Press, 1957), p. 9.

[2] See Fritz Redlich, *Molding of American Banking: Men and Ideas* (1947 and 1951; reprint, New York: Hafner, 1968), p. 35, and Hammond, *Banks and Politics,* pp.144–45.

[3] In 1794 there were only five chartered banks in the British Isles, while there were eighteen in the United States (Hammond, *Banks and Politics,* p. 6). See also Benjamin J. Klebaner, *Commercial Banking in the United States: A History* (Hinsdale, Ill.: Dryden Press, 1974), pp. 2–7.

[4] Hammond, *Banks and Politics,* p. 146.

[5] Quoted in Hammond, ibid. p. 66.

[6] H. Rooksby Steele, "An Architectural History of the Bank of England," *Journal of the Royal Institute of British Architects* 33 (17 July 1926): 502–4. See also John Summerson, *The Architecture of the Eighteenth Century* (London: Thames and Hudson, 1986), pp.144–45.

[7] The Bank of North America endured until 1929.

[8] Harold Kirker, *The Architecture of Charles Bulfinch* (Cambridge: Harvard University Press, 1969). Bulfinch also remodelled a house for a bank.

[9] Redlich, *Molding of American Banking,* p. 37.

[10] Robert Rosen, *A Short History of Charleston* (San Francisco: LEXICOS, 1982), p. 21.

[11] The directors had first applied to the legislature for a charter in the fall of 1796, but the bill of incorporation was defeated (J. Mauldin Lesesne, *The Bank of the State of South Carolina: A General and Political History* [Columbia: University of South Carolina Press, 1970], pp. 7–8). The 1801 charter became the model for all bank charters issued by South Carolina during the antebellum period.

[12] Competition from the Bank of the United States branch would have created the need for a fine building, although the federal bank did not erect its own building until 1800. It was designed by Gabriel Manigault and subsequently became the city hall.

[13] Roger G. Kennedy, *Architecture, Men, Women and Money in America 1600–1860* (New York: Random House, 1985), p. 147.

[14] The resemblance to the Brewton House was originally stronger, for the limestone stringcourse above the second-floor windows of the bank has disappeared, slightly altering the appearance of the elevations.

[15] In his discussion of Charleston culture and building, Roger Kennedy observes that "her oligarchs looked to Europe, and to the past, for their standards of behavior and of architecture. Elsewhere, even in Savannah, Americans were beginning to move with greater self-confidence toward cultural independence" (*Architecture,* p. 157).

[16] The bank purchased Josiah Barker's house in 1804, allowing him to live there rent free for a period "not exceeding two years." The building was remodelled for banking purposes, which included the procuring of "stone & other materials for the vaults" (*1804–1979: A Remarkable Account* [Nantucket: Pacific National Bank, 1980], pp. 4–5).

[17] Clay Lancaster, *The Architecture of Historic Nantucket* (New York: McGraw-Hill, 1972), p. 96.

[18] Clay Lancaster, *Nantucket in the Nineteenth Century* (New York: Dover, 1979), p. 43.

[19] Although the brick and brownstone would have come from the American mainland, Nantucket historian Edouard Stackpole (interview by author, 2 July 1987) believes the slate came from an unidentified stockpile originally from Britain.

[20] The building originally followed an L-shaped plan, with only two bays fronting on Main Street. Subsequent additions added another three bays (stepped back slightly) to the Main Street elevation and altered the subsidiary west and north elevations. With the restoration of the semicircular portico in the twentieth century, the main façade appears much as it was, although Lancaster in *The Architecture of Nantucket,* p. 96, believes that the spaces around the windows were originally stuccoed or painted a near-white to contrast with the brickwork. The bank now owns the exquisite little Masonic Hall (1802), which abuts it on Main Street and which it has restored and uses as the trust department.

[21] Hammond, *Banks and Politics,* p. 6.

[22] Ibid., p. 121.

[23] Lois A. Craig et al., *The Federal Presence: Architecture, Politics, and National Design* (1978; reprint, Cambridge: MIT Press, 1984), pp. 4–6.

[24] Quoted by William H. Pierson, Jr., *American Buildings and Their Architects,* vol. 1: *The Colonial and Neo-Classical Styles* (Garden City: Anchor, 1976), p. 296.

[25] Talbot Hamlin, *Greek Revival Architecture in America* (1944; reprint, New York: Dover, 1964), p. 18.

[26] James O. Wettereau, "The Oldest Bank in the United States," *Transactions of the American Philosophical Society* 43, pt. 1(1953): 72.

[27] Sandra L. Tatman and Roger W. Moss, "Samuel Blodget, Jr.," *Biographical Dictionary of Philadelphia Architects: 1700–1930* (Boston: Hall, 1985).

[28] Wettereau, "The Oldest Bank," p. 72.

[29] Matthew Baigell, "James Hoban and the First Bank of the United States," *Journal of the Society of Architectural Historians* 28 (May 1969): 135, and Fiske Kimball, "The Bank of Pennsylvania, 1799," *Architectural Record* 44 (August 1918): 133.

[30] Blodget was greatly distressed that less costly brick had to be substituted for marble on the subordinate elevations.

[31] Quoted in Wettereau, "The Oldest Bank," p. 73.

[32] Kimball, "Bank of Pennsylvania," p. 135.

[33] From a letter by Latrobe to Samuel Fox, president of the bank, in Talbot Hamlin, *Benjamin Henry Latrobe* (New York: Oxford, 1955), p. 155.

[34] Quoted in Samuel Wilson, Jr., "Benjamin H. Latrobe," in *Macmillan Encyclopedia of Architects* (New York: Free Press, 1982).

[35] Wettereau, "The Oldest Bank," p. 71.

[36] Ibid.

[37] Fiske Kimball, "The Bank of the United States 1818–1824," *Architectural Record* 58 (December 1925): 581.

[38] Marcus Whiffen and Frederick Koeper, *American Architecture 1607–1976* (London: Routledge and Kegan Paul, 1981), p. 164.

[39] Hamlin, *Greek Revival Architecture*, p. 70.

[40] Agnes Addison Gilchrist, *William Strickland, Architect and Engineer: 1788–1854* (1950; enl. ed. reprint, New York: Da Capo, 1969), p. 32.

[41] Whiffen and Koeper, *American Architecture,* p. 153. Latrobe accused Strickland of plagiarism.

[42] Quoted in Gilchrist, *Strickland,* p. 32.

[43] Quoted in Bates Lowry, *Building a National Image: Architectural Drawings for the American Democracy, 1789–1912* (New York: Walker, 1985), p. 39.

[44] Quoted in Craig, *The Federal Presence*, p. 53. Cooper's novel, *Home as Found,* was published in 1838, not in 1828 as stated in Craig. The Temple, or Tower of the Winds, an octagonal tower on the western slope of the Acropolis, was also illustrated in Stuart and Revett's *Antiquities of Athens.*

[45] Bray Hammond, "The Second Bank of the United States," *Transactions of the American Philosophical Society* 43, pt. 1 (1953): 82.

[46] Ibid., p. 83.

[47] The battle has been documented by many historians as "the Bank War."

[48] Hammond, "The Second Bank," p. 84.

[49] Hammond, *Banks and Politics,* p. 169.

[50] The design was formerly erroneously attributed to Gideon Shryock.

[51] The Bank of Louisville was merged into the Southern National Bank in 1899 (John Jay Knox, *A History of Banking in the United States* [1903; reprint, New York: Augustus M. Kelley, 1969], p. 637). The building, now a National Historic Landmark, remained in use under various names until 1930, when it became vacant for several years. It was restored in 1937 by the Louisville Credit Men's Association, who added the rear portion of the existing building. In 1972 it was renovated when the Actors Theatre moved in.

[52] Arthur Scully, Jr., *James Dakin, Architect: His Career in New York and the South* (Baton Rouge: Louisiana State University Press, 1973), p. 30.

2. *Canadian Banks — Late Georgian Through the 1850s*

[1] Inspired by the feudal system and involving the dependency of tenants on a seigneur or landowner, the seigneurial system was officially abolished in 1854.

[2] The Clearances refer to the large-scale evictions of small tenant farmers carried out in the nineteenth century by landlords attempting to improve agriculture in the Scottish Highlands.

[3] J.M.S. Careless, *Canada: A Story of Challenge* (Toronto: Macmillan of Canada, 1963), p. 147.

[4] The first of these, the Canada Banking Company, may have operated briefly, but quickly disappeared.

[5] The first bank to actually operate under a charter in Canada was the Bank of New Brunswick in Saint John, which began business under a charter granted by that province in 1820.

[6] As Adam Shortt has shown, the articles of association and subsequent charter of the Bank of Montreal correspond closely to Hamilton's charter for the first Bank of the

United States, serving as the foundation of the Canadian banking system. In addition, the Montreal Bank's officers were sent to gain experience in the recently established second Bank of the United States [5]. "The Early History of Canadian Banking," *Journal of the Canadian Bankers' Association* 4 (October 1896): 1–19.

7 Hammond, *Banks and Politics,* p. 640.

8 Merrill Denison, *Canada's First Bank* (Toronto: McClelland & Stewart, 1966), 1: 5; 118.

9 John Bland, "Loyalist Architecture in Montreal," unpublished typescript, 1987, p. 17.

10 The building contract is quoted in Michelle Nolin-Raynauld, "L'Architecture de la Banque de Montréal à la Place d'Armes" (M. A. thesis, Université de Montréal, August 1983), p. 5.

11 As quoted from the building contract in Denison, *Canada's First Bank,* 1: 119.

12 Nolin-Raynauld, "La Banque de Montréal," pp. 5–6. The exterior masonry was required to resemble that of a building being built nearby on St. Paul Street for the mercantile house of Maitland, Garden & Auldjo.

13 These cast, mainly clay, panels were purchased in England in 1819. Research by Ida Darlington, former archivist and librarian of the London County Council, was published as "'FROST and DAMPS have no effect,'" in the Bank of Montreal *Staff* (April 1965), pp. 2–6, 44. Miss Darlington's article includes the entry in a Coade firm order book for these panels, which cites the craftsmen as Dubbin and Panzetti. The panels are based on stock designs attributed to British sculptor John Bacon.

14 The building contract for the Montreal Bank was signed on 23 January 1818, while the notice inviting architects to design the second Bank of the United States was published in May 1818. Thus the directors of the Montreal Bank did not "turn their backs" on the nationalistic Greek Revival in the United States, as Denison suggests in *Canada's First Bank,* 1: 119.

15 John Bland singles out such roofs as important distinguishing features of Montreal Loyalist architecture in "Loyalist Architecture in Montreal," p. 11.

16 Edward Allen Talbot, *Five Years' Residence in the Canadas: Including a Tour through Part of the United States of America, in the Year 1823* (London: Longman, et al., 1824), 1: 71.

17 For a recent study of the early banking history of Upper Canada, see Peter Baskerville, *The Bank of Upper Canada: A Collection of Documents* (Toronto: The Champlain Society with Carleton University Press, 1987).

18 It was built at the corner of George Street and Duke Street, which is now Adelaide Street East.

19 William Dendy and William Kilbourn, *Toronto Observed: Its Architecture, Patrons, and History* (Toronto: Oxford University Press, 1986), p. 25.

20 All but the bank have been demolished.

21 Of the fifteen members of the bank's first board of directors nine were either members of the Executive or Legislative Council or held important government positions. See W. S. Wallace, "The Place of the Bank in Canadian History," *Journal of the Canadian Bankers' Association* 30 (October 1922): 116.

22 Eric Arthur, *Toronto: No Mean City* (Toronto: Toronto University Press, 1974), pp. 37–38.

23 Dendy and Kilbourn, *Toronto Observed,* p. 25.

24 *The Northern Traveller, and Northern Tour, with Routes to the Springs, Niagara, & Quebec, and the Coal Mines of Pennsylvania, also Tours of New England* (New York: J. and J. Harper, 1830).

25 The oldest surviving building that housed a bank in Canada is a warehouse on Water Street in Halifax, erected by Nova Scotia's leading merchant, Enos Collins, about 1812. A part of this warehouse served as the office of the private yet powerful Halifax Banking Company from 1825 to 1903, when it was absorbed by the Canadian Bank of Commerce.

26 Incorporated as the Commercial Bank of the Midland District, the name was later changed to the Commercial Bank of Canada (Max Magill, "The Failure of the Commercial Bank," in *To Preserve and Defend: Essays on Kingston in the Nineteenth Century,* ed. Gerald Tulchinsky [Montreal: McGill-Queen's University Press, 1976], pp. 169 and 363, n. 1).

[27] Thomas quickly became one of the most important architects in British North America, eventually also opening offices in Hamilton and Halifax. He designed such major Toronto buildings as St. Michael's Cathedral and St. Lawrence Hall.

[28] Neil Einarson, "Abstracts from the 10th Annual Meeting: William Thomas," *Society for the Study of Architecture in Canada Bulletin* 9 (July 1984): 5. See also Neil Einarson, "William Thomas," in *The Canadian Encyclopedia* (Edmonton: Hurtig, 1985).

[29] In the late 1860s the façade was extended by one bay to the east, continuing Thomas's design.

[30] Besides the Commercial Bank of the Midland District, two other important bank buildings erected in the 1840s, the Gore Bank in Hamilton and the Bank of British North America in Montreal, also featured Greek Revival elements, but applied to conventional Georgian designs.

[31] See Gunter Gad and Deryck Holdsworth, "Building for City, Region, and Nation," in *Forging a Consensus: Historical Essays on Toronto,* ed. V. L. Russell (Toronto: University of Toronto Press, 1984), pp. 277–78.

[32] Nolin-Raynauld, "La Banque de Montréal," pp. 15–16.

[33] Denison, *Canada's First Bank,* 2: 20, and Nolin-Raynauld, "La Banque de Montréal," p. 24.

[34] By 20 July 1845, designs and one model had been received from nine competitors as well as various line sketches from the British Linen Company, "with Copies of the Elevation & Plans of their own Banking House." Nolin-Raynauld, "La Banque de Montréal," pp. 25–26.

[35] The pediment sculpture, by the noted Scottish sculptor John Steele, is different from the illustration: the escutcheon of the Bank of Montreal, flanked by a pair of Indians, occupies the center; the sculpture proposed in the engraving was "Britannia," the "trademark" of the Bank of England.

[36] Nolin-Raynauld, "La Banque de Montréal," p. 36. It is known that the foundations were laid the preceding autumn. The contracts between the master-carpenters and masons were signed in February and March of 1846 (pp. 47 and 50).

[37] Wells was "to make such changes as might be necessary, supply working drawings, draw up specifications, and superintend construction." Denison, *Canada's First Bank,* 2: 21.

[38] Nolin-Raynauld, "La Banque de Montréal," p. 71.

[39] Alfred Sandham, *Ville-Marie, or, Sketches of Montreal, Past and Present* (Montreal: George Bishop, 1870), p. 353. The first Bank of Montreal building [7] was sold in 1847 to La Banque du Peuple, the first bank established by French-Canadians. Initially a private enterprise, it received a charter in 1844, but failed in 1894.

3. *American Banks — Mid and Late Victorian*

[1] Martin Mayer, "The Banking Story," *American Heritage* 35 (April–May 1984): 31.

[2] According to Hammond, *Banks and Politics,* p. 600, the term was first used in 1836.

[3] Knox, *Banking in the United States,* pp. 701–702.

[4] Hammond, *Banks and Politics,* p. 195.

[5] Lee was in partnership with Edward C. Jones from 1852 to 1857, but Lee is credited with the design of the bank. See Beatrice St. Julien Ravenel, *Architects of Charleston* (Charleston: Carolina Art Association, 1945), p. 225.

[6] The 1857 article is partially quoted in W. A. Clark, *The History of Banking Institutions Organized in South Carolina Prior to 1860* (Columbia: State Company for the Historical Commission of South Carolina, 1922), pp. 169–70. Brownstone was used for the façade and continues about 4 feet around the corner on the south wall. The contractors for the building were Lopez and Trumbo.

[7] Mills Lane, *Architecture of the Old South: South Carolina* (Savannah: Beehive Press, 1984), p. 234. The interior has been altered by the insertion of a second floor.

[8] Clark, *History of Banking Institutions,* p. 169.

[9] Quoted in Winston Weisman, "Commercial Palaces of New York: 1845–1875," *Art Bulletin* 36 (December 1954): 287.

[10] Quoted in ibid., p. 286.

[11] The design of Stewart's Store is attributed to Ottavian Gori, an Italian marble cutter.

[12] Constance M. Greiff, *John Notman, Architect* (Philadelphia: The Athenaeum of Philadelphia, 1979), pp. 127–28.

[13] Weisman, "Commercial Palaces," p. 290.

[14] Belden L. Daniels, *Pennsylvania — Birthplace of Banking in America* (Harrisburg: Pennsylvania Bankers Association, 1976), pp. 91–92.

[15] Turpin C. Bannister, "Bogardus Revisited — Part I: The Iron Fronts," *Journal of the Society of Architectural Historians* 15 (December 1956): 12.

[16] Cast-iron façades were seen in New York at the end of the 1840s, but actually the first in North America appeared on a bank erected in 1828 in the Pennsylvania frontier coal-mining village of Pottsville. Designed by the noted Philadelphia architect John Haviland, the walls and vaults of the Miners' Bank were of brick, but the front was faced with cast-iron plates which were painted and sanded to resemble the stone which had originally been intended. Ibid., p. 15.

[17] *Biographical Souvenir of the States of Georgia and Florida, Containing Biographical Sketches of the Representative Public, and Many Early Settled Families in these States* (Chicago: F. A. Battey, 1889), and John S. Lupold, "William H. Young," in *Dictionary of Georgia Biography* (Athens: University of Georgia Press, 1983).

[18] Nancy Telfair [Louise Gunby DuBose], *A History of Columbus, Georgia, 1828–1928* (Columbus: Historical Publishing Company, 1929), p. 124, and F. Clason Kyle, *Images; a Pictorial History of Columbus, Georgia* (Columbus: Historic Columbus Foundation, 1986), p. 39.

[19] Young was responsible for the only other cast-iron-fronted edifice erected in Columbus before the war: the Gunby Building, located on Eleventh Street, subsequently known as the Reich Building. Telfair, *History of Columbus*, pp. 198–9.

[20] Young made the shipping arrangements and gave detailed instructions on how his order was to be sent by water to Columbus. Louise D. Byrd, "Family Lore Sheds Light on Bank's Origins." Letter to the editor, *Columbus Ledger*, 5 March 1985, and Louise Byrd, telephone interview by author, 6 October 1987.

[21] "National Register of Historic Places Inventory — Nomination Form: The Bank of Columbus [Georgia]," prepared by Elizabeth Z. Macgregor and Carole Stevens (19 June 1974). An important tenant, however, also occupied the building during the war years and managed to survive: the Georgia Home Insurance Company, a pioneer fire-insurance company founded in 1859, of which the enterprising Young was an organizer. This business occupied space to the rear of the banking quarters, acquiring the entire building by auction in 1869. The insurance company then apparently remodelled the interior and completed the upper floors. "Georgia Home Insurance Co. One of South's Oldest," *Industrial Index*, Columbus Centennial Number published in Columbus 22 (18 April 1928): 117.

[22] John Lupold, telephone interview by author, 6 October 1987.

[23] In 1986 First Alabama Bank opened a commercial loan office in the building. Although not a full-fledged bank, it represents an initial step in anticipation of interstate banking.

[24] Charles Brilvitch, *Walking Through History: The Seaports of Black Rock and Southport* (Fairfield: Fairfield Historical Society, 1977), pp. 35–36. I am grateful to William M. and Mary Martha Sherts for alerting me to this publication.

[25] "Historic American Buildings Survey, Southport Savings Bank," prepared by Jan E. Cigliano, January 1979. HABS No: CONN-315, p. 2.

[26] One of the earliest brick structures in Southport, it was originally built as a branch of the Connecticut Bank of Bridgeport. In 1851 the Southport Bank was independently chartered and occupied the building from 1852 until 1903, becoming the Southport National Bank in 1865. Before the Southport Savings Bank constructed its own building, it was also housed here. "Historic American Buildings Survey, Connecticut Bank, Mill River Branch," prepared by Jan E. Cigliano, December 1978. HABS No: CONN-319, p. 1, and *Southport Savings Bank, Southport, Connecticut, 100th Anniversary, 1854–1954* (Southport: Southport Savings Bank, 1954), unpaginated.

[27] Original building specifications for the masons' and carpenters' work for the Southport Savings Bank, dated 13 September 1864, as copied in HABS, Southport, pp. 7, 3.

[28] I am grateful to the Danbury Scott-Fanton Museum and Historical Society for providing me with photocopies of illustrations and other material in their collection relating to Austin's Danbury Bank, now unrecognizable following alterations.

[29] HABS, Southport, p. 3.

[30] Ibid., pp. 13–14.

[31] This was the Miners' Bank in Pottsville, Pennsylvania. See n. 17 above.

[32] Brilvitch, *Walking Through History,* pp. 39–40.

[33] The Act was amended in 1864 and renamed the National-Bank Act in 1874.

[34] Quoted in Klebener, *Commercial Banking in the United States,* p. 54.

[35] Quoted in ibid., p. 63.

[36] Daniels, *Pennsylvania — Birthplace of Banking in America,* pp. 177–78.

[37] Fritz Redlich in *Molding of American Banking,* p. 221, notes that quoting from Benjamin Franklin and his *Poor Richard's Almanack* was common in the advertising material for the early savings banks.

[38] Daniels, *Pennsylvania — Birthplace of Banking in America,* p. 180.

[39] The city's first commercial bank was a branch office of the Bank of Pennsylvania, which opened in 1803. The first savings bank was the Pittsburgh Savings Fund Company, which was incorporated in 1834, later becoming the Farmers Deposit Bank.

[40] Tatman and Moss, "Isaac Harding Hobbs," *Philadelphia Architects.*

[41] William T. Schoyer, *A Century of Saving Dollars: 1855–1955* (Pittsburgh: [The Dollar Savings Bank], 1955), p. 40.

[42] Quoted in ibid., p. 46.

[43] The first study of Sargent and his work is Betsy H. Woodman, *Newburyport's Rufus Sargent (1812–1886): An Architect Rediscovered* (n.p.: 1987). I am grateful to Mrs. Woodman for sharing with me her knowledge of Sargent.

[44] Quoted in ibid., p. 334.

[45] The Bank of New York bank was executed between 1856 and 1858 by Vaux and Withers; the addition in 1879–1880 was by Vaux and Radford.

[46] For his City Hall in Peabody of 1882–83, Sargent used the Second Empire style more overtly, although he produced a far less elegant building.

[47] The 1903 expansion and remodelling was carried out by Boston architect Edwin Dodge. The handsome present interior dates from this remodelling.

[48] Samuel Bowles, *Across the Continent: A Summer's Journey to the Rocky Mountains, the Mormons, and the Pacific States, with Speaker Colfax* (Springfield, Mass: Samuel Bowles & Co. and New York: Hurd & Houghton, 1866), pp. 294–95. The original name Wells, Fargo & Co. was gradually modified to Wells Fargo & Company.

[49] Harold Kirker, *California's Architectural Frontier* (Layton, Utah: Gibbs M. Smith, 1986), p. 33.

[50] B. Stout of Sonora was engaged to erect the building. Constructed later in the year were a flanking one-story brick warehouse and two frame rooms at the back to serve as a dining room and kitchen. In 1861 Daegener built a smelting room, or assay office, in the rear.

[51] Otheto Weston in *Historic Buildings of Columbia: "Gem of the Southern Mines"* (Columbia, CA: n.p., 1966) notes that this unassuming, one-story structure was nevertheless considered one of the most beautiful banks on the gold trail with its steps of Columbia white marble and counters of imported Honduras mahogany inlaid with black walnut.

[52] Barbara Eastman, "Wells Fargo Express Company at Columbia," *The Quarterly of the Tuolumne County Historical Society* 4 (January–March 1965): 118–21. Eastman records that Daegener was advertising himself as a banker and assayer in 1867 and that the 1880 census describes his successor, Henry Sevening, as banker rather than Wells Fargo agent.

[53] Orvel B. Johnson, "Columbia Historic State Park, Columbia, California: Restoration of Wells Fargo and Company's Express Office 1952–1953" (Distributed by California State Division of Beaches and Parks, January 1955), p. 1.

[54] These scales had arrived at about the same time as the safe.

[55] Weisman, "Commercial Palaces," p. 298.

[56] For a discussion of the distinction between Ruskinian and High Victorian Gothic, see Eve Blau, *Ruskinian Gothic: The Architecture of Deane and Woodward, 1845–1861* (Princeton: Princeton University Press, 1982).

[57] Few of these buildings have escaped destruction or mutilation. This is especially tragic in the case of those designed by Furness, one of the most powerfully individualistic American architects of all time.

[58] "Syracuse Savings Bank . . . . architecture worth saving" (n.p.).

[59] Quoted in Montgomery Schuyler, "A Great American Architect: Leopold Eidlitz," in *American Architecture and Other Writings by Montgomery Schuyler,* eds. William H. Jordy and Ralph Coe (Cambridge: Harvard University Press, Belknap Press, 1961), 1: 172.

[60] Ibid., 1: 168, and Robert A. M. Stern, Gregory Gilmartin, and John Massengale, *New York 1900: Metropolitan Architecture and Urbanism 1890–1915* (New York: Rizzoli, 1983), p. 177.

[61] The interior of the bank has been renovated several times. In 1928–29 the entire front portion of the second floor was removed to create a double-storied banking hall.

[62] The walls are constructed of buff Ohio sandstone with accents of red New Jersey sandstone. The builder was John Moore, who also built the Colorado State Capitol.

[63] Born in rural Georgia, Root was a graduate in civil engineering from New York University. The Chicago poet Harriet Monroe, who was Root's sister-in-law and biographer, observed: "The mathematics of his profession interested him as deeply as its art." *John Wellborn Root: A Study of His Life and Work* (1896; reprint, Park Forest, Ill.: Prairie School Press, 1966), p. 114.

[64] Until the Civil War, houses and public buildings in Cleveland had been strongly influenced by the New England origins of the early settlers. After railroads replaced canals just before the war, the city developed strong trade ties with Chicago, which began exporting her rapidly evolving commercial architecture as early as the mid-eighties. Donald Hoffmann in *The Architecture of John Wellborn Root* (Baltimore: Johns Hopkins University Press, 1973), p. 97, notes: "In the few years between 1886 and 1894, the Chicago idea was carried to Kansas City, Cleveland, San Francisco, Tacoma, St. Louis, Atlanta, Salt Lake City, and Buffalo."

[65] "Society for Savings Building. Cleveland, Ohio" (1891), unpaginated.

[66] Hoffman, *The Architecture of Root,* p. 121.

[67] "Society for Savings Building," unpaginated. A four-story addition was added at the rear in 1949.

[68] Monroe, *Root,* p. 123.

[69] "Society for Savings Building," unpaginated.

[70] Monroe, *Root,* p. 82.

[71] The panels were restored at the time of the bank's centennial in 1949 by Louis P. Szanto and Andrew B. Karoly, who also painted two new murals in the same style and size as the originals for the new east end of the banking room. The banking floor was a showpiece for the decorative arts — stained glass, ironwork, wall painting, and wood carving. Some of this was lost as a result of renovations over the years, and the colors differ somewhat from the original scheme, but the late-Victorian flavor remains. In 1988 a downtown redevelopment project, Society Center, was announced, entailing a flanking fifty-five-story office tower designed by Cesar Pelli and restoration of the old banking floor.

[72] The Princeton Bank became the Princeton Bank and Trust Company in 1916. Now controlled by Horizon Bancorp, the institution was renamed the Princeton Bank in 1982.

[73] The letting of the contract was reported in the *Princeton Press* on 16 May 1896. According to the *Press,* the building was to measure 34 by 52 feet, with a basement containing two offices, a first floor for the banking room and vault, and a second and third floor containing apartments. I am indebted to Constance M. Greiff for this information. See also Constance M. Greiff, Mary W. Gibbons, and Elizabeth G. C. Menzies, *Princeton Architecture: A Pictorial History of Town and Campus* (Princeton: Princeton University Press, 1967).

[74] Upper Pyne was demolished in 1964.

75 Montgomery Schuyler, "Architecture of American Colleges," *Architectural Record* 27 (February 1910): 160.

76 Montgomery Schuyler wrote approvingly of this building in "A Picturesque Skyscraper," *Architectural Record* 5 (January–March 1896): 299–302. Also, Stern et al., *New York 1900,* p. 457, n. 83, states that a plate of the "Wolfe Building, Maiden Lane, Corner of William Street, New York, H. J. Hardenbergh, Architect," was published in *Architecture and Building* 23 (July 13, 1895): plate.

77 Stern et al., *New York 1900,* p. 365.

78 Stern et al. discuss the "old family" connotations of the Dutch Revival style in New York's West End in ibid., p. 365.

4. *Canadian Banks — Mid and Late Victorian*

1 By 1867 there were thirty-five chartered banks in Canada, three times the number operating in the 1840s. Among them they had a total of 127 branches. By 1900 there were still thirty-five chartered banks, but 708 branches. See Michael Bliss, *Northern Enterprise: Five Centuries of Canadian Business* (Toronto: McClelland and Stewart, 1987), pp. 258, 267.

2 The Corinthian portico of the Bank of Montreal [10] was echoed in a new head-office building constructed for the Bank of New Brunswick in 1878–79 in Saint John, although whether deliberately or not is unknown.

3 This structure, built in 1833, was probably designed by the English-born architect Thomas Rogers. See J. Douglas Stewart, "Thomas Rogers," in *Dictionary of Canadian Biography* . I am grateful to Professor Stewart for alerting me to the earlier bank, which still exists at 44 Princess Street in an altered state. When the Commercial Bank failed in 1867, the building on King Street was sold to the Merchants Bank of Canada and in 1899 became the property of Regiopolis College. Three subsequent owners occupied the building between 1914 and 1936, when it was purchased by the present owner, the Empire Life Insurance Company, for their head office.

4 Margaret S. Angus, "City Hall and the Community," in *Kingston City Hall* (Kingston: Corporation of the City of Kingston, 1973), p. 12.

5 Frederick H. Armstrong, "William Hay," in *Dictionary of Canadian Biography.*

6 A one-story extension fronting on King Street was added in 1931.

7 J. Douglas Stewart, "Architecture for a Boom Town: The Primitive and the Neo-Baroque in George Browne's Kingston Buildings," in *To Preserve and Defend: Essays on Kingston in the Nineteenth Century,* ed., Gerald Tulchinsky (Montreal: McGill-Queen's University Press, 1976), p. 37.

8 A. B. Jamieson, *Chartered Banking in Canada* (Toronto: Ryerson Press, 1953), p. 9. Thus, as Hammond observes, "the established pattern was not abandoned; nor from that time has any important banking innovation of the Americans been taken over by the Canadians." (*Banks and Politics,* p. 662). Savings banks also were not a success in Canada. See E. P. Neufeld, *The Financial System of Canada: Its Growth and Development* (Toronto: Macmillan of Canada, 1972), pp. 41–42.

9 Shirley E. Woods, Jr., *The Molson Saga: 1763–1983* (Toronto: Doubleday Canada, 1983), pp. 149–150.

10 About $100 million was invested in the construction of 1600 miles of railway in British North America during the 1850s (Bliss, *Northern Enterprise,* p. 190).

11 Molsons Bank ultimately established 125 branches across Canada before being taken over, in 1925, by the Bank of Montreal.

12 Although the capital was moved to Toronto in 1850, the popular government architect Browne had settled permanently in Montreal in 1854, practicing with his son John James. The Molsons building was carried out under the supervision of "George and John Jas. Browne, Esqs., Architects."

13 *The Stranger's Illustrated Guide to the City of Montreal* (Montreal: D. Ross, 1865), p. 23.

14 Woods, *The Molson Saga,* pp. 174–75.

15 An addition was earlier made to the rear of the bank by Taylor & Gordon in 1900.

[16] Bliss, *Northern Enterprise,* p. 216. Before the transcontinental railroad was in place, communication among the far-flung provinces and territories was more difficult than with the more accessible United States and even Britain. One newcomer arriving in the pre-railroad era described conditions vividly: "Canada was then in many respects a *terra incognita,* consisting of half-a-dozen provinces, knowing about as much of each other as they did of the South Sea Islands, . . . " *The Centenary of the Bank of Montreal:1817–1917* (Montreal: The Bank of Montreal, 1917), p. 38.

[17] Denison, *Canada's First Bank,* 2: 228.

[18] The British North America Act of 1867 gave the Parliament of Canada exclusive legislative authority in all matters pertaining to currency and coinage, banking, incorporation of banks, and the issue of paper money. During the first session of the first Parliament, an Act was passed authorizing all banks incorporated by any of the Provinces included in the Dominion to open branches and do business throughout the Dominion.

[19] Denison, *Canada's First Bank,* 2: 181.

[20] This building, designed by Kivas Tully and built in 1845, had been constructed after the Bank of Montreal was allowed to reestablish branches in what is now Ontario after the union of Upper and Lower Canada.

[21] Dendy and Kilbourn, *Toronto Observed,* p. 114. The significance of this bank was first analyzed by Howard Shubert in "The Development of the Banking Hall in Canada" (M. Ph. Thesis, Department of History of Art, University of Toronto, 1983), pp. 33–41. Shubert notes on p. 33 that the Union Bank in Halifax (1863) had the highest banking room — 22 feet — until the Bank of Montreal was constructed.

[22] Quoted in Dendy and Kilbourn, *Toronto Observed,* p. 114. This description dates from 1886.

[23] Preliminary research indicates that Taylor's firm was responsible for at least ten branch banks for the Bank of Montreal, excluding alterations and additions to existing buildings and buildings and additions for other bank clients. He was not the first such bank architect in Canada, however. James H. Springle, one of the winners in the Bank of Montreal competition of 1845, was subsequently responsible for plans for Bank of Montreal branches in Belleville, Brockville, and Cobourg, Ontario. See Nolin-Raynauld, "La Banque de Montréal," p. 27.

[24] E. J. Lennox's Richardsonian Romanesque Toronto City Hall was not begun until 1889 and not completed until 1899.

[25] Beaumont (1853–1910), who arrived in Canada from London in 1888, subsequently built up an extremely successful practice in Montreal.

[26] The Montreal bank also housed until 1899, in addition to the messenger, the Canadian Society of Civil Engineers, which had been established in 1887. The building currently serves as a branch of the Guardian Trust.

[27] The building no longer stands.

[28] Both have been torn down.

[29] The architect was W. H. Williams of Portland, Oregon.

[30] "British Columbia Letter. No. I," *Canadian Architect and Builder* 12 (March 1899): 50.

[31] These included the house (now demolished) of the General Manager of the Bank, E. S. Clouston.

[32] Quoted in Harold D. Kalman, *The Railway Hotels and the Development of the Château Style in Canada* (Victoria: University of Victoria Maltwood Museum, 1968), p. 6.

[33] Ibid., pp. 30–31.

[34] Ibid., p. 19.

[35] The Bank of British Columbia, for example, could not long withstand competition from the eastern banks. It was taken over by the Toronto-based Canadian Bank of Commerce in 1900.

[36] Quoted in Carl Berger, *The Writing of Canadian History* (Toronto: Oxford University Press, 1976), p. 67.

5. *American and Canadian Banks — Beaux-Arts Classicism*

[1] Leland M. Roth, "McKim, Mead, and White," in *Macmillan Encyclopedia of Architects.*

[2] Among those who designed notable bank buildings were John Carrère, Thomas Hastings, Edward York, Philip Sawyer, Walter Bliss, William Faville, and Ernest Barott. The influence of McKim, Mead & White and their followers also extended to England. Charles H. Reilly, head of the School of Architecture at the University of Liverpool, who published a monograph on the firm in 1924, wrote in 1935 that the great classical banking hall was a feature that British banks had adopted from America after the First World War. Charles H. Reilly, "Banks," *Architectural Record* 78 (September 1935): 104. See also Reilly, "Some Impressions of Canadian Towns," *Journal, Royal Architectural Institute of Canada* 6 (July-September 1924): 89, for differences between Canadian and London banks.

[3] "Province of Quebec Association of Architects: Proceedings of the Annual Convention," *Canadian Architect and Builder* 6 (October 1893): 104.

[4] The 1893 panic stemmed from uncertainty over the federal government's willingness and ability to maintain the gold standard.

[5] Stern et al., *New York 1900,* p. 178.

[6] "Business transactions in 1892 went beyond that of any other year in the history of the country. All records were broken in trade." (Oscar Schisgall, *The Bowery Savings Bank of New York: A Social and Financial History* [New York: American Management Associations, 1984], pp. 71–72).

[7] The Butchers and Drovers Bank was a long-established commercial institution that had generously provided rent-free space for the Bowery Savings Bank when it first opened.

[8] Fanny Gong, Associate Principal, Swanke Hayden Connell Architects, who, together with John Peter Barie, oversaw the restoration, suggests that sophisticated modern lighting has somewhat intensified the drama and richness of the interior. (Interview by author, 1 October 1987).

[9] The area now holds the officers' platform as well as the original wooden check-writing desks.

[10] Schisgall, *The Bowery Savings Bank,* p. 67.

[11] Ibid., p. 77.

[12] This bank was designed by York & Sawyer. Like the earlier bank, it has been designated a City of New York Landmark.

[13] Andrew Taylor, letter to the editor, *Journal of the Royal Institute of British Architects* 34 (20 November 1926): 64.

[14] *A Monograph of the Works of McKim, Mead & White, 1879–1915* (1915–1920; reprint, New York: Benjamin Blom, 1973), p. 68, and Leland M. Roth, *McKim, Mead & White, Architects* (1983; reprint, New York: Harper & Row, 1985), pp. 298–301.

[15] Andrew Taylor stated in letter to *JRIBA*: "It was their custom then for each partner to identify himself with individual buildings, and Mr. Mead and I therefore collaborated on this building, sharing the remuneration equally, and our relations all through were of the happiest." Letters from Taylor to the firm concerning the Bank of Montreal project in the McKim, Mead & White Archive in the New-York Historical Society are all addressed to Mead.

[16] The 1859 renovations are discussed in Nolin-Raynauld, "La Banque de Montréal," pp. 140–53. During 1885 and 1886 Andrew Taylor's firm had carried out further alterations and additions to the bank. See "Bank of Montreal, Montreal," *Canadian Architect and Builder* 6 (January 1893): 3.

[17] Roth, *McKim, Mead & White,* p. 300. Behind and at a cross axis to the old bank, the addition, which faced Craig Street, parallel to and lower than St. James Street, was in fact separated from the old bank by a narrow city lane, but linked by the hall-bridge extending from the old building. Now part of Rue St. Antoine, Craig Street is the more familiar appellation.

[18] Percy E. Nobbs, *Present Tendencies Affecting Architecture in Canada* (Montreal: McGill University Press, 1930), p. 4.

[19] Ye Gargoyle [Percy E. Nobbs], "Montreal Notes," *Canadian Architect and Builder* 17 (July 1904): 111.

[20] Stephen Leacock, "Meet Mr. Wegg, Banker," *Hellements of Hickonomics in Hiccough of Verse Done in Our Planning Mill* (New York: Dodd, Mead, 1936), pp. 64–65.

[21] The Bank of California, according to Bancroft's *History of California,* "sprang full armed from the head of Jove, . . . Its board of directors was composed of the heads of the largest houses in San Francisco; the oldest and strongest banker on the coast [Mills] was its president and its cashier [Ralston] was considered a marvel of ability, and the ablest financier in California." Quoted by Neil C. Wilson in *400 California Street: A Century Plus Five* (San Francisco: Bank of California, 1969), p. 20.

[22] "The Bank of California: Nothing Seemed Impossible," *Portfolio* 1 (San Francisco: Bank of California, Summer 1984): 13.

[23] Wilson, *400 California Street,* p. 66.

[24] Roth, *McKim, Mead & White,* p. 302.

[25] Montgomery Schuyler, "A Modern Classic," in *American Architecture and Other Writings by Montgomery Schuyler,* eds. Jordy and Coe, 2: 588–97. The Trust's influence also spread to Canada, as evidenced by the Bank of Toronto (now Toronto-Dominion) branch at the corner of St. Catherine and Guy streets in Montreal, constructed in 1908 to the designs of the Canadian firm Ross & MacFarlane.

[26] During the restoration process, the lighting in the banking hall was improved and the clutter of teller wickets and office cubicles was removed. Simpler, peripheral marble teller counters and check-writing stands were then installed.

[27] Redlich, *Molding of American Banking,* p. 175.

[28] Ibid., p. 382.

[29] Harold van B. Cleveland and Thomas F. Huertas, *Citibank 1812–1970* (Cambridge: Harvard University Press, 1985), p. 33.

[30] As Leland Roth notes, Stillman was "attracted to the Rogers work not only because of its long Ionic portico on Wall Street but also because it filled an entire city block and few New York banks could claim the distinction of being freestanding buildings" (*McKim, Mead & White,* p. 304).

[31] "America's Largest Banking Institution in Its New Quarters," *Architectural Record* 25 (February 1909): 140.

[32] A.C. David, "Private Residences for Banking Firms," *Architectural Record* 14 (July 1903): 13–17, and Montgomery Schuyler, "The New National Park Bank ," *Architectural Record* 17 (April 1905): 319–28. In addition to Donn Barber's glorious National Park Bank (1904), which formerly stood at 214 Broadway, *Architectural Record* reviewed the low-rise Knickerbocker Trust (1902–04) at Fifth Avenue and Thirty-fourth Street and the Chemical National Bank by Trowbridge & Livingston at 80 Chambers Street. The new Morgan structure was erected on the site of the much higher Drexel Building, which had previously housed the firm.

[33] At the time the J. P. Morgan & Company building was constructed, the House of Morgan dominated a combination that held a total of 341 directorships in 112 of the leading financial and other corporations in the country with aggregate resources or capitalization of $22,245,000,000. The combination controlled thirty-four banks and trust companies, ten insurance companies, thirty-two transportation companies, twenty-four industrial and commercial companies (including U. S. Steel), and twelve public utility companies. See Lewis Corey, *The House of Morgan* (New York: Grosset and Dunlop, 1930), p. 356.

[34] Morgan's son-in-law, Herbert L Satterlee, records that Morgan intended to acquire two antique columns to place on either side of the door but died before he could do so, in *J. Pierpoint Morgan: An intimate Portrait* (New York: Macmillan, 1939), p. 561.

[35] Although Morgan had employed McKim to design his elegant library on East Thirty-sixth Street in 1902, McKim had died in 1909, three years after Stanford White. Moreover, the relationship between Morgan and McKim had ended in acrimony because of cost overruns and delays in completing the library. (David Wright, Registrar and Archivist, Morgan Library, telephone interview by author, 15 July 1987). The partnership of Trowbridge & Livingston, active from 1899 to the early 1940s, designed primarily for the affluent in and around New York.

[36] Satterlee, *Morgan,* p. 561. The entrance to the New England Trust, completed in 1907, was originally on one of the flanks, not on the corner.

[37] Frederick Lewis Allen, *The Great Pierpont Morgan* (New York: Harper, 1949), p. 7.

[38] John J. Klaber, "Some Recent Bank Plans: The Work of Thomas Bruce Boyd,"

Architectural Record 37 (February 1915): 115. Klaber describes the original disposition of all the interior, which has undergone modification.

[39] Eric Arthur, "The R. A. I. C. Exhibition in Montreal," *Journal, Royal Architectural Institute of Canada* 10 (December 1933): 203.

[40] David Spector, *Monuments to Finance: Three Winnipeg Banks* (Winnipeg: Historical Buildings Committee, 1980), p. 6.

[41] Bliss, *Northern Enterprise,* p. 263.

[42] The front was extended in 1930 by adding three matching bays.

[43] The bank's name has been removed, since the building no longer belongs to the bank.

[44] Kip Park, *The Historic Winnipeg Restoration Area: An Illustrated Guide to Winnipeg's Historic Warehouse District* (Winnipeg: Heritage Winnipeg, 1983), p. 16. Toronto-based Darling & Pearson were so important in the architectural development of Winnipeg that they opened a branch in the city. Pearson had been Darling's partner since 1895.

[45] The bank prospered sufficiently to engage in the costliest land transaction of 1927, when the extra frontage on Portage Avenue was purchased for the westward extension.

[46] Donald Creighton, *Canada's First Century* (Toronto: Macmillan of Canada, 1970), pp. 105–6.

[47] The Grand Valley towns include Brantford, Paris, Gault, and Kitchener-Waterloo.

[48] Larry L. Kulisek, "Windsor, Ont.," in *The Canadian Encyclopedia* (Edmonton: Hurtig, 1985).

[49] I am grateful to John J. M. Pratt and Gerald T. Bloomfield for sharing their knowledge of Kahn's work in Walkerville. See also Pratt, "Albert Kahn at Willistead: Problems of Interpretation" (M. A. Thesis, Cornell University, 1978), and Gerald T. Bloomfield, "Albert Kahn and Canadian Industrial Architecture 1908–1930," *Society for the Study of Architecture in Canada Bulletin* 10 (December 1985): 4–10.

[50] Thomas Adams, *Rural Planning and Development* (Ottawa: Commission of Conservation, 1917), p. 171; quoted in Bloomfield, "Albert Kahn and Canadian Industrial Architecture," p. 9, n. 20.

[51] Kahn's firm at this time was known as Albert Kahn, Architect, Ernest Wilby, Associate.

[52] For a time the U. S. government used the bank for its foreign banking business.

[53] An addition was added at the rear in 1917.

[54] Further research may reveal other branches based on Kahn's design.

6. *American and Canadian Banks — Prairie Style*

[1] Louis H. Sullivan, *The Autobiography of an Idea* (New York: Dover, 1956), p. 326, quoted in James Morton Fitch, *Architecture and the Esthetics of Plenty* (New York: Columbia University Press, 1961), p. 97.

[2] Louis H. Sullivan, *Kindergarten Chats and Other Writings* (New York: George Wittenborn, 1947), p. 37.

[3] Hugh Morrison, *Louis Sullivan: Prophet of Modern Architecture* (1935; reprint, New York; Norton, 1962), p. 206.

[4] See H. Allen Brooks, *The Prairie School: Frank Lloyd Wright and His Midwest Contemporaries* (1972; reprint, New York: Norton, 1976), pp. 7–13, for distinction between Chicago School and Prairie School.

[5] Carl K. Bennett, "A Bank Built for Farmers: Louis Sullivan Designs a Building Which Marks a New Epoch in American Architecture," *The Craftsman* 15 (November 1908): 176–85.

[6] Larry Millett, *The Curve of the Arch: The Story of Louis Sullivan's Owatonna Bank* (St. Paul: Minnesota Historical Society Press, 1985), p. 9.

[7] Bennett, "A Bank Built for Farmers," p. 183.

[8] Quoted in Millett, *The Curve of the Arch,* p. 2 and n. 3, pp. 177–78.

[9] The bank building itself occupied a 68-foot square on the corner of a 68-by-154-foot lot. An adjoining complementary two-story shop and office building produced revenue for the bank.

[10] For Sullivan Nature was synonomous with God.

[11] Sullivan to Bennett, 4 January 1910, quoted in Millett, *The Curve of the Arch,* p. 85.

[12] Morrison, *Louis Sullivan,* p. 209.

[13] Bennett, "A Bank Built for Farmers," p. 185.

[14] The mural on the east wall was reduced in size in 1958 when a new opening was cut through.

[15] Owatonna advertised itself as the "Butter Capital of the World." Millett, *The Curve of the Arch,* p. 6.

[16] Address to the Chicago Architectural Club, 30 May 1899, quoted in Morrison, *Louis Sullivan,* p. 260.

[17] Brooks, *The Prairie School,* p. 134.

[18] Peter B. Wight, "The Winona Savings Bank and Winona National Bank Building Winona, Minn., George W. Mayer, Architect," *Architectural Record* 41 (January-June 1917): 48.

[19] Wim de Wit, "The Banks and the Image of Progressive Banking," in *Louis Sullivan: The Function of Ornament,* ed. Wim de Wit (New York: Norton, 1986), pp. 158–97.

[20] Winona already boasted the two-year-old Sullivanesque Merchants Bank of Winona by Purcell, Feick and Elmslie. (Elmslie had left Sullivan in 1909.)

[21] Wright did not exploit this interplay in either of his two banks.

[22] See Brooks, *The Prairie School,* p. 205.

[23] Incorporated in 1874 as the Winona Savings Bank, this bank established the Winona National Bank as its commericial affiliate in 1916. The two institutions were consolidated in 1928 and renamed the Winona National and Savings Bank. I am very grateful to Sylvester J. Kryzsko, former president of the bank, for supplying me with historical information.

[24] The capitals of the portal columns were based on the American, not Egyptian, lotus flower and leaf.

[25] Wight, "The Winona Savings Bank," p. 48.

[26] Bliss, *Northern Enterprise,* p. 268, and Deryck Holdsworth and Edward Mills, "Pioneer Prefab Banks on the Prairies," *Canadian Geographic Journal* 96 (April–May 1978): 67.

[27] Edward Mills and Deryck Holdsworth note in "The B. C. Mills Prefabricated System: The Emergence of Ready-made Buildings in Western Canada" (Ottawa: Canadian Historic Sites, 1974), p. 144, that although the Bank of Montreal and the Winnipeg-based Northern Bank purchased house prefabs to use as branch buildings and managers' accommodations in British Columbia, it was the Canadian Bank of Commerce that exploited their potential.

[28] Following the earthquake and fire of 1906, the Bank of Commerce sent two prefabs to San Francisco. See Victor Ross, *A History of the Bank of Commerce* (Toronto: Oxford University Press, 1922), 2: 294–95.

[29] Holdsworth and Mills, "Pioneer Prefab Banks," p. 69, and Mills and Holdsdworth, "The B. C. Mills Prefabricated System." I am also grateful to Chris Lea of Toronto for sharing his unpublished paper, "Chain Store Banking in the Prairies," written in 1982 while he was an undergraduate at the University of Toronto.

[30] The first wooden prefabricated bank may have been designed and prepared for the South Australian Company by the London carpenter and builder John Manning, who advertised this and other buildings for emigrants to "South Australia and Other Colonies" in the *South Australian Record,* 13 January 1838. It is unknown if the bank was ever built. See Gilbert Herbert, *Pioneers of Prefabrication: The British Contribution in the Nineteenth Century* (Baltimore: Johns Hopkins University Press, 1978), pp. 15–17.

[31] The bank termed these three models its "Prairie Type" branches.

[32] Ross, *Bank of Commerce,* 2: 490.

[33] Heather Robertson, *Grass Roots* (Toronto: James Lewis & Samuel, 1973), p. 39.

[34] Walker was travelling on the newly completed Canadian Northern Railway, for which the Canadian Bank of Commerce served as bank.

35 Mavis Y. Kaminsky, "Canadian Imperial Bank of Commerce," in *Through the Years: A History of Innisfree and District* (Innisfree: Innisfree History Book, 1986), p. 23.

36 In the early 1940s the upstairs was modernized and converted into a manager's apartment, although the current manager lives off the premises.

7. *American and Canadian Banks — Twenties and Thirties*

1 Paul Warburg, who served on the first Federal Reserve Board, was possibly more than any other individual responsible for the basic features of the Act.

2 The Act called for not less than eight but not more than twelve cities to be Federal Reserve cities and left it to an organizing committee to determine the exact number and location and to divide the nation into districts.

3 Klebaner, *Commercial Banking in the United States,* pp. 106–7, and *The Federal Reserve System : Purposes and Functions* (Washington: Board of Governors of the Federal Reserve System, 1984), pp. 4–6.

4 About 355 million troy ounces as of 1983.

5 Following the official retirement in 1919 of the surviving original partner Mead, the firm continued under junior partners.

6 "The Federal Reserve Bank of New York: Historic Landmark." Pamphlet from the Public Information Department, Federal Reserve Bank of New York, October 1978.

7 Robert A. M. Stern, Gregory Gilmartin, and Thomas Mellins, *New York 1930: Architecture and Urbanism Between the Two World Wars* (New York: Rizzoli, 1987), p. 174. The building was first occupied in 1924, although the eastern-most portion of the block fronting on William Street was only acquired in 1933, the final phase of construction being completed in 1935.

8 When Root died in 1891, the firm was renamed D. H. Burnham & Company. When Burnham died in 1912, it was reorganized as Graham, Burnham & Company. In 1917 this firm was dissolved and the partnership of Graham, Anderson, Probst & White was formed.

9 The chief designer was Pierce Anderson, who possessed an A.B. from Harvard, a postgraduate degree in engineering from Johns Hopkins, and the coveted *diplôme* of the Ecole des Beaux-Arts.

10 Two additional stories were added after the 1928 merger.

11 When the Board of Trade Building was completed in 1930 at the head of LaSalle, one of the notable financial vistas of all time was achieved, indicative of Chicago's new position as a major financial center.

12 Escalators have replaced the original stairs and subtle electric fixtures the skylight.

13 The murals were completed in 1924. Guerin's work includes the murals in the Lincoln Memorial in Washington and, before its destruction, Pennsylvania Station in New York.

14 "Description of Murals." Typescript from the archives of Continental Illinois Bank.

15 The total scheme is discussed in "Finance in Epigram: A Wall Street Sermon by C. W. Barron." Unpublished typescript provided by Continental Illinois Bank.

16 The architects' Chicago Union Station was simultaneously under construction.

17 In 1929 the new bank, operating under a state charter, was renamed the Continental Illinois Bank and Trust Company. It became Continental Illinois National Bank and Trust Company of Chicago when it received a federal charter in 1932.

18 "Bank Building Text (Rev.)." Draft dated 14 April 1975 provided by Continental Illinois Bank, pp. 8–9.

19 Cervin Robinson and Rosemarie Haag Bletter, *Skyscraper Style: Art Deco New York* (New York: Oxford University Press, 1975), p. 12.

20 Ralph T. Walker, "The Barclay-Vesey Telephone Building, McKenzie, Voorhees & Gmelin, Architects," *American Architect* 130 (5 November 1926): 395 as quoted in Stern et al., *New York 1930,* p. 566.

21 Ralph T. Walker, "Architecture of To-Day: An American's View," *Creative Art* 5 (July 1929): 460–65 as quoted in Stern et al., *New York 1930,* p. 568.

[22] Walker's firm, which at its high point in 1928 had had more than three hundred employees, had by 1931 shrunk to a mere twenty-five, a typical drop throughout North America for those architectural firms that managed to keep their doors open at all. Dean Everett V. Meeks served as consulting architect for the Irving Trust Building.

[23] Ralph T. Walker, *Ralph Walker, Architect* (New York: Henahan House, 1957), p. 35.

[24] Ibid., p. 36.

[25] Stern et al., *New York 1930,* p. 568.

[26] Ralph T. Walker, "The Relation of Skyscrapers to Our Life," *Architectural Forum* 52 (May 1930): 694.

[27] The first branch was established in Winnipeg in 1893. Beginning in 1898 the bank began opening more branches and initiated a series of acquisitions, acquiring the Bank of British Columbia, the Halifax Banking Company, the Merchants Bank of Prince Edward Island, and the Eastern Townships Bank, the latter giving them a Quebec presence.

[28] The architect, R. A. Waite, had designed the Ontario Legislative Buildings earlier in the decade.

[29] For legal reasons, the bank was cited in contemporaneous publications as the work of Darling & Pearson with York & Sawyer as consulting architects. Darling & Pearson was now headed by John A. Pearson following Darling's death in 1923.

[30] Even in New York, the testing ground for current skyscraper design, the appropriate form for skyscrapers with setbacks was still evolving in 1927.

[31] See Philip Sawyer, "The Problem of Building a Bank," *Architectural Forum* 48 (June 1928): 792, showing two preliminary schemes for the Canadian Bank of Commerce that exhibit a composition more similar in kind to the Royal Bank.

[32] It has recently been carefully restored.

[33] Quoted in Margaret E. McKelvey and Marilyn McKelvey, *Toronto: Carved in Stone* (Toronto: Fitzhenry & Whiteside, 1984), p. 25.

[34] The architects were I. M. Pei & Associates with Page & Steele as associated architects, the latter a Canadian firm.

[35] The Halifax architect Andrew R. Cobb was associated with Lyle on the Halifax project.

[36] In 1946, the year after Lyle died, the Bank resumed the project, handing the plans over to Mathers & Haldenby, who worked in association with Beck & Eadie, Lyle's successor firm. The exterior was simplified with much of Lyle's sculpture program omitted.

[37] Geoffrey Hunt, *John M. Lyle: Toward a Canadian Architecture* (Kingston, Ontario: Agnes Etherington Art Centre, Queen's University, 1982), p. 24.

[38] John M. Lyle, "The Bank of Nova Scotia Building, Halifax," *Journal, Royal Architectural Institute of Canada* 9 (January 1932): 5, 13.

[39] John M. Lyle, "Canadian Decorative Forms," *Journal, Royal Architectural Institute of Canada* 9 (March 1932): 70.

[40] *"Wanted — a Suitable Building for The Bank of Nova Scotia."* A Bank of Nova Scotia Heritage Series Publication (Toronto: Bank of Nova Scotia, 1986), p. 8. See also John M. Lyle, "Canadian Art Goes Native," *American Architect* 140 (December 1931): 34–39.

[41] Hunt, *John M. Lyle,* p. 111.

[42] The Bank of Nova Scotia, designed by John Lyle, and the Bank of Commerce, by Darling & Pearson, were erected on Sparks Street in the early twenties.

[43] " . . . the result being that the building is all-Canadian in design and also entirely Canadian in methods employed" (*Ottawa Evening Journal,* 30 March 1932 [Bank of Montreal Archives]).

[44] "The New Bank of Montreal Building, Ottawa, Ont.: Barott & Blackader, Architects," *Journal, Royal Architectural Institute of Canada* 9 (September 1932): 207.

[45] Robert A. M. Stern, *George Howe: Toward a Modern Architecture* (New Haven: Yale University Press, 1974), p. 117.

[46] The second building on his list is Richard Neutra's Lovell House (1927–29) in Los Angeles. William H. Jordy, *American Buildings and Their Architects,* vol. 4: *The Im-*

pact of European Modernism in the Mid-Twentieth Century (Garden City: Anchor, 1976), pp. 87–88.

[47] In 1930 Howe also remodelled this bank. See James F. O'Gorman, *The Architecture of Frank Furness* (Philadelphia: Philadelphia Museum of Art, 1973), p. 191. PSFS is currently part of the Meritor Financial Group.

[48] At the time of its construction PSFS was only exceeded in height by the City Hall. The observation tower later became a TV relay station.

[49] No longer, as Jordy observes, could "the eye glut itself on the extravagant textures, ornament, or bulk permitted by the Bacchic materialism of Beaux-Arts esthetics" (*The Impact of European Modernism,* p. 122).

[50] Paul Goldberger, *The Skyscraper* (New York: Knopf, 1982), p. 97.

[51] Jordy, *The Impact of European Modernism,* pp. 90–91. Jordy notes, "to venture into modern architecture in the United States in 1929 was not only risky, but lonely as well" (p. 102).

[52] Richard Webster, *Philadelphia Preserved,* Catalog of the Historic American Building Survey (Philadelphia: Temple University Press, 1976), p. 118.

8. *American and Canadian Banks — Modernism and Late Modernism*

[1] Alfred H. Barr, Jr., in Henry-Russell Hitchcock and Philip Johnson, *The International Style: Architecture since 1922* (New York: Norton, 1932), p. 13.

[2] Stern, *George Howe,* p. 154.

[3] Jordy, *The Impact of European Modernism,* p. 181.

[4] The name Manufacturers Hanover Trust Company was adopted in 1961 following a merger of Manufacturers Trust Company and the Hanover Bank.

[5] "Lantern on Fifth Avenue," *Progressive Architecture* 54 (June 1973): 108.

[6] Christopher Woodward, *Skidmore, Owings & Merrill* (New York: Simon & Schuster, 1970), p. 13.

[7] "Manufacturers Trust Company Builds a Conversation Piece on Fifth Avenue," *Architectural Record* 116 (November 1954): 154.

[8] The views of the escalator and the screen have been obscured by recent interior modifications and by tall tropical plants.

[9] Henry-Russell Hitchcock, Introduction to Ernst Danz, *Architecture of Skidmore, Owings & Merrill, 1950–1962* (New York: Praeger, 1963), p. 12. Interior designer Eleanor LeMaire worked on this first SOM bank. Just after this commission, however, SOM set up its own interiors department.

[10] John Donald Wilson, *The Chase: The Chase Manhattan Bank, N.A. 1945–1985* (Boston: Harvard Business School Press, 1986), p. 7.

[11] Wilson's recent study of Chase records that "the board sought out Skidmore, Owings and Merrill, the firm that had recently completed for Manufacturers Trust a branch on Fifth Avenue of modern design which was attracting favorable attention. More than any other architects, they were regarded as having a concept of what the future architecture of the city should be" (ibid., p. 104). The plans rejected in 1953 were submitted by Shreve, Lamb & Harmon.

[12] Crawford Wheeler, "The Chase Manhattan Story," a series of oral history interviews with leading Chase officers of the period 1930–1955 (Chase Archives, February 1963), quoted in Wilson, *The Chase,* pp. 103–4.

[13] David Rockefeller, interview quoted in Wilson, *The Chase,* p. 105.

[14] Hitchcock, Introduction to *Architecture of SOM,* p. 7.

[15] Woodward, *Skidmore, Owings & Merrill,* p. 15.

[16] Rockefeller's mother, Abby Aldrich Rockefeller, was the principal founder of the Museum of Modern Art.

[17] Wilson, *The Chase,* pp. 111–12, and David Rockefeller, interview by Linda Edgerly, 23 October 1980, Chase Archives.

[18] In 1982, the firm had offices as well in Washington, Boston, and Denver. There were 35 general partners, 93 associate partners, and 212 associates.

[19] An article, "Banking By Automobile," in *Scientific American* 157 (September 1937): 151, reported that "what is reputed to be the first drive-in bank in the world has recently been opened at Vernon, a suburb of Los Angeles." This early facility, which is no longer exists, was heavily protected by an electric gateway—virtually a portcullis—and bullet-proof glass. A rival claim is made for Dallas architect George Dahl, who is also said to have designed the first drive-in bank in the world, the Hillcrest State Bank in Dallas, "circa 1938" (Michael McCullar, "Profile: George L. Dahl, FAIA Dallas Designer, Innovator, Entrepreneur," *Texas Architect* 30 [November-December 1980]: 73). The Bank of Montreal pioneered drive-in banking in Canada at the Broadway and Granville District Branch in Vancouver, opened in June 1950.

[20] Both banks have undergone subsequent modifications, including a 1,200-square-foot addition to the Bank of Montreal designed by the Parkin firm in 1967.

[21] *Toronto Daily Star,* 29 October 1956.

[22] See also Gunter Gad and Deryck Holdsworth, "Large Office Buildings and Their Changing Occupancy: King Street, Toronto, 1880–1950," *Society for the Study of Architecture in Canada Bulletin* 10 (December 1985): 19, 22–25.

[23] The four banks are the Canadian Imperial Bank of Commerce, the Bank of Montreal, the Bank of Nova Scotia, and the Toronto Dominion Bank.

[24] A third tower, the Commercial Union, was added later at the northeast corner of Wellington and York streets, and a fourth, the IBM Tower, was added on a site on the south side of Wellington Street in 1985.

[25] Lambert became president and chairman of the board in 1961 and chairman and chief executive officer in 1972.

[26] Robert W. Collier, *Contemporary Cathedrals: Large-Scale Developments in Canadian Cities* (Montreal: Harvest House, 1974), pp. 124–25.

[27] Ibid., p. 125.

[28] R. P. Patterson, "The Toronto-Dominion Centre" (term paper for Art History Course 211, Woodsworth College, University of Toronto, 29 November 1983. Typescript in the Toronto Dominion Bank Archives), p. 2.

[29] Ibid., p. 3.

[30] Ibid., p. 5.

[31] Mildred F. Schmertz, "Canadians Build an Office Complex by Mies van der Rohe in Toronto," *Architectural Record* 149 (March 1971): 105.

[32] William Dendy, *Lost Toronto* (Toronto: Oxford University Press, 1978), p. 99.

[33] Schmertz, "Canadians Build an Office Complex," p. 106.

[34] These two buildings are in fact linked by two low glassed-in corridors and have curtain walls of glass and steel-reinforced aluminum.

[35] Macy DuBois, "Toronto-Dominion Centre: A Critique," *Canadian Architect* 12 (November 1967): 33.

[36] "GAF's remarks: Katharine Kuh Dinner: December 2, 1970." Typescript courtesy of Gaylord Freeman's office, p. 1.

[37] C. William Brubacker, interview by author, 16 June 1987.

[38] The tapered form is, in fact, composed of a series of straight members.

[39] Karl Plath, "First National still Graces Chicago Loop after 20 Years," *Chicago Tribune,* Sunday 8 March 1987, sec. 16. (The 20 years refer to the cornerstone-laying ceremony.)

[40] The gift of Mr. and Mrs. William Wood Prince.

[41] Gaylord Freeman, interview by author, 17 June 1987.

[42] Ibid. and "GAF's remarks," pp. 2–3.

[43] Freeman has characterized it as "a modest eclectic collection of mosaics, drawings, paintings, sculpture, tapestry and other art forms, ranging from the Fifth Century, B.C. to some on which the paint is hardly dry" ("GAF's remarks," p. 4).

[44] Nan Robertson, "Banking on Art As the Bottom Line," *New York Times,* 9 June 1977, sec. 3.

[45] "Federal Reserve in Suspense," *Architectural Forum* 130 (January-February 1969): 100.

[46] The new office tower, which was originally to be called Commerce House, was commissioned in 1972 and renamed Rainier Bank Tower two years later. Rainier Bank, letter to the author, 27 January 1987, and Minoru Yamasaki, *A Life in Architecture* (New York: Weatherhill, 1979), p. 168.

[47] Yamasaki, *A Life,* p. 168. In January 1989 following a merger, the name was changed to Security Pacific Bank Washington.

[48] Sally B. Woodbridge and Roger Montgomery, *A Guide to Architecture in Washington State: An Environmental Perspective* (Seattle: University of Washington Press, 1980), p. 127.

[49] Goldberger, *The Skyscraper,* p. 128.

[50] Peter Wood, 21 September 1987.

[51] Susan Pigg, "Toronto Set to Approve Bank Tower," *Toronto Star,* 21 June 1984.

[52] Bliss, *Northern Enterprise,* p. 394.

[53] Dendy and Kilbourn, *Toronto Observed,* p. 283.

[54] Ray Smith, "Revolutions in Bank Designs," *Interiors* 136 (April 1977): 66–79.

[55] A series of press releases in the archives of the Bank of Canada issued between 1964 and 1971 give some idea of the serpentine progress of the undertaking.

[56] Leon Whiteson, *Modern Canadian Architecture* (Edmonton: Hurtig, 1983), p. 197.

9. *American Banks — Postmodernism*

[1] Charles Jencks, *The Language of Post-Modern Architecture* (New York: Rizzoli, 1977), p. 9. This was the Pruitt-Igoe project, which Oscar Newman discussed in his influential *Defensible Space: Crime Prevention Through Urban Design* (New York: Macmillan, 1973).

[2] Much of the information on the old and new building has been obtained from Debra Hilbert, "A Building That Speaks to its Community: The East Cambridge Savings Bank" (term paper for Art History Course 798, Boston University, 8 December 1982. Typescript in the East Cambridge Savings Bank Archives).

[3] The sculptor was Paul Fjelde and the painter was Alfred Rasmussen.

[4] The two have now formed their own partnership, Schwartz/Silver Architects, Inc.

[5] The carpet and furniture in the new wing were furnished by a decorator selected by the bank and were not chosen by the architects.

[6] Robert Campbell, "Gem of a Bank for Cambridge," *Boston Globe,* Sunday 13 August 1978.

[7] Warren Schwartz and Robert Silver, telephone interview by author, 15 December 1987.

[8] In 1982 the firm name, Johnson/Burgee Architects, was changed to John Burgee Architects with Philip Johnson.

[9] Goldberger, *The Skyscraper,* p. 124.

[10] Ibid., p. 153.

[11] "Together, We Have Changed Houston's Skyline," *Prime Interest,* by Republic-Bank Houston 7 (October 1983): 1.

[12] Pilar Viladis in "Gothic Romance," *Progressive Architecture* 8 (February 1984): 1, reports that Johnson/Burgee's original design was "quite sympathetic to *le style Pennzoil,*" but that the bank wanted something more distinctive.

[13] As Pilar Viladis points out, ibid., p. 3.

[14] Ledoux's design for the House of Education at Chaux served as the prototype for the firm's University of Houston School of Architecture, completed in 1985.

[15] Kendall/Heaton Associates were the associate architects on the project.

[16] William L. Livingston, Senior Associate, Gensler and Associates Architects, interview by author, 13 October 1987.

[17] *Philip Johnson/John Burgee Architecture 1979–1985* (New York: Rizzoli, 1985), p. 6.

[18] Ada Louise Huxtable, *The Tall Building Artistically Reconsidered: The Search for a Skyscraper Style* (New York: Pantheon, 1984), pp. 68–69.

[19] Harwood K. Smith & Partners served as associate architect and 3D/International as interior architect on the project.

[20] "The New Greed Takes Center Stage," *New York Times,* 3 January 1988, sec. 2.

[21] "Momentum Place Introduces New Concept in Design of Bank Buildings." Press release dated 1 September 1987 provided by MBank, p. 1. The project was a joint venture of Cadillac Fairview Urban Development, Inc. and MBank Dallas.

[22] Ibid., p. 2.

[23] In 1988 the North Carolina-based NCNB Corporation entered into an agreement with the Federal Deposit Insurance Corporation under which they manage a new bank, NCNB Texas National Bank, formed through the restructuring of the subsidiary banks of First RepublicBank Corporation. In March 1989 the Ohio-based Banc One Corporation entered into an agreement with the FDIC to purchase twenty of the twenty-five MBanks (including MBank Dallas) operating in Texas. Momentum Place currently serves as headquarters for Bank One, Texas.

[24] "Guest Speaker: Cesar Pelli: Pieces of the City," *Architectural Digest* 45 (August 1988): p. 36.

[25] "The Architectural Process: Norwest Center Cesar Pelli Minneapolis," (Norwest Corporation and Gerald D. Hines Interests, 1986), unpaginated.

[26] Ibid.

[27] Ibid.

[28] Ibid.

[29] Interview by author 10 November 1988.

[30] Sharon Schmickle, "Norwest's Design Lets IDS Retain Tallest Title," *Minneapolis Star and Tribune,* 30 July 1986, sec. A.

10. *Conclusion*

[1] These plans, for the Bank of Pennsylvania and the State Bank of Louisiana, are in Hamlin, *Latrobe,* pp. 153, 527.

[2] Hammond, *Banks and Politics,* p. 4.

[3] This was the Security State Bank of Madison, Wisconsin, now the Marine Bank Dane County.

[4] Banks were, however, leaders in commissioning skyscrapers in Canada. The West's first skyscraper was the ten-story steel-framed Union Bank in Winnipeg (1903) by Darling & Pearson, while in the East Toronto led the way with Traders Bank (1905–6) by Carrère & Hastings.

[5] David Pearce, *The Great Houses of London* (New York: Vendome Press,1986), p. 13.

[6] Quoted in Rod McQueen, *The Money Spinners* (Toronto: MacMillan, 1983), p. 4.

SELECTED BIBLIOGRAPHY

Banks, Banking, and General — United States

Bennett, Carl K. "A Bank Built for Farmers: Louis Sullivan Designs a Building Which Marks a New Epoch in American Architecture." *The Craftsman* 15 (November 1908): 176–85.

Brooks, H. Allen. *The Prairie School: Frank Lloyd Wright and His Midwest Contemporaries.* 1972; reprint, New York: Norton, 1976.

Craig, Lois A. et al. *The Federal Presence: Architecture, Politics, and National Design.* 1978; reprint, Cambridge: MIT, 1984.

Daniels, Belden L. *Pennsylvania — Birthplace of Banking in America.* Harrisburg: Pennsylvania Bankers Association, 1976.

Goldberger, Paul. *The Skyscraper.* New York: Knopf, 1982.

Hammond, Bray. *Banks and Politics in America from the Revolution to the Civil War.* Princeton: Princeton, 1957.

——— "The Second Bank of the United States." *Transactions of the American Philosophical Society* 43, pt. 1 (1953): 80–85.

Hitchcock, Henry-Russell, and Philip Johnson. *The International Style: Architecture since 1922.* New York: Norton, 1932.

Huxtable, Ada Louise. *The Tall Building Artistically Reconsidered: The Search for a Skyscraper Style.* New York: Pantheon, 1984.

Jordy, William H. *American Buildings and Their Architects.* Vol. 4: *The Impact of European Modernism in the Mid-Twentieth Century.* Garden City: Anchor, 1976.

Kimball, Fiske. "The Bank of Pennsylvania, 1799." *Architectural Record* 44 (August 1918): 132–39.

——— "The Bank of the United States 1818–1824." *Architectural Record* 58 (December 1925): 581–94.

Klebaner, Benjamin J. *Commercial Banking in the United States: A History.* Hinsdale, Ill.: Dryden, 1974.

Knox, John Jay. *A History of Banking in the United States.* 1903; reprint, New York: Augustus M. Kelley, 1969.

Lowry , Bates. *Building a National Image: Architectural Drawings for the American Democracy, 1789–1912.* New York: Walker, 1985.

Millett, Larry. *The Curve of the Arch: The Story of Louis Sullivan's Owatonna Bank.* St. Paul: Minnesota Historical Society, 1985.

Pierson, William H., Jr. *American Buildings and Their Architects.* Vol. 1: *The Colonial and Neo-Classical Styles.* Garden City: Anchor, 1976.

Redlich, Fritz. *Molding of American Banking: Men and Ideas.* 1947 and 1951; reprint, New York: Hafner, 1968.

Sawyer, Philip. "The Problem of Building a Bank." *Architectural Forum* 48 (June 1928): 785–802.

Stern, Robert A.M., Gregory Gilmartin, and John Massengale. *New York 1900: Metropolitan Architecture and Urbanism 1890–1915.* New York: Rizzoli, 1983.

Stern, Robert A.M., Gregory Gilmartin, and Thomas Mellins. *New York 1930: Architecture and Urbanism Between the Two World Wars.* New York: Rizzoli, 1987.

Weingarden, Lauren S. *Louis H. Sullivan: The Banks.* Cambridge: MIT, 1987.

Wettereau, James O. "The Oldest Bank in the United States." *Transactions of the American Philosophical Society* 43, pt.1 (1953): 70–79.

Wit, Wim de, ed. *Louis Sullivan: The Function of Ornament.* New York: Norton, 1986.

Banks, Banking, and General — Canada

Bliss, Michael. *Northern Enterprise: Five Centuries of Canadian Business.* Toronto: McClelland & Stewart, 1987.

Collier, Robert W. *Contemporary Cathedrals: Large-Scale Developments in Canadian Cities.* Montreal: Harvest House, 1974.

Dendy, William. *Lost Toronto.* Toronto: Oxford, 1978.

Dendy, William, and William Kilbourn. *Toronto Observed: Its Architecture, Patrons, and History.* Toronto: Oxford, 1986.

Denison, Merrill. *Canada's First Bank.* 2 vols. Toronto: McClelland & Stewart, 1966.

Gad, Gunter, and Deryk Holdsworth. "Building for City, Region, and Nation." In *Forging a Consensus. Historical Essays on Toronto,* ed. V.L. Russell, pp. 272–319. Toronto: University of Toronto, 1984.

———— "Large Office Buildings and Their Changing Occupancy: King Street, Toronto, 1880–1950." *Society for the Study of Architecture in Canada Bulletin* 10 (December 1985): 19, 22–25.

Holdsworth, Deryck, and Edward Mills. "Pioneer Prefab Banks on the Prairies." *Canadian Geographic Journal* 96 (April-May 1978): 66–69.

Ross, Victor. *A History of the Bank of Commerce.* 2 vols. Toronto: Oxford, 1920–22.

Tulchinsky, Gerald, ed. *To Preserve and Defend: Essays on Kingston in the Nineteenth Century.* Montreal: McGill-Queen's, 1976.

Whiteson, Leon. *Modern Canadian Architecture.* Edmonton: Hurtig, 1983.

Architects

Gilchrist, Agnes Addison. *William Strickland, Architect and Engineer: 1788–1854.* 1950; enl. ed. reprint, New York: Da Capo, 1969.

Hamlin, Talbot. *Benjamin Henry Latrobe.* New York: Oxford, 1955.

Hitchcock, Henry-Russell. Introduction to Ernest Danz, *Architecture of Skidmore, Owings & Merrill, 1950–1962.* New York: Praeger, 1963.

Hunt, Geoffrey. *John M. Lyle: Toward a Canadian Architecture.* Kingston, Ontario: Agnes Etherington Art Centre, Queen's University, 1982.

Monroe, Harriet. *John Wellborn Root: A Study of his Life and Work.* 1896; reprint, Park Forest, Ill.: Prairie School Press, 1966.

Morrison, Hugh. *Louis Sullivan: Prophet of Modern Architecture.* 1935; reprint, New York: Norton, 1962.

Philip Johnson/John Burgee Architecture 1979–1985. New York: Rizzoli, 1985.

Ravenel, Beatrice St. Julien. *Architects of Charleston*. Charleston: Carolina Art Association, 1945.

Roth, Leland M., *McKim, Mead & White, Architects*. 1983; reprint, New York: Harper & Row, 1985.

Scully, Arthur, Jr. *James Dakin, Architect: His Career in New York and the South*. Baton Rouge: Louisiana State University, 1973.

Stern, Robert A.M. *George Howe: Toward a Modern Architecture*. New York: Yale, 1974.

Wagg, Susan. *Ernest Isbell Barott, Architect: An Introduction*. Montreal: Centre Canadien d'Architecture/Canadian Center for Architecture, 1985.

Walker, Ralph T. *Ralph Walker, Architect*. New York: Henahan House, 1957.

Woodman, Betsy H. *Newburyport's Rufus Sargent (1812–1886): An Architect Rediscovered*. N.p., 1987. Originally printed as two articles in the *Essex Institute Historical Collections,* October 1986 and January 1987.

Woodward, Christopher. *Skidmore, Owings & Merrill*. New York: Simon & Schuster, 1970.

Yamasaki, Minoru. *A Life in Architecture*. New York: Weatherhill, 1979.

Dictionaries and Encyclopedias

The Canadian Encyclopedia. Edmonton: Hurtig, 1988 ed.

Macmillan Encyclopedia of Architects. New York: Free Press, 1982.

Tatman, Sandra L., and Roger W. Moss. *Biographical Dictionary of Philadelphia Architects*. Boston: Hall, 1985.

Withey, Henry F., and Elsie Rathburn Withey. *Biographical Dictionary of American Architects (Deceased)*. Los Angeles: New Age, 1956.

LIST OF ARCHITECTS

Anderson, Peirce (1870–1924)
Austin, Henry (1804–91)
Baldwin, Dr. William Warren (1775–1844)
Barott, Ernest Isbell (1884 1966)
Birkerts, Gunnar (1925–)
Bliss, Walter Danforth (1873–1956)
Blodget, Samuel, Jr. (1757–1814)
Browne, George William Richardson (1811–85)
Brubacker, Charles William (1926–)
Bunshaft, Gordon (1909–)
Burgee, John Henry (1933–)
Burnham, Daniel Hudson (1846–1912)
Curry, Samuel George (1854–1942)
Dakin, James (1806–52)
Darling, Frank (1850–1923)
Elmslie, George Grant (1871–1952)
Erickson, Arthur (1924–)
Fredenburgh, Harold (1933–)
Graham, Ernest Robert (1866–1936)
Gries, John M. (1827–62)
Hay, William (1818–88)
Hobbs, Isaac H. (1817–96)
Howard, John (1803–90)
Howe, George (1886–1955)
James, Thomas M. (1875–1942)

Johnson, Philip Cortelyou (1906–)
Kahn, Albert (1869–1942)
Latrobe, Benjamin Henry (1764–1820)
Lee, Francis D. (1826–85)
Lescaze, William Edmund (1896–1969)
Livingston, Goodhue (1862–1925)
Lyle, John MacIntosh (1872–1945)
Maher, George Washington (1864–1926)
Manny, Carter H., Jr. (1918–)
McKim, Charles Follen (1847–1909)
Mead, William Rutherford (1846–1928)
Merrill, John O. (1896–1975)
Mies van der Rohe, Ludwig (1886–1969)
Murphy, Charles Frank (1890–1985)
Owings, Nathaniel A. (1903–84)
Parkin, John Burnett (1911–75)
Parkin, John Cresswell (1922–89)
Pearson, John Andrew (1867–1940)
Pei, Ieoh Ming (1917–)
Pelli, Cesar (1926–)
Perkins, Lawrence Bradford (1907–)
Probst, Edward (1870–1942)
Rattenbury, Francis Mawson (1867–1935)
Rogers, Isaiah (1800–69)
Root, John Wellborn (1850–91)
Sargent, Rufus (1812–86)
Sawyer, Philip (1868–1949)
Schwartz, Warren Richard (1943–)
Silsbee, Joseph Lyman (1845–1913)
Silver, Robert Harold (1946–)
Skidmore, Louis (1897–1962)
Stone, William E. (died 1905)
Strickland, William (1788–1854)
Sullivan, Louis Henry (1856–1924)
Taylor, Andrew Thomas (1850–1937)
Thomas, William (1799–1860)
Trowbridge, Samuel Breck Parkman (1862–1925)
Walker, Ralph (1889–1973)
Wells, John (1789–1864)
White, Howard Judson (1870–1936)
White, Stanford (1853–1906)
Williams, Warren Haywood (1844–88)
Yamasaki, Minoru (1912–)
York, Edward Palmer (1865–1927)
Zerafa, Boris Ernest (1933–)

WHERE ONE STANDS
AND WHEN
ONE STANDS THERE

Anne Wilkes Tucker

A seasoned architectural photographer approaches the moment of making a photograph with an acquired sense of its expressive possibilities. Like a baseball slugger batting against his own previous-best effort, he knows what he has done before and what he can do well. But he also knows what he has never done, either because earlier attempts failed, or because he simply cannot exhaust the possible solutions to his photographic challenges.

Solving photographic problems, then, depends on his trained intuition and on his ability to ask critical questions. Standing before each of these banks, he intuitively asks what is the building's architectural significance, what about it distinguishes it as a bank, and how he can make compelling photographs from this subject. More generally, he asks what it symbolizes within the environment in which it stands and for the time in which it was built.

Equally relevant to the photographer is the axiom articulated by photographer/historian G. E. Kidder Smith: "Given reasonable sunshine, the two main determinants are *where* one stands and *when* one stands there." [1] Where a photographer stands and what equipment he uses determines whether he is photographing an architectural detail, the whole façade, or the building in relation to its neighbors. It also determines how the subject is framed and from what altitude and angle of view the picture is taken. It distinguishes what the photographer wishes us to notice and what he obscures or excludes from view. In other words, it graphically reveals his interpretation of the facts before him.

This essay addresses the basic challenges of architectural photography.

Too, it reviews special problems encountered by this project's photographers. Some problems were dictated by the scale and location of each building; others were consequences of the photographer's interpretive aims.

The projects' photographers were given few fixed guidelines. Each was assigned specific buildings to photograph and was asked to document their façades. The photographer was given a sheet outlining the historical and architectural significance of each building. However, because these photographers were chosen for their interpretive skills in dealing with buildings as objects and as metaphors, it seemed counterproductive to be more directive.

Considerable thought was given to selecting the banks for each photographer. The decision was influenced by previous work that had been done on his or her own initiative. For instance, Robert Bourdeau was assigned to photograph Molsons Bank in Montreal. His subjects in recent years have included Maya pyramids and Yucatec churches. Since he has been drawn particularly to structures of heavy, weathered stone, he was assigned buildings constructed of stone. The walls of Molsons Bank offered a great variation of projecting and receding planes and carved detail which, combined with reflected light off adjoining buildings, attracted Bourdeau. He conveys an impression of "inner radiance" coming from the sandstone which animates the photographs and communicates a quality of spirituality also found in Bourdeau's subjects of entirely personal choice.

Another match based on prior work was George Tice to J. P. Morgan & Company and the Wall Street environment. Tice is a master of provocative juxtapositions. He thought that Wall Street with its tightly situated, contrasting architectural styles was a choice assignment. He framed the austere elegance of J. P. Morgan & Company against the ornate Corinthian columns and sculpture on the New York Stock Exchange's façade. By comparison, the Beaux-Arts Stock Exchange building is teeming.

In a view down Wall Street, Tice contrasts the towering Bankers Trust building and two of the financial district's more modest, as well as most historic, buildings: Trinity Church and Federal Hall, where George Washington was inaugurated. The latter structure is a one-story, Doric-columned temple. It nests among its tall neighbors, shimmering in full sunlight.

Assigning Edward Burtynsky to photograph skyscrapers involved more of an intuitive leap for the project organizers. Burtynsky had not previously photographed tall buildings. Rather he documented railcuts and open-pit mining excavations in the United States and Canada. In both series, he surveys vast, man-altered landscapes, reducing their chaotic complexity to coherent, visual images. Coping with the gigantic scale of this industrial architecture created by miners and railroad engineers prepared Burtynsky to approach the towering skylines of 1970s boom towns such as Toronto, Houston, and Minneapolis.

The photographers in this project had to explore their feelings and assumptions about banks, in general, and specifically about the banks which were assigned to them. Their photographs document the wide variety of sizes, shapes, and materials used in bank architecture. Some banks deliberately resemble homes and blend unobtrusively with their neighbors, others aggressively dominate their townscape. The constant qualities are that banks appear secure, respectable, and prosperous.

Serge Hambourg understood this when he saw the Nantucket Pacific Bank. "In photographing this small building," he wrote, "I wanted to preserve its 'intimate' character, but to also make it seem, by photographing it from low to high, to have a certain grandeur because a bank must be imposing." [2] David Miller's notes reflect a certain dislike for banks' conservative appearances and what he regards as authoritarian practices. It therefore wasn't surprising that his photograph of the manager's office in the Bank of British Columbia has the aura of a school principal's office.

Committed to the referential capacity of photography, most photographers of architecture strive for dramatic rendition within the bounds of accurate documentation. They see invention as a matter of degree and of balance. Interpretation is a conjunction between their personal vision of the building and their respect for the architect's artistry.

In finding their own interpretive position, they may seek out what others value, or perhaps revile, in a building. If the structure is historic, they may note relevant historical details, as for instance, when George Tice photographed J. P. Morgan & Company. He included the pockmarks inflicted in 1920 when a presumed anarchist, attacking what he felt to be the structural embodiment of the actual and symbolic power of Morgan's bank and its Wall Street address, ignited a wagonload of explosives. Paul Strand addressed the same sense of immense power and influence in 1915 in his photograph of Morgan's bank. Its massive, deeply recessed, two-story windows dwarf nearby pedestrians.

Photography is not a easy medium for conveying abstract concepts directly. Instead, in photography, as in architecture, universal statements are figuratively expressed in evocative details; symbolism is embodied in structural forms and materials. Phyllis Lambert, the founder/director of the Canadian Centre for Architecture, recognized this when she wrote about buildings as a formal expression of a society's needs, values, and aspirations. "While structural soundness and functional suitability are requirements of a good building," she wrote, "the ordering of the materials and the means of construction, consciously or not, also represent abstract concepts. In architecture at its finest, symbolism is inherent in the way the building is put together." [3] Mies van der Rohe addressed the same concept more tersely in his often-quoted aphorism, "God is in the details."

Architectural photographers seek to communicate a sense of each institution's cultural significance, as well as its function, and the structural relevance of its materials and methods. For photographers working by commission, the clients' desires variously affect the image-making. For instance, architects encourage photographers to highlight those features that reflect the architects' aspirations while complying with conventions of architectural display. Architectural magazines set guidelines according to their design image. Writers need illustrations for their texts.

This does not mean that all commissioned architectural photography is obsequious nor that it lacks personal expression. In his designs, an architect seeks to maintain a balance between the practical and the artistic sides of his efforts. This interplay continues into architectural photography. Its natural issue is that professional photographers may have less latitude in selecting and interpreting the visual facts before them. The most talented photographers regard this as one of their considerable number of challenges.

Façade

To photograph a building's façade is to portray its public face. Generally, these photographers photographed the façade at street level, standing directly across from the main entrance. The majority of buildings were less than five stories high, and from street level they could be encompassed in one image without distortion. If the photographer so desired, smaller buildings could be isolated from their neighbors. The larger buildings required the photographer to stand further away to capture the entire façade. As a result, neighboring structures also appear. For skyscrapers, it meant including much of the city's skyline—which is appropriate given a skyscraper's proportionally larger impact on its neighbors.

A sense of control and stillness results when the photographer stands directly in front of a building to photograph. The design and ornamental details are unified in the image, particularly if the building is symmetrical. A frontal approach also makes a building more imposing, especially when taken from street level. When a façade fills the picture frame, it looms over the viewer. In architectural photography, as in portraiture, the closest, straight-on view is inherently confronting. As photographer Paul Hester observed, "A flat façade stares back at you." [4]

Serge Hambourg recognized that this was the most appropriate approach for the National Farmers' Bank in Owatonna. "Square and massive," he wrote, "it is imposing in its volume but distinguished in its conception and refined in its details." A frontal view emphasizes the basic box-like shape of this bank, which is symmetrically broken by the imposing semicircular window and refined by terra cotta medallions and blue glass bands. The frontal view conveys both the bank's basic stability and its glorious embellishments.

In response to the symmetry of other buildings, James Iska and Len Jenshel also chose frontal approaches to document the second Bank of the United States and the Bank of South Carolina, respectively. Iska worked with the symmetry; Jenshel worked against it.

In commissioning the Second Bank of the United States, its directors sought an edifice of classical form. Its architect, William Strickland, based the design on the Parthenon but made it more severe by eliminating elaborate pediment sculpture. Set up on a marble platform, the building is solid, austere, and stately. Iska elaborates on the façade's elevation, as well as its status as a tourist attraction, by including two pedestrians who are gazing upward at the façade.

Iska's frontal approach to both north and south porticos is appropriate to the building's spare simplicity. The porticos are architecturally identical, but their appearance and spirit verge dramatically because Iska photographed them in different seasons and varying light. Lighting plays a significant role in the overall effect conveyed by a frontal view. Full sunlight makes a bold impression. Shadows, overcast light, or billowy clouds will soften the result, as will shimmering reflections in windows.

Len Jenshel generally chose the gentler approach. In his photographs of the bank in Southport, Connecticut, and of both banks in Charleston, he let greenery drop into the frame, breaking the hard structural edges. By investing the space around the Bank of South Carolina with leaves and traffic signs, Jenshel undermined the satisfying effect of its symmetry. He was "a bit set back by the coldness and squareness of this bank," so he set out to soften it with the plants and by photographing it at dawn when the stained glass above the door would show up best. Later he considered the possibility that portrayal in the midday sun would have been more faithful to the simplicity and intellectual rigor of the Federal style.

In Cleveland and at the Bowery Savings Bank in New York, Jenshel utilized the normal urban clutter — street lights, traffic, pedestrians — to moderate an unchallenged, direct approach. In his photographs of Bowery Savings, the environment had a metaphorical as well as formal purpose for Jenshel. He observed that, "people's first association to the word 'Bowery' is not 'Bank' or 'Street', but 'bum.' And it is so that this classical temple rises out of the dirt, the noise, and the homeless strewn on its very portals. The irony is that one cannot remove that seedy reality, even while marveling at this architectural masterpiece. We must remember that it was a bank serving wage earners and small depositors, not the wealthy." In this environment, the bank can be regarded as a moral tale about thrift.

Environment

Other photographers also choose to establish the site context for their banks by moving back to include the neighborhoods. Banks are frequently in the center of town, reflecting their prominence in the commercial endeavors that fuel the rise and growth of cities. Normally, cities have a "Banker's Row" where the major banking institutions vie to build the largest and most attractive edifices. In the small towns, too, banks are often the most impressive structures. The photographers wished to communicate that sense of prominence which bankers sought to convey by their sites as well as by appropriate architectural design.

George Tice included the horses and carriages on Place d'Armes in Montreal to indicate the historical status of the Bank of Montreal's location. The carriages convey that the Place d'Armes and the Church of Notre Dame across from the bank are tourist attractions. With the Syracuse Savings Bank, Tice chose perspectives and lenses to make obvious the spaciousness of the bank's setting. The bank stands across from a plaza, at the intersection of a major boulevard and what was the Erie Canal. The canal has been filled in, but the sense of openness that its width afforded the bank remains, as does the significance of the bank's prominent location on two major thoroughfares.

Sometimes the bank's original site is relatively well preserved. Because the First and Second Banks of the United States and the Farmers and Mechanics Bank are in a historic neighborhood in Philadelphia, the architectural encroachment of modern times is minimal. By including part of the Second Bank's main portico in his image of the Farmers and Mechanics Bank, Iska suggests the commercial value of having one's own place on "Banker's Row." He also suggests the additional value of distinctive appearance within this attractive grouping by establishing the distinct differences in architectural taste reflected by the Second Bank of the United States as compared to the Farmers Bank.

Conversely, historic bank buildings are frequently surrounded by towering modern neighbors. Robert Bourdeau makes it clear that the then-vacant and unkempt Commercial Bank of the Midland District in Toronto cannot compete with the glistening modern buildings around it which offer modern conveniences and vistas. In printing the photograph, he accentuates the contrasts between the dark time- and weather-worn façade of the Commercial Bank and the shiny, undulating glass façade of the Royal Bank Plaza. He reinforces the contrast of "old" and "new" by also including the needle-like CN Tower in the distance.

In photographing Manufacturers Trust on New York's Fifth Avenue, James Iska had a similar problem—a small building amid towering neighbors—but here the incongruity was inverted. The bank was the "new" building. Its discreet size and glass-curtain construction were calculated to appeal to customers as open and friendly rather than as massive and austere. It went against the convention that solidity and scale were necessary to promote business and public confidence.

Showing the building in its context was Iska's main objective. Therefore, he was obliged to photograph from the greatest distance he could achieve. This also satisfied his second prerequisite: to have the camera in the midst of midday Manhattan traffic, indicating one of the busiest areas of the city and thereby the value of the real estate on which they had built this moderately scaled structure.

With architectural progress and the advent of bank-skyscrapers, the skyline view became more practical and photographically preferable to street-level approaches. For a building more than ten stories high, the photographer is forced to climb with it, seeking the nearest roof, balcony, or clean window in a nearby building. To translate into his photographs the scale, weight, and mass of the structures, Edward Burtynsky chose an elevated distance from which the bank building was prominent, and the surrounding buildings functioned primarily to locate the bank within the city. Specifically, he sought locations from which the bank was the apex of a pyramid, with the rest of the city falling away from its sides. He wanted it to appear rooted, as if its great mass had grown out of the city—which, in a financial sense, it could be said to have done.

Getting permission to photograph from the desired vista can require persistent initiative, ingenuity, and diplomacy. Some of the photographers were particularly adept at securing desired locations. Catherine Wagner even gained the participation of a construction crew whose crane was in her camera's line of vision to the Rainier Bank in Seattle. The crew gave her a headphone, and she instructed the crane operator where she needed him to position his crane for the best possible pictorial effect. Too, by including the construction cranes, she conveys that another modern tower will join the Rainier Bank building on the skyline, and connotes an ongoing relationship between the bank and other businesses.

New York's congested financial district offered similar challenges. An almost insolvable problem for the project was to convey the sixty-story Chase Manhattan building as the giant it was when completed in 1961, rather than as it now stands, somewhat eclipsed by other buildings. Three photographers evolved three different tactics. Wagner chose a view where the midsection of the bank tower broke above some of the smaller buildings to one side. To exclude newer neighboring skyscrapers, she opted to show only a portion of Chase Manhattan. Conversely, John Pfahl accepted the contemporary situation of Chase Manhattan in relation to it neighbors. He photographed in Brooklyn looking across the East River. Chase Manhattan is central to his view, but the World Trade Center towers top the skyline.

Aerial photography offered another solution. From a helicopter, Marilyn Bridges could document the sense of imbalance between the Chase Manhattan tower and the contiguous Federal Reserve Bank while excluding its taller neighbors. In her photographs, the Chase appears to be reaching skyward. This feeling is created because only the thrusting upper stories of the skyscraper are lit by sunlight; its base and neighboring medium-height buildings appear earth-bound in shadow, foothills in mountain twilight.

Light

Compared to less stationary subjects, architecture offers both advantages and disadvantages to the photographer. Time-dependent factors of patination and use — such as light, weather, neglect, and ordinary habitation — cause striking changes in appearance, but the architectural presence of each building remains available for contemplation and for interpretive efforts to capture its essence.

Light was a central concern in both exterior and interior photographs but is more controllable in the latter situation. For exterior light of choice, there is little the photographer can do but plan according to the season and to wait for the right weather. In winter the sun is lower, its light is harsher, striking vertical elevations at an almost perpendicular angle. During summer, the sun is higher and its light grazes surfaces more softly. Depending on the season, the desired façade may receive direct sunlight for only fifteen or twenty minutes a day, or not at all. A façade facing due north would not get direct sunshine from mid-September to mid-March in most American cities. Consequently, many of the project's photographers had to rely on light reflected from other buildings to illuminate the surface of a bank.

The photographers of the Classical Revival buildings as well as those of other styles in the present project sensed that raking light would best articulate a bank's features. Classical architecture is designed as a romance of light and stone; nineteenth-century architecture students learned how to create shade (graded edges) and shadows (sharp edges) with concave and convex surfaces and with architectural elements. Flat, noon light makes rounded forms appear linear or planar. Angled light gives depth and texture to surfaces and separates sculptured details and planes. However, too much angle on the light source creates deep shadows under sculptured forms. To modify this effect while photographing the richly carved Farmers and Mechanics Bank, Iska chose light coming from a 45-degree angle but on a somewhat hazy day.

Iska quickly learned that the appearance and spirit of the Second Bank of the United States changed dramatically depending on the quality of light. On a sunny afternoon he watched the shadow of a sycamore tree move along the columns on the south portico. Eventually, he decided that his best photograph showed the bank's southeast corner with all but one column in shadow. The forms of the shaded columns are softly molded and quietly solid; the end column is seemingly fragile in its vibrating sheath of light. The contrast reveals the building's spirited romance with light.

Shadow is as useful a tool as light. It can soften, hide, or accentuate elements of architecture. Serge Hambourg used long shadows in the foreground to lead the viewer toward the brilliantly lit Institute for Savings in Newburyport and the Nantucket Pacific Bank. The shadows obscure distracting foreground details while portraying both banks in graciously spacious settings.

If a photographer is working in color, the angle and quantity of light falling on a building can alter our perception of its color. This is most notable in David Duchow's two photographs of the Bank of Montreal branch on Front Street in Toronto. On a rainy day, the Ohio sandstone is at its most visually diffident. In raking sunlight the same building glows; its ornate façade regains the splendor intended by its architect.

Edward Burtynsky prefers to photograph near sunset or sundown because in this period all densities of color blend in such a way that no one color dominates another. Neither the front nor side of the building is masked by shadow. Moreover, its mass and volume, as well as its architectural detailing, are clearly revealed. In Burtynsky's photograph of the RepublicBank Center, the warm, yellow-crimson light of sunrise accomplishes the above effects and heightens the color of the bank's red granite exterior, bathing its neighbors in the same hue. Thus, the building's color, as well as its height, signifies its dominant presence.

Only two of the photographers in this project worked at night; both were photographing glass-curtain-wall buildings and wanted to capture the dramatic shifts in such buildings from opacity in daylight to transparency at night. George Tice photographed the Toronto-Dominion Centre in overcast daylight, sunset, twilight, and late-evening darkness. The complex of four black towers dominates Toronto's downtown district. In bright daylight, the black glass is impenetrable. The towers and their smooth-skinned neighbors remain somber with absorbed soft, flat light through a grey day. At sunset on a clear day, they begin to glisten. As the sunlight fades, interior lights sparkle through the glass curtain walls, transforming the buildings into a lattice of steel beams. This set of photographs establishes that no one photograph of the Toronto-Dominion Centre can describe it definitively.

Obstacles and Interruptions

Sometimes when light is most advantageous, other conditions, such as traffic, are not. Both John Pfahl and David Duchow wrote about working around the traffic — or more specifically, with the traffic around them.

Pfahl photographed the Princeton Bank from a small pedestrian island, where two other streets intersect Nassau Street, Princeton's main thoroughfare. Since the best light on the bank building coincided with rush hour, exposures were confined to sporadic gaps in the traffic pattern. The resulting photograph reveals no hint of this commotion. Rather it conveys the feeling of quiet.

Duchow achieved a different result when he photographed the Bank of Montreal West End Branch under similar circumstances. There was a single fifteen-minute span when light was reflected onto the façade. While seizing this golden moment for art and architecture, he was obliged to contend with not only the traffic but pigeons and sea gulls, as well as curious and sometimes aggressive drunks. While the bank's exterior richness is evident, some of the seedy residue of vagrants is conveyed in the littered gutters and an overflowing trash bin.

Nearby construction poses another frequent problem, particularly in urban areas. Sometimes, scouts failed to mention scaffolding that covered a rear portico, the massive road repair at the front door, or the window cleaners who were scheduled for the same day. The photographers either had to work around the obstructions or make another trip.

David Miller contrasted the general shabbiness of the neighborhood and traffic barricades surrounding the Philadelphia Saving Fund Society building with the modernist elegance of its stainless steel and granite exterior at street level. When Miller was positioned twenty stories above the street for an elevation shot, the construction and traffic became miniscule. In his skyline view Miller carefully juxtaposed the neon initials PSFS that cap the building and Philadelphia's other famous icon, the statue of William Penn on City Hall. He includes in the distance the new building designed by Helmut Jahn, which is the first skyscraper that Philadelphia has allowed to rise higher than the statue of William Penn.

Interiors

When a photographer moves from the exterior to the interior of a building, his professional problems change. Inside he must address the flow of space (how do spaces form and interconnect), accesss (how it feels to move through the halls), and significant details (what do the decorative and structural details convey). Yet it is particularly difficult for photographs to transmit a sense of the flow and enclosure of interior spaces.

One solution is to seek high resolution of interior details. In this instance, all details become significant ones which would be lost if the photographer softens the lens' focus or permits a shallow depth of field. Unlike portraying a person, where the photographer may focus on the sitter's cheekbones and let the background blur, the architectural photographer takes pains to record the bank seal at his feet, as well as the window details in the distance. A wealth of receding details implies volume traversed.

Cameras are best at recording solid forms and the nature of materials. In interiors, as well as exteriors, the expressive impact arises from selectively emphasized details. But while safety-deposit boxes, armed guards, and other security measures most clearly indicate the bank's primary function, photographs of utilitarian spaces in a building's interior are often less arresting than photographs of interior-decorative details; photographs of the vaults and desks, for example, were less compelling than those of sculpted details, entrance lamps, murals, and door frames. The latter objects were more likely to have been designed to be expressive as well as functional. The former had only to be functional and generally were selected, but not designed, by the architect for this bank.

Significant interior detailing noticed by photographers include Jenshel's record of the carved American eagles on the interior arch of the main doorway at the Bank of South Carolina, and his photograph of the shrine-like setting for a founder's portrait over a check writing table in Bowery Savings.

Serge Hambourg also focused on expressive interior details. In photographing the banking hall at Winona Savings and Winona National Bank, he included a stuffed lion which lords it over the balcony rail. The lion is both the bank's emblem and, in this instance, serves a double role as a hunting trophy of one of the directors. Hambourg's project notes were as poetic as his pictures. He photographed the chandeliers in Owatonna as "penetrating a space made of lace" and the base of the exterior columns in Winona as "crushed onto the ground like a large elephant's feet."

At the Wells, Fargo & Co. Express Office in Columbia, California, Catherine Wagner recognized that the safe and the gold scales symbolized what the office meant to the miners. It wasn't the stature of the building but the accuracy of measurement and security of their gold in the safe that attracted the miners as customers. David Miller noted the enticement-to-save-then-spend implicit in someone at the Bank of British Columbia posting a travel advertisement for Hawaii near the entrance to safety-deposit boxes. It's an observation typical of Miller to juxtapose the vaults (locked-up) and the islands (escape).

The construction and decorative materials in banks can be strikingly lavish. This is arguably good business practice: "A beautiful bank building . . . begets public confidence," wrote Louis Lamb in a 1905 essay in the *Banker's Monthly*.[5] And, banks are well-situated, economically and socially, to mobilize resources in the construction of their quarters. Most observers perceive the ongoing prosperity connotation of the color gold, so it has been used generously in banks. Gold or polished bronze, in fact, have been used in the doors and the seal in the banking hall of the Bank of Nova Scotia; the mosaics in Irving Trust Company; the safe, capitals, and ceiling in Bowery Savings; the gold-glass, exterior wall of the Royal Bank of Canada in Toronto; and the gold-trimmed, coffered ceilings in the Canadian Bank of Commerce in Toronto.

The photographers assigned to these banks remarked upon and documented each of these uses. Jenshel described the main hall of Bowery Savings as having "a golden pervasiveness that bathes everything." He employed this gold hue together with elaborately carved capitals and window casings, and highly reflective, polished surfaces to transmit the impression of a wondrous place which one might want to visit without having any business to transact.

Susan Wagg points out in her essay, "Whereas the interior of the Bowery Savings Bank is warm and inviting, the remodeled Bank of Montreal interior is cool and intimidating. It is clear given the unprecedented vastness and grandeur of the banking hall . . . that it was still Canada's preeminent financial institution."[6] Agreeing with Wagg, the photographer David Miller found the McKim, Mead, & White renovation "out-of-human scale, off-putting, and imposing," and those feelings are reflected in his photographs. The marble columns soar upward in a regal procession from the main door to the banking hall. The ample spaces and refined interior appointments are dramatically grand and not conducive to lingering after conducting one's business.

People

A criterion guiding almost all architectural design is suitability for use by people. However, in most architectural photography, and particularly in interior views, people are absent. There are many explanations for this. Most often, photographers are inhibited by technical limitations. Extended periods of time are needed to expose film properly in dimly lit interior spaces, periods longer than most people can or will be still. If people move during a long exposure, they appear either as a blur or not at all. Iska was grateful for two gentlemen who sat quietly during the two-minute exposure necessary for his photograph of the Continental Illinois banking hall. He included them to provide human scale.

Beyond the technical limitations, photographers cite other reasons for excluding people from interior views. People distract the viewer from the primary subject — the architecture. Clothing and hair styles quickly date a picture. New buildings haven't been occupied and are without the wear or personal touches of those who inhabit the spaces. Finally, a building's tenant may request that its employees and clients not be photographed.

Yet many photographers regard signs of life as enriching an architectural photograph. When he was documenting the work of Louis Sullivan in the 1950s, John Szarkowski realized, "As I began to work, I found, to my own surprise, that I was seeing this building not with the decorous disinterest with which a photographer is supposed to approach a work of formal architecture, but as a real building, which people had worked in and maimed and ignored and perhaps loved, and which I felt was deeply important. I found myself concerned not only with the building's art-facts but with its life-facts." [7]

In reviewing Szarkowski's photographs, Hugh Morrison recognized this approach had value as commentary. He wrote, "People and automobiles and clocks and wires, and above all the sordid clamor of advertising signs, make you see these as real buildings, sometimes overwhelmed, sometimes still triumphant in their existence. . . . Yet you come to realize that these same sordid, vulgar, cheap, surroundings were then, when Sullivan worked, just the same, and part of what he contended with and what his life was all about." [8]

Szarkowski recognized that Sullivan's bank served its customers, so he included them as part of the life of the building. The farmers lined up in Szarkowski's photograph of the Owatonna banking hall exemplify bank customers as Sullivan may have envisioned them. The beefy men in worn overalls contrast sharply with the similarly massive, yet delicately molded, door-head above them. Thus Szarkowski also addressed an aspect of what the bank symbolizes, the transcendent power of beautiful forms in everyday life.

Conclusion

The eleven photographers commissioned for this project are practiced and sophisticated artists. All are knowledgeable in the intricacies of their craft; each is broadly familiar with the history of the medium. They learned to photograph from mentors, personal experiences, and lessons accumulated by a regard for the photographs of others.

Each balances his desire to make compelling pictures with his intention to make useful documents. Of first importance are how clearly he perceives the subject and the intensity with which he can convey his revelations. What he can technically master is secondary, but it is inseparably intertwined with the delivery of ideas. If the procedural solutions are inappropriate, then the content is compromised.

These decisions distinguish one artist's photographs from others' and constitute his individual style of photography. For instance, the difference between Bourdeau's intimate, 8- x 10-inch black-and-white contact prints and Burtynsky's shimmering 20- x 24-inch color enlargements is a matter of whispered versus bold engagement. The adroit containment of abundant detail in Bourdeau's relatively small prints conveys his search for a bank's dignity as expressed in materials and details. Burtynsky's confident, graphic compositions celebrate the monumental character of skyscrapers and communicate his impressions of their full scenic glory. The scale of the prints is essential to project the immense mass and lofty dominance of skyscraper banks.

In addressing the inherent challenges and special problems encountered by these photographers, I hope to have clarified the responsibilities and skills required of an architectural photographer. Describing his aims leads inherently to discussions of the buildings themselves because the photographer is interpreting and evaluating as well as describing the building. For the public as well as the field of architecture, a fine photographer is a visually articulate guide, conversant in the subject of buildings as art and as metaphors of cultural values.

[1] "Architectural Photography with the Small Camera," *The Encyclopedia of Photography.* Edited by Willard D. Morgan. Greystone Press, New York, 1962. Vol. II, p. 245.

[2] Project notes. Unless noted otherwise, all quotations from the photographers are from project notes and letters in the archives of The Museum of Fine Arts, Houston, and of the Parnassus Foundation.

[3] Phyllis Lambert, "The Record of Buildings as Evidence," *Court House: A Photographic Document,* Horizon Press, New York, p. 10.

[4] Conversation with author, January 15, 1988.

[5] "Where the Money Was: The Making of America's Temple Banks," unpublished lecture by Neil Harris.

[6] Wagg essay, p. 93.

[7] *The Idea of Louis Sullivan.* Minneapolis: University of Minnesota Press, 1956, unpaginated.

[8] Untitled book review, *Journal of the Society of Architectural Historians,* XVII:2 (Summer 1958), p. 30.

INDEX